Every Citizen A Soldier

Number 146

WILLIAMS-FORD

TEXAS A&M UNIVERSITY

MILITARY HISTORY

SERIES

Every Citizen A Soldier

THE CAMPAIGN FOR

UNIVERSAL MILITARY TRAINING

AFTER WORLD WAR II

WILLIAM A. TAYLOR

TEXAS A&M UNIVERSITY PRESS

COLLEGE STATION

Library of Congress Cataloging-in-Publication Data

Taylor, William A., 1975– author.

   Every citizen a soldier : the campaign for universal military training after
World War II / William A. Taylor.—First edition.

        pages cm — (Williams-Ford Texas A&M University military history series ;
number 146)

   Includes bibliographical references and index.

   ISBN 978-1-62349-146-8 (cloth : alk. paper)—(ISBN 978-1-62349-169-7 (e-book)
1. Draft—United States—History—20th century. 2. Military education—United
States—History—20th century. I. Title. II. Series: Williams-Ford Texas A&M
University military history series ; no. 146.

   UB343.T395 2014

   355.2'25097309044—dc23

                                                            2014008382

To my parents

RICHARD A. TAYLOR

and

L. DIANE TAYLOR

THE TRAINEE COMES HOME

The trainee has given up a year to his country. In return he has acquired confidence that as long as he and other boys like him are prepared for the eventuality of combat, they can look forward to a prosperous future untroubled by war.

His military training has had valuable by-products. His interests have broadened. He has learned how to play new sports and developed new hobbies. The specialist and technician training he received may develop into a vocation. He has learned the habit of concentration in study which will be of great advantage if he continues in school. The ability he has acquired to adjust himself socially to the personalities of people with diverse backgrounds has made him more tolerant and understanding. He has learned to assume responsibility and exercise leadership. He has had an experience in democracy.

He looks a man. Outdoor living, exercise, regular hours, and well-balanced meals have strengthened him and given him endurance. He is physically fit and mentally alert—ready to take on his new job or school work with the satisfaction of recent accomplishments. He should be proud, for he is a responsible citizen now, prepared to defend his country if ever the need arises.

— War Department

Contents

Illustrations

Preface

I often remember a story my grandfather told me when I was a child. As soon as America formally entered World War II, he wanted desperately to enlist. Being only seventeen years old, he had to obtain the approval of his parents. After a good deal of pleading and probably a little arm-twisting, he finally convinced them to sign his paperwork and dutifully reported to the local recruiting office. After waiting in line for what seemed like hours, he finally made his way to the front, where he timidly stood looking up at a raised table. It was from behind this fortified position that a board of three military officers—one from the army, one from the navy, and one from the Marine Corps—quizzed volunteers about their intentions and informed them of the outcomes. When given permission to speak, my grandfather clearly explained that he was there for one purpose and one purpose only: to join the navy voluntarily. To his surprise, instead of instant approval of such a laudable goal, the board began conversing. "Joe," the army officer bellowed to the navy officer, "you got the last two, I'm taking this boy in the army." My grandfather, awestruck and in disbelief, blurted out, "You can't do that, I want to join the navy!" With a slight grin on his face and his official stamp raised high in the air, the army officer retorted, "Boy, you're in the army now!" and slammed the stamp home on the papers formally placing my grandfather in the army. This event would officially start the journey that would send him to far-off and unimagined places throughout the European theater.

As a child, the story was just that—a story. As all good grandfathers do, mine repeated it countless times. For some reason I never tired of hearing it. The repetition of the account slowly ingrained itself into my consciousness. Later in life, the anecdote interested me more and more. I began to contemplate the delicate relationship between national security requirements and individual liberties in American democracy. Reflection on this balance led me to a related question: Do defense planners in American democracy face constraints in terms of ensuring their national security goals, since they must be mindful of the revered status of individual liberty within American society? The question revealed to me an irony. American defense planners were extremely successful at cultivating military power, especially in the modern military era beginning with World War II, and created what is undoubtedly the most powerful military force in the world today. I wondered how this could be the case. Unlike totalitarian regimes, American military leaders always had to balance their demands for security with assurances that individual liberties would not be infringed upon. I began to seek a case study that would be fertile ground to examine some of these important issues concerning the development of American military power within the confines of American society. I soon became fascinated with army policy and planning for the post–World War II era. As a result, I landed on 1943 as a point of departure.

Even though 1943 witnessed such interesting events as the introduction of Frank Sinatra, the Broadway premier of *Porgy & Bess,* and the notorious zoot suit riots, Americans focused the bulk of their attention overseas. Even so, at the same time that Allied forces were completing their invasions of Sicily and Italy, army planners at home were sowing the seeds of a campaign that would last the better part of five years. It was their campaign for universal military training, or UMT. The campaign centered on securing legislation that would require every eighteen-year-old male in the United States to undergo a year of military training and then become part of a citizen reserve army. The importance of such a campaign is multifaceted and has four main dimensions.

First, this narrative is important because it illustrates what can best be termed strategic fixation. Army leaders settled on UMT because of its strategic value, primarily for the creation of a trained citizen reserve that would speed mobilization and secondarily for its value as a deterrent against potential adversaries in an uncertain international environment. Unable to convince others—especially critics in American society and an unenthusiastic Congress—of the merits of their policy, army leaders rigidly stuck with their plan even in the face of repeated setbacks. As the chances of success clearly diminished following the war, they became entrenched in their insistence on UMT. In essence, they lost sight of the fact that strategy is never far removed from policy, which is never far removed from politics. In a democracy, policy cannot be produced in a vacuum. Instead, it is part of a triumvirate made up of policy, politics, and society. Army leadership failed to adapt their policy to the political realities of securing their plan and the implications of it for American society. As a result, they entered the early Cold War devoid of any viable strategic alternatives to UMT. As such, this story evidences the dangers of organizational calcification caused by overwhelming strategic consensus among senior military leaders on one possible plan.

Second, this account is significant because it demonstrates the delicate balance in American democracy between civilian and military control of policy. Throughout the period, army leaders drove the campaign for UMT without clear guidance from civilian leaders in the executive branch. As history unfolded, President Truman became most closely associated with UMT, even though War Department planners had already been working on UMT for several years before his arrival as commander-in-chief. There were supporters of UMT in Congress and among civilian elites outside of government, but the primary drivers of the campaign resided in the halls of the War Department. In fact, army leaders often walked a fine line between providing strategic input to civilian leaders in the policy process and propagandizing for their desired policy with the executive branch, the Congress, and the American public as a whole. Such actions would lead to congressional hearings in 1947 and 1948 that chastised army leaders for overstepping their bounds in the democratic process. Overall, most senior politicians who supported UMT did so late in the campaign and after significant prodding from army leaders. Instead of senior civilian leaders setting broad strategic guidelines and army leaders devising the best means to achieve them, the UMT narrative reveals the process turned upside down. Army leaders drove policy on their own.

The elation of pending victory in World War II vaulted the status of army leaders to the pinnacle of American society. To the victors go the spoils, and the stars of generals shone brightly by 1943. Military leaders such as George C. Marshall ascended to dominance and became increasingly influential in the policy making process. *Time* named Marshall "Man of the Year" in both 1943 and 1947. The rise of military leaders to policy control also had interesting and important side effects. As army leaders marketed their strategic vision of UMT, they were caught in a conundrum. Critics of UMT often highlighted potential social ills that would result from such a drastic change. In answering these charges, army leaders sometimes subtly shifted their emphasis from military utility to social benefits. To their credit, the alteration by army leaders was usually negligible as they attempted to stay true to their cause. Even so, small ripples can cause large waves. Politicians, most notably in the Truman administration, found such shifts attractive. As a result, the US

Army's campaign for UMT following World War II underwent a meta-morphosis. Military utility gave way to the broader positive impact of UMT on American society as politicians entered the campaign, led by President Truman himself. What began as a measure to speed mobilization gave way to a plan to eradicate illiteracy, improve public health, and inculcate citizenship.

Third, this history is vital because of its ultimate outcome. The death of UMT in 1948 was also the birth of the Cold War draft. From 1948 until 1973, selective service was the law of the land. It is crucial to remember that UMT was at the time the one seriously contemplated alternative to selective service. The juxtaposition of the two choices reveals much about American society during the mid-1940s. Supporters of UMT within the army, most notably John M. Palmer, touted UMT as the truly American policy because of its universal nature and democratic application. Army leaders publicized the sociological advantages of opening leadership advancement within the army to a broader audience under a system of UMT than was possible under the expansible army concept of Emory Upton that was in vogue during the interwar period. In contrast, many people at the time—both supporters and critics of UMT—saw selective service as the less fair but more efficient military option, especially as international tensions heightened in the spring of 1948. The debate surrounding the two options exposed much about how various Americans viewed the appropriate balance between national security and individual liberty in America following World War II.

Finally, as we look at American society today, we cannot help but be struck by a much different landscape than that of 1943. The fact that the UMT story seems so far removed from American society of today reveals that America of 1943 was a strange and interesting society. Americans at the time seriously contemplated something many today would label draconian. Yet we live in an America that has directly witnessed military manpower shortages in far-flung places such as Iraq and Afghanistan. Such deficiencies have increasingly resulted in the outsourcing of military personnel functions. Beginning with relatively mundane personnel functions such as cooking and equipment maintenance, this trend has continued until private military contractors have become involved in training combat troops. Eventually, this drift has led to extremes, such as the engagement of military contractors in combat operations while under the direction of private corporations instead of governments. Such developments raise important ethical considerations about the privatization of force and illuminate the importance of public debate regarding military manpower policy. In addition, a paradox exists in American society today relative to military manpower policy. As Americans' views of a citizen's obligations to government have shrunken dramatically (imagine a poll today on UMT, for example) our expectations of government's obligations to its citizens have increased in reverse proportion. In an age when the size and power of government seem to be increasing daily, questions about whether there should be limits to government power and where those limits should be seem more appropriate than ever. Finally, the reemergence of national service policy relates directly to earlier attempts to secure both national service and universal military training. At a time when individual citizens can and should do more to be part of something bigger than themselves, it is instructive to look to our past at the much higher levels of sacrifice previous American citizens advocated. The fact that most polls in the mid-1940s illustrated consistently high levels of public support for what would be considered severe today highlights a much different American society immediately following World War II. A better understanding of earlier attempts by national security planners to achieve universal military training will illuminate both the promise and the dangers inherent in discussions of national service policy today.

In the end, the story of the US Army's campaign for universal military training from 1943 to 1948 is important because it highlights strategic considerations that were meant to improve America's national security in the postwar world but in many ways undermined preparedness through strategic fixation, the inversion of civilian and military control of policy, and the establishment of peacetime selective service at the outset of the Cold War. As a result, the story reveals much about American society as it found itself trying to heal from a traumatic war while at the same time seeking to define its newfound position as a fledgling military superpower and prepare itself for what had to be a daunting and uncertain future.

Such a historical case study can also be instructive in opening a debate about the broader considerations of balancing national security goals with the traditional values of American democracy. Americans in the post-9/11 world in many ways face the same ethical quandaries that Americans confronted in the aftermath of World War II. In both instances, the world those Americans had previously known seemed shattered. The world had changed forever. Fear of the unknown drove many to demand serious changes in order to augment American military power and prepare for any eventuality. Others cautioned restraint and focused on the inherent strength of traditional American values of liberty and freedom. Ultimately, America chose not to institute UMT in the aftermath of World War II. It will yet be determined what America will decide today with regard to the challenges it faces in the long-term aftermath of 9/11.

Acknowledgments

The staffs at various archives and libraries were helpful in guiding me through a maze of primary sources. Richard L. Boylan at the National Archives at College Park, Maryland, assisted me in getting started and introduced me to the pertinent army records. Randy Sowell and David Clark at the Harry S. Truman Library and Museum in Independence, Missouri, aided me in finding records detailing the inner workings of the Truman administration and the records of the President's Advisory Commission on Universal Training. Janice Davis provided excellent photographs depicting the activities of the Universal Military Training Experimental Unit located at Fort Knox from an album given to President Truman by advocates of UMT. Paul Barron and Jeffrey Kozak at the George C. Marshall Research Library in Lexington, Virginia, helped me locate records detailing Marshall's close friendship with John M. Palmer and the impact it had on the UMT campaign. They also located compelling photographs depicting some of the key personalities in this story.

Four research grants aided me in conducting in-depth primary source research at various archives and libraries. An ABC-Clio research grant from the Society for Military History afforded me extra time at the Marshall library. Pat Carlin of ABC-Clio awarded the grant and provided administrative assistance and backing. A George C. Marshall/Baruch fellowship funded an additional extensive research trip to the Marshall library. Joanne D. Hartog and Alice J. Lee were instrumental in administering the grant smoothly. A Truman Library Institute research grant allowed a final visit to the Truman library prior to completion of the book. Michael Devine made me feel welcome at the library, and Lisa A. Sullivan provided excellent support and help throughout the grant. Finally, an Angelo State University Faculty Research Enhancement Program grant aided this project. Katie Plum imparted many insights into the grant process and furnished significant aid in the application for and administration of the grant. Angelo State University proved itself supportive of faculty endeavors, as exemplified by the Office of Sponsored Projects and the Center for Innovation in Teaching and Research.

This book began in work I did for my doctoral dissertation at George

Washington University. I thanked my dissertation advisor, Ronald H. Spector, and committee members Lawrence J. Korb and Edward D. Berkowitz there, but I want to recognize their help here as well. Professor Berkowitz provided his notes on Wilbur J. Cohen's role on the President's Advisory Commission on Universal Training and also imparted a fascination with Hollywood that I took with me from the university. Leo P. Ribuffo and William H. Becker served as additional readers and offered considerable guidance. My previous work at other institutions also prepared me for this undertaking. Jon T. Sumida at the University of Maryland, College Park, taught me the rigors of deciphering policy choices and shaped my understanding of strategy—especially Clausewitz. Craig L. Symonds at the United States Naval Academy first introduced me to historical scholarship.

The entire staff of Texas A&M University Press has been professional, supportive, and encouraging. Mary Lenn Dixon believed in this project from the start and has been a joy to work with. Patricia Clabaugh, Holli Koster, Katherine D. Duelm, Paige Bukowski, and Taylor Phillips were always helpful. Peer reviewers William T. Allison and Peter R. Mansoor provided sage advice and insightful guidance. I am both humbled and honored to receive their very positive endorsements.

Two dear friends and former US Naval Academy roommates, Ronald P. Wisdom and Lt. Cdr. Brian J. Haggerty, opened their homes to me during my research at the Truman library. I am grateful to them and their families. My parents, Richard A. Taylor and L. Diane Taylor, to whom I dedicate this work, offered immeasurable assistance throughout. Most important, my wife Renee deserves special thanks. She patiently endured not only my incessant fascination with events long past, but also my attending graduate school while carrying a heavy workload. As a result of both school and work, she shouldered an extra share of family responsibilities caring for our two wonderful children, Madison and Benjamin. She carried the burden gracefully and was a constant source of encouragement. Without her patience, this work never would have been completed.

Even with such a supportive cast around me, I alone am responsible for any errors contained in this work.

Every Citizen a Soldier

1   A Grave Decision

This nation faces a grave decision—whether or not to continue in peacetime the drafting of its young men for military training. The proposal concerns not only every boy and parent, but every citizen of this country. It involves our national postwar security and the world's postwar peace.

Bills proposing universal training are before Congress now. Behind them are leading military and naval authorities. More than two thirds of the GIs, voting in secret polls, approve the idea. All polls show the general public approves it. But some important educational and religious bodies oppose it or at least favor postponing the decision until after the war. The Army and Navy want action now—while the people are alert to our defense needs and before we backslide into postwar apathy.

—*Washington Post*

The "grave decision" was determining the best method of securing America's national security immediately following World War II. One plan to do that was to make every eighteen-year-old male in America undergo one year of mandatory military training. The army called this plan universal military training, or UMT. Beginning in 1943, US Army leaders such as John M. Palmer, Walter L. Weible, George C. Marshall, and John J. McCloy mounted a sustained and vigorous campaign to establish a system of universal military training in America. Fearful of repeating the rapid demobilization and severe budget cuts that had accompanied peace following World War I, these army leaders saw UMT as the basis for their postwar plans. As a result, they marketed UMT extensively and aggressively. The core justification for UMT was its strategic rationale based on improving mobilization through the creation of a General Reserve. However, boosters of UMT found that their attempts to overcome the objections voiced by many educators, labor leaders, and clergy often had unintended consequences.[1]

In 1945, the campaign became politicized as President Truman championed UMT for reasons that differed from the purely strategic concept that army leaders had created. President Truman portrayed UMT as improving national health, combating illiteracy, and inculcating citizenship. Army leaders focused their attention on establishing the UMT Experimental Unit at Fort Knox, Kentucky, to fine-tune implementation and to demonstrate the program's utility to the nation. President Truman

Army Chief of Staff George C. Marshall, ca. 1945.
(Courtesy George C. Marshall Foundation, Lexington, Virginia)

established a President's Advisory Commission on Universal Training composed of well-known civilians who unanimously advocated UMT. Focus then shifted to the potential impact UMT would have on American society. One specific example was concern over the program's impact on race relations. Since army leaders proposed locating the majority of the training camps in the South, critics questioned whether UMT would promote segregation in a new and unprecedented way.

In 1948, the campaign for UMT climaxed as supporters attempted to seize on heightened international tensions as a rationale to pass UMT legislation without delay. Such appeals cut two ways. In the end, advocates had to admit that their primary goal contributed little to immediate national security. A weary but alarmed Congress approved selective service instead of UMT as the short-term answer for the army's manpower dilemma. This paradox resulted in the begrudging acceptance of selective service by advocates of UMT because it was the more efficient although less democratic option available.

Senior army planners envisioned UMT as the cornerstone of their postwar defense establishment. Because of its importance to their postwar vision, they actively sought its enactment. Two presidents, first Roosevelt and then Truman, approved of the concept and sought to influence its passage in Congress. Opinion polls consistently revealed that a majority of Americans favored the general idea. In spite of all of this, the plan did not come to fruition. For more than five crucial years, 1943–48, an intense public debate raged as various individuals and groups sought to influence the ultimate formation of the postwar defense establishment.[2] To varying degrees, religious groups, labor organizations, and education leaders fought against the plan. Military authorities and veterans' organizations supported the proposal. What follows is the story of the military policy underlying the plan's initial formation, the supporters of the plan and their vision of the postwar environment, the marketing of the plan, the details of the plan, and the opposition to the plan. In addition, this book explores the acceptance of the plan by the Truman administration and the metamorphosis that ensued, the debate over the social impact of UMT that followed the politicization of UMT, especially regarding segregation, and the final push for UMT amidst international crisis using all the combined resources of the army and the presidency that failed in 1948. UMT's failure resulted in a paradox that vaulted selective service above UMT because of its value as a short-term fix to the nation's preparedness concerns.

As soon as World War II began, American military leaders began to plan for two related yet distinct missions. Most turned their attention to overcoming the daunting challenges that confronted American military forces on battlefields around the globe. Some, however, began to craft the American military establishment that would exist after the smoke of battle had dissipated. As the war raged on and Allied victory slowly became a distinct probability, additional leaders deliberated on the significant issues facing the American military machine as it transitioned from total war to an uncertain and tense peace.[3]

One of the most immediate challenges for military planners was the issue of demobilization. The American public was clamoring for the speedy return of soldiers. In addition to that immediate challenge, finding the appropriate military manpower policy for postwar America became a crucial task. Military planners increasingly discussed the concept of UMT as the centerpiece for the postwar military manpower policy. Military thinkers crafted detailed plans for the training. Army leaders implemented a pilot program at Fort Knox, Kentucky, to test the concept. Starting in 1943 and continuing for more than five years, a contentious public debate raged over the plan and its potential impact on America. Even though there were high levels of support for the plan, it polarized American society in many unexpected ways. Finally, in 1948 Congress effectively killed the plan by burying it in the legislative process and instead chose to fill its military manpower needs through a peacetime selective service system.

The strategic origins of the plan for universal military training, the debate surrounding it, the metamorphosis the plan underwent, why it ultimately failed, and the impact of that failure on the postwar national security establishment are an integral and important part of US military history in the post–World War II period. From 1943 to 1948, supporters, detractors, and undecided observers of the UMT proposal not only debated it as a significant policy change, but also examined it as a major social issue with far-reaching implications for America. Military planners during the war envisioned universal military training as the primary means to transition from the wartime footing of World War II to the postwar security environment. The early but still palpable rivalry between the United States and the Soviet Union, along with the uncertainty created by huge advances in military capability such as long-range strategic bombing and the atomic bomb, characterized that security environment. The congressional defeat of the UMT proposal and the immediate aftermath of the legislative debacle in 1948 hold important implications for the history of postwar America.

UMT was a military policy that developed within the context of advancing military technology, the rise of strategic bombing, the destruction of a total war, the advent of the atomic age, and the introduction of the early Cold War. Within that context, US military planners contemplated heightened postwar military manpower requirements. This was a product not only of rapidly advancing military technology, but also of the changed postwar international political landscape. The United States was not completely at peace following World War II but rather was in a new and uncertain position of world leadership and an uneasy state of tension with the Soviet Union. Augmenting such an increased conventional threat was realization on the part of military planners that the advent of long-range strategic bombing and the atomic bomb significantly shortened parameters for mobilization planning. Prior to this development, American military planners felt confident that they could maintain a small professional army. If war erupted, the professional army could conduct a holding action while the military mobilized a much larger citizen army in six-, twelve-, eighteen-, and twenty-four-month increments. However, if an enemy possessed the striking power necessary to unleash a quick and devastating attack on the United States and intended to use such power, mobilization over such a long period became problematic in the minds of military planners. Many leading military thinkers argued that UMT was the best way to resolve the dilemma because it would create a pool of trained manpower *prior to* the outbreak of hostilities. Once fighting erupted, military leaders could call upon this General Reserve to go through a much-shortened refresher training phase before deployment, as these troops had already completed a year of military training. In this regard, UMT was one option envisioned to address the strategic realities of the postwar era.

Once military thinkers created, proposed, and marketed the policy, a coalition of supporters—including military leaders, veterans, the American Legion, the Veterans of Foreign Wars, and the executive branch—pushed vigorously for some form of the plan. A coalition of opposition formed that included pacifists, religious leaders, academia, and organized labor. According to numerous public opinion polls, the majority of Americans consistently supported the concept of UMT throughout the debate, even if they disagreed over the best method of implementing it. Even so, UMT suffered defeat. This book will explore why.

In many ways, the origins of UMT as a military policy and the struggle over it that ensued reveal a great deal about the military in American democracy. National security can trump individual liberty in a democracy for a limited time, but only when leaders clearly articulate a direct and immediate threat. However, there is danger in such an approach. The story of UMT reveals a paradox. As proponents of the plan, both in the army and in the Truman administration, argued that the heightened tensions of international crisis in the spring of 1948 evidenced the need for UMT, they quickly became captive to their own rhetoric. Opponents countered that if the world was as immediately dangerous as they said, they could not afford the delay required to implement their preferred long-term solution of UMT. Instead, supporters of UMT had to concede that selective service was more useful in the existing crisis, and thus selective service vaulted over UMT as the more immediately productive option. In the end, the long-term military utility of UMT could not address the short-term crisis that erupted in the spring of 1948.

The story of UMT reveals that in American democracy, military training is secondary to the broader societal goals of economic development and educational achievement. Supporters and even some opponents of UMT ultimately saw military training as somewhat beneficial, but the consensus failed to support it at the perceived expense of these broader societal goals. Finally, the defeat of UMT suggests that military training is not considered a prerequisite for citizenship in American democracy. UMT had its highest chance of success when the debate centered on military utility. When discussions shifted to the broader benefits of military training to citizenship, the push for UMT lost momentum and eventually faltered. In the end, citizenship and military training existed as separate entities during this time in American history.

No other published book-length history has focused exclusively on UMT.[4] The present book contributes to the existing literature in several unique ways. First, it highlights the broad support that the UMT proposal held all the way through 1948. A general consensus existed as to the value of UMT as an idea. It was not a long shot, as some portray it, but rather a seriously contemplated military policy that garnered widespread support throughout the military, the government, and American society in general. It was disagreement on the details of implementing any particular plan that fractured the accord.

Second, in this book I show that UMT was a significant change to American military thinking. UMT envisioned completely overturning traditional American military manpower policy and longstanding mobilization practices. The plan came close to doing just that.

Third, this book challenges the notion that UMT was an aberration. The reason that UMT appeared in the immediate postwar era was no accident. The dual context of military changes, such as the rise of long-range strategic bombing and the advent of atomic weapons, and political changes, such as the uncertainty of the postwar era and the ascendance of the United States to a position of world leadership, not only produced an environment that made the UMT proposal attractive, but also made it relevant to US military planners at the time. In this book, I examine in detail the origins of the UMT proposal as a military policy based on improving mobilization through the creation of a General Reserve. Of course, as debate ensued over the desirability of UMT, both advocates and opponents introduced a wide array of social, moral, legal, economic, and constitutional arguments either for or against it. This book explores those arguments but does not lose sight of the fact that UMT was at its origins a military policy even when it was being marketed as something else.

Fourth, this volume challenges the notion that UMT was simply a pet project of President Truman. It explores earlier support for the proposal among army leaders such as John M. Palmer and George C. Marshall, whose plans for UMT garnered wider and earlier support than did President Truman's. Most important, unlike previous works that deal with UMT tangentially, this book tells the complete story, which includes the details of the plan, the struggle over it, the political transformation of the plan, and its ultimate failure.

In this book, I broaden the analysis of UMT by examining the public debate over it that occurred in American society over the course of several years. I have researched government sources in depth, but I have also analyzed the significant amount of primary sources that depicted UMT as a broader social issue at that time. These primary sources included the records of various special interest groups, books, journals, magazines, and newspapers. Only by examining the government records in more depth in order to outline the specifics of the plan and the campaign for it and by examining the nongovernmental records in detail in order to summarize the public debate that swirled around UMT in American society can one hope to tell the complete story. This book is unique in that it does just that. In broader terms, such an exploration also illuminates the relationship of the military to American society during the mid-1940s.

I have three specific goals for this book. First, I examine the actual details of the plan for UMT. The core concept for UMT revolved around a strategic shift in American mobilization planning for a future war. In this volume, I consider the key mobilization calculations that in many ways gave birth to the UMT proposal. Specific military records at the National Archives outline relevant mobilization time frames and the total number of men available both with UMT implemented and without UMT implemented. I explore details such as who would be required to participate and who would be exempted. I analyze how many men would be trained, as well as where they would be trained. More important, I describe what training the men would actually receive under the UMT plan. The military records at the National Archives hold substantial details outlining the specifics of the training on a week-by-week basis. In addition, the army actually established an experimental UMT program at Fort Knox, Kentucky. The army collectively labeled this battalion of its youngest recruits the "beardless wonders" or the "one-shave-a-month boys."[5] In this book, I inspect the experimental Fort Knox training program in order to ascertain its role in the broader campaign for UMT.

Analyzing the specifics of the training is critical, because one of the fundamental reasons for the UMT proposal was to speed mobilization through the creation of a General Reserve. Some military thinkers at the time disagreed that UMT could accomplish that goal. They argued that the training would be ineffective in two distinct ways. First, they contended that the training would be too general in nature and in case of war might lead masses of poorly trained men to their slaughter. Others claimed that even if the training were technically and tactically sufficient at the time, it would be quickly forgotten by the trainees or outdated by tactical or technological change and therefore irrelevant when eventually needed in a future war. For these reasons, the perceptions of military planners regarding the sufficiency of the training are critical.

Finally, this volume examines how much UMT would actually cost according to calculations made by military planners at the time. Analyzing this portion of the UMT proposal is important, as critics attacked UMT for its high cost within an environment of shrinking defense budgets and calls for broad-based tax cuts. As the push for UMT unfolded, cost calculations by supporters of the plan continually lessened in the hopes of securing congressional approval, while the cost calculations of dissenters continually rose to achieve the opposite effect.

I also tell the story of the people involved. I explore the advocates campaigning for UMT, opponents who resisted the proposal, and uncommitted observers who sought to evaluate the plan's usefulness. In examining the origins and supporters of the UMT proposal, I focus on its strategic impetus. Certain individuals and groups saw UMT as a solution to the national security problems America faced at the time. Advocates touted strategic necessity, readiness, and deterrence as reasons UMT would benefit America. Throughout, it is important to ascertain the level of support for UMT that existed within the Roosevelt administration and compare that to the level of support given to UMT once Truman assumed the presidency. Determining whether UMT was simply a pet project of Truman's or whether it garnered broader support from military leaders, politicians, and others is important to establish the far-reaching significance of the issue at the time.

Opposed to supporters of UMT were individuals and groups who saw the proposal as creating more problems than it solved. Examples of reasons for opposition included increased militarization of American society, moral subversion of trainees, and weakening of labor unions and by extension the American economy as a whole. In addition, an unlikely group of dissenters appeared. Some military authorities themselves began to question the UMT proposal on practical grounds. They questioned its high costs and the tactical usefulness of the training to America's future national security in an era of increasingly complex military technology.

Overall, scrutinizing the varied reasons that some individuals and groups passionately supported or opposed UMT is vital for this book. It investigates not only why individuals and groups took certain stances on UMT but also how they communicated their support or opposition to others and to American society at large. In addition, it explores how these interested individuals and groups influenced the political process and their relative success at doing it. Overall, this book tells the accounts of military strategists, true believers in UMT, political opportunists who saw UMT as a means to other ends, critics who felt America was stronger without UMT, and the many observers who were not sure of the proposal's usefulness but saw the debate as vital nonetheless. The struggle that they engaged in over this important issue forms a crucial aspect of the overall story.

In this volume, I explore change over time not only in support for the UMT proposal but also change over time in the actual UMT proposal. One way to explore such change over time is to look at support for UMT across elections and evaluate any discernable changes in the actual proposal surrounding and especially following elections. As a result, I evaluate the impact of the 1946 midterm election on support for the UMT proposal and on the UMT proposal itself. The election shifted control of both houses of Congress to the Republican Party, which was clearly less supportive of President Truman's agenda. By analyzing the election, I evaluate domestic political concerns and how they impacted military policy formation in the postwar period.

Finally, I examine why the UMT proposal was not successful. Military leaders—including prominent ones, such as Marshall and Eisenhower—supported UMT to varying degrees. In addition, multiple special interest groups, such as the American Legion, the Veterans of Foreign Wars, and the Citizens Committee for UMT, strongly supported the proposal. President Truman also came to support UMT passionately. In addition to this backing—or perhaps because of it—the UMT proposal garnered significant popular support during the time period. Most poll numbers reveal public approval for UMT at the time consistently hovering around 65 to 70 percent.[6]

The high levels of popular advocacy flowed from two distinct sources. First, America's recent experience with World War II illustrated to many Americans the direct threat to American national security that even geographically remote countries could pose in the modern age. It seemed that the globe had shrunk and that America no longer could afford to ignore the problems of Europe or other strategic regions. In addition to these military issues, the perceived values and responsibilities of citizenship hit a crescendo during this period. Advocates of UMT often related the responsibilities of citizenship to military training. They urged UMT as not only a plan that would fortify American military power, but also one that would strengthen American society as a whole. In the end, these two factors—military concerns regarding recent World War II experience and the rising wave of citizenship sentimentality—were viewed as sufficient motivations to push UMT toward successful implementation. They were not. This book explores why that was the case.

In addition to filling a fundamental void in historical scholarship, this work is also important because it uses the specific context of the UMT debate to explore broader important questions about American military power and the place of the military within American society. It considers such important issues in three ways. First, it examines the proper balance between national security and individual liberty within American democracy. In the wake of World War II, most Americans undoubtedly agreed that their country had some basic national security needs. These same Americans probably also agreed that individual liberty was an essential fiber in their national character. However, individuals and groups disagreed vehemently regarding the proper balance of these two important concepts.

Second, the book surveys the place and role of military training within American society through the words and actions of various individuals and groups. Some groups—such as most army planners, veterans' groups, and some special interest groups—saw military training as eminently beneficial for both the individual and the nation at large. Other groups disagreed strongly. These groups included pacifists, most religious leaders, certain members of academia, leaders of labor unions, and even some military authorities. Pacifists argued that military training undermined the prospects of peace by militarizing the entire American population. They compared the UMT proposal to fascism and argued that military training was a necessary evil best reserved for imminent military threats. Religious leaders pointed out that military training undermined the morality of young men by placing them in training camps that festered with immorality. According to such critics, these youths were exposed to a myriad of tantalizing temptations in such environments and were far away from parental supervision and other forms of moral instruction. Many education leaders saw the UMT proposal as stifling college attendance. In addition, many argued that military training was less valuable to national security than a general education that resulted in a well-educated populace. Labor leaders feared that military training would sap the economy. These critics contended that by siphoning young workers away from the factories and towards the military camps, unions, the labor force, and ultimately the entire economy would suffer a slowdown. Finally, some military leaders came to see UMT as undesirable because the training that it would impart had little practical value. All of these groups voiced differing views of the place of military training in American society. This book investigates those views and why individuals held them.

Third, this book assesses the relationship between citizenship and military training within American democracy. Promoters of UMT continually and consistently touted military training as a civic duty. They drew a close connection between citizenship and soldiering. Opponents disagreed. They argued that citizenship was simply being used as a rhetorical and political tool to garner support for the UMT proposal. This book assesses the relationship between citizenship and military training from 1943 to 1948 and examines the differing views with regard to it. Overall, it uses the specific story of the campaign for UMT following World War II to illuminate some of these broad and important issues surrounding military power in American democracy.

In the end, the story of the campaign for UMT after World War II is a story about the best of intentions going awry. Army leaders diligently sought to enhance American national security but eventually became obsessed with their self-prescribed solution, UMT. This obsession paralyzed army strategic planning by fixating the gaze of senior army leaders on a distant prize that they would never obtain. In the hopes of achieving their crown, army planners marketed UMT, and eventually politicians joined the campaign, resulting in a metamorphosis. UMT evolved into something quite different from what it started out as. It became a panacea for all of the social ills of American society. Like snake-oil salesmen, politicians argued that it would cure the problems of public health, educate the illiterate, and ameliorate class distinctions. But all of this is to come. The story starts with the arrival of a prophet who converts the nonbelievers and makes disciples of them all.

2   The Spirit of 1920

Despite our very best efforts, we failed utterly in persuading the Senate that the universal military training should be included in the National Defense Act. The opposition to it was overwhelming. We had no chance. The comment most frequently heard in opposition to the provision was, "Oh, what's the use of imposing such an obligation upon young men in time of peace? There will never be another war." That was the spirit of 1920, as you may remember. Now, twenty years later, I find myself assuming the effort, this time with a better chance of success.
—James W. Wadsworth

I shall never forget one man of this group as he sat on his bunk just before marching to the train. He swore profusely. He cursed those in authority for allowing our country to be so unprepared. He accused them of being murderers for sending him into active service with no training. He wanted to know why they all had not had military training in peacetime so that if they must fight they would know how and stand some chance—an equal one—for their lives. . . . Therefore, universal service and compulsory military training is the only sane, safe, and humanitarian answer to our dilemma.
—Montana World War I veteran

The concept of UMT was not new. In fact, a similar idea had been widely discussed and partially implemented before, during, and shortly after World War I. It was known as the Plattsburg Movement, due to the location of one of its main training camps at Plattsburg, New York. Its ultimate theoretical goal was universal military training, and it provided for first students and then businessmen to attend voluntary training camps to receive basic military training. As the movement gained momentum, its leaders organized the Military Training Camps Association (MTCA). During World War I and immediately following, the MTCA interacted with policy makers to crusade for training camps and universal military training. One leader of the Plattsburg Movement was Maj. Gen. Leonard Wood, commanding general of the Department of the East and former army chief of staff. Wood held a steadfast philosophical commitment to preparedness. His staunchness presaged the same basic desire for preparedness that the leaders of the campaign for UMT following World War II held. Wood liked to say, "It is a great deal better to get ready for war and not have war, than it is to have war and not be ready for it." He proposed, "My personal opinion is we must eventually adopt some system not unlike the Swiss and the Australian, under which all of our youth, all of our men, will receive a basic military training which will make it possible for them to become, quickly, reasonably efficient soldiers." His aide-de-camp, Halstead Dorey, went even further, declaring, "Of course, anything short of universal training is from our point of view a make-shift."[1]

The leaders of the Plattsburg Movement were pragmatic. They often compromised their long-range theoretical goals in order to achieve tangible short-term victories. As a result, their focus tended to be on intermediate steps towards universal military training, such as voluntary training camps and federalizing the militia. In addition, there was a significant social difference why Wood felt that universal military training would be useful, as compared to the thoughts of his World War II successors. In addition to the military benefits, Wood suspected that it would help to "Americanize" the masses of immigrants reaching America's shores. He contended, "We are taking in enormous numbers of alien people. They come in racial groups, they live in racial groups and they go to racial schools and are fed by a dialect press. We native-born citizens have too little contact with them and do little to make them good citizens. I think some system of universal training would have a great influence in this direction." Such sentiments conveyed a specific historical context that existed in American society during the 1920s but was less relevant in the 1940s.[2]

Ultimately, the Plattsburg Movement failed in its attempt to secure UMT. There were several reasons for that failure, chief among them the general acceptance that World War I, although tragic, was so horrific that it served as a great deterrent to future war. It was the war to end all wars. This sentiment represented one aspect of "the spirit of 1920." As the *Washington Post* reported later, "Universal military service was widely discussed after the first world war, but failed to make much headway against the comfortable idea that there would not be another major war."[3] Even though they failed to achieve their ultimate goal of UMT, the leaders of the Plattsburg Movement ushered in a mindset shift among regular army officers. Serving under Wood was a younger generation of officers that interacted positively with the Plattsburgers and became converts to the goal of universal military training. Included in this younger generation of military officers were George C. Marshall and

George C. Marshall and John M. Palmer in General Marshall's office.
(Courtesy George C. Marshall Foundation, Lexington, Virginia)

John M. Palmer. There were also notable civilian converts of the Plattsburg Movement, such as Franklin D. Roosevelt, John J. McCloy, and
Robert P. Patterson. Eventually these men and others like them would
lead the campaign following World War II that sought to achieve many
of the same objectives that the Plattsburg Movement had pursued more
than twenty years earlier. This group represented the other aspect of "the
spirit of 1920." They saw in post–World War I America an opportunity
lost. They lamented what they argued was a lack of preparedness that
invited aggression. This context would inform their decisions as they
hoped to avoid the same "mistakes" following World War II.

Even with general similarities, though, it is important to note that
there were some major contextual differences between the Plattsburg

Movement and the campaign for UMT following World War II. First, the Plattsburg Movement was to some degree an aristocratic movement in which elites voluntarily participated in military training. Their goal was to attend military training primarily for the purposes of officer training. Their work paid dividends. Many of the Plattsburgers served as officers in World War I and greatly sped America's military mobilization for that conflict. In contrast, the campaign for UMT following World War II focused not on officer reserves, which were usually well manned, but on enlisted reserves, which were in constant disarray. The proponents of UMT following World War II sought a program that would be truly universal and democratic in scope in order to achieve maximum military preparedness. There were political differences as well. The Plattsburg Movement garnered most of its political support from the Republican Party. The push for UMT following World War II was supported mostly by the Democratic Party. Finally, the Plattsburg Movement had little support within the army or the administration. The Plattsburgers' strongest military ally, Wood, conflicted with Newton D. Baker, secretary of war. Baker eventually reassigned Wood. In addition, President Wilson did not support UMT. One major obstacle to UMT during the World War I era was the general acceptance among army officers of the views of Emory Upton. The senior leadership of the army still clung dogmatically to his philosophy that civilian soldiers were practically useless in war. A little background on Upton is instructive.[4]

Emory Upton had been an important personality in the army for many years. Born in 1839, Upton graduated in 1861 near the top of his class at West Point. His career during the American Civil War was a meteoric ascent. In four years, he advanced from a second lieutenant to a twenty-five-year-old brevet major general. Even though he commanded troops on the battlefield, Upton's ultimate impact on the army would be as a military theorist and reformer. He published several books on military organization, tactics, and policy. Although his writings on organization and tactics saw wide publication immediately, his final book, *The Military Policy of the United States,* went unpublished during his lifetime, which tragically ended by suicide in 1881. It was not until 1904, under the direction of Elihu Root, secretary of war, that *The Military Policy of the United States* was published and circulated widely throughout the army. In it, Upton argued that citizen soldiers performed poorly and were not reliable for the foundation of the army. Instead, professional soldiers should serve in the army in peacetime and lead the army in wartime. In time of war, citizens should be added to professional army units to serve under the guidance of professional officers. Upton's concept of a professional, expansible army dominated the thinking of senior army leaders prior to World War I. The experience of World War I, but especially World War II, altered the thinking of many younger professional army officers on this point and made UMT a more attractive military policy after World War II. This shift in officer thinking combined with the tremendous prestige army officers held as a result of victories in World War II to allow them more influence to advocate a plan that focused on citizen soldiers. As a result, the campaign for UMT following World War II was actually initiated by the army, even though the movement would also engender a great deal of tacit support within both the Roosevelt and the Truman administrations.

In addition to the Plattsburg Movement's overall context of voluntary military training in America, another effort immediately following World War I attempted to make UMT national policy in America. That effort was the passage of the National Defense Act of 1920. The campaign to pass UMT as part of the National Defense Act of 1920 announced the arrival of a key figure in the US Army's campaign for UMT: John M. Palmer. Palmer's military career began when he graduated from West Point in 1892. In June 1910 he graduated from the General Staff College at Fort Leavenworth, Kansas. A year later he became one of the first general staff officers in America. Shortly after his arrival in Washington, DC, the army chief of staff, Wood, assigned Palmer to work on a comprehensive plan to organize American land forces. Palmer applied himself to the project with zeal. His efforts produced an account entitled *Report on the Organization of the Land Forces of the United States.* Henry L. Stimson, secretary of war, published it in his annual report for 1912. In August of that year, Palmer fell victim to a curious new law that army slang referred to as the Manchu law. The Manchu law provided that any officer with less than two years' service with troops out of the past six years had to return to an active regiment. Since Palmer's tour at Leavenworth counted against him—this part of the law was later changed—his time in a staff position was up. In an ironic twist that only military orders could provide, the Manchu law ousted Palmer from Washington, DC, and sent him close to Manchuria for service with his regiment in Tientsin, North China. Late in 1915 Palmer returned from "exile" and was reassigned in early 1916 to General Staff duty in Washington, DC. Throughout 1916 he worked closely with the Military Training Camps Association on their push for UMT.[5]

Palmer's early work on UMT came to a screeching halt with the outbreak of World War I. In the spring of 1917, Gen. John J. Pershing selected Palmer as one of his assistant chiefs of staff, and the two of them set sail for Europe on May 27. Palmer served as first assistant chief of staff of the American Expeditionary Force (AEF) and later commanded an infantry brigade in the 29th Division in the Meusse-Argonne offensive in 1918. Following the armistice on November 11, 1918, General Pershing chose Palmer to fulfill a request for a General Staff officer to work on plans for a permanent national military system.[6]

Late in the summer of 1919, Palmer attended an important meeting that would connect two central figures in the campaign for UMT. It was a meeting of the Military Training Camps Association in the Willard Hotel in Washington, DC. The keynote speaker was James W. Wadsworth Jr., chairman of the Senate Military Committee. Wadsworth was the consummate politician. He devoted his entire life to issues of government, with national military policy standing out as his one true passion. Above all else, Wadsworth zealously advocated UMT. In many ways, his family background and varied political experience made him uniquely qualified to become the leading political proponent of a proposal that would have to transcend many obstacles if it were to succeed.

Wadsworth came from a leading family of Geneseo, New York. His great-grandfather, James Wadsworth, was born in Durham, Connecticut, and had graduated from Yale University in 1787. Following graduation, Great-grandfather Wadsworth had acquired large real estate holdings on the bank of the Genesee River in New York and had even traveled to Europe with the help of such notable public figures as Robert Morris, Aaron Burr, and Dewitt Clinton to promote investment in the American economy by European capitalists. From 1800 until his death in 1844, James Wadsworth was a community leader in Geneseo, New York, focusing his efforts on improving the education system and establishing a public library.

Senator Wadsworth's grandfather, James S. Wadsworth, garnered the family even more fame as a result of his military exploits in the American Civil War. Commissioned a brigadier general in the US Army, he became a brevet major general for his gallant actions at Gettysburg and during the Wilderness Campaign. The senator's father, James Wolcott Wadsworth Sr., was born in Philadelphia, Pennsylvania, in 1846 and by 1864 was serving on the staff of a major general in the Union Army. In 1875, James W. Wadsworth Sr. became supervisor of Geneseo, starting what would become a long political career. In 1878, he became a member of the New York General Assembly. Two years later he became comptroller of New York. Following that, he served two separate terms in the US House of Representatives, from 1881 to 1885 and again from 1901 to 1907.[7]

James Wolcott Wadsworth Jr. was born on August 12, 1877, in Geneseo. He graduated from Yale University in 1898. After graduation, he entered the family farming business. In 1902 he married Alice Hay, daughter of renowned American diplomat John Hay. In 1906, Jim launched his own political career, becoming first a member of the New York General Assembly and then eventually its speaker. In 1915 he transitioned to national politics with his election as a US senator from New York, and he served there until 1927. In 1933 he won election as a representative from New York in the US House of Representatives, where he served until 1951.[8]

Even though Palmer had never met Wadsworth before, the senator greatly impressed him. Wadsworth was forming a special subcommittee under his own direction with the intention of creating an improved permanent military system based on the feedback and recommendations of a wide range of military men, including enlisted men, junior officers, senior officers, professional soldiers, and citizen soldiers. On October 9, the subcommittee summoned Palmer to appear before it. The seven senators had been examining witnesses for several weeks and were little interested in Palmer's testimony until he surprised them with his answer that the proposed War Department military system was "not in harmony with the genius of American institutions." When asked to explain, he went through a detailed two-day exposition of his philosophy on military manpower policy, including a passionate appeal for UMT. The subcommittee liked his theory so well that they unanimously implored Wadsworth to write Newton D. Baker, secretary of war, and request that Palmer be reassigned from the General Staff to special duty with the Senate Military Committee as its military advisor. From then until the spring of 1920, Palmer worked relentlessly with Wadsworth on what was to become the National Defense Act of 1920.[9]

Although the act originally contained a strong provision for UMT,

Democratic opposition to UMT forced a last-minute revision eliminating UMT and replacing it with a weak provision for voluntary training. Even without UMT, the National Defense Act of 1920 provided an organizational framework for a citizen army and reorganized the National Guard and reserves. The act provided for the military training of all males between the ages of eighteen and twenty-one for a period of either four or six months. The supporters of UMT knew that such a short training period would be ineffective militarily but nevertheless planned to secure it as a foothold in order to solidify acceptance of the broad principle of UMT. Once this intermediate goal had been accomplished, they planned to lengthen the training "in order to make it reasonably effective in a military sense." Accordingly, supporters of UMT wrote the training provision into the law. Two things conspired against the military training provision in the National Defense Act of 1920. One was the mistaken notion that World War I was "the war to end all wars," and the other was partisan politics.[10]

Wadsworth highlighted the impact of World War I on the legislation. In a letter recalling the obstacles the National Defense Act of 1920 faced, Wadsworth singled out what he termed "the spirit of 1920" as insurmountable. As he wrote, "The comment most frequently heard in opposition to the provision was, 'Oh, what's the use of imposing such an obligation upon young men in time of peace? There will never be another war.'" The unprecedented nature of World War I, evidenced by the extremely high costs in terms of casualties, national debts, and broken militaries, led many to believe that such a thing could never happen again. UMT became unnecessary in a world hopeful that it had experienced its last war. Politics also played a role in defeating the universal military training provision of the National Defense Act of 1920. Wadsworth characterized the situation as "partisan in character with the minority united solidly against universal training and the majority sadly divided." In the face of these two major obstacles, the Senate Committee on Military Affairs dropped the military training provision to ensure passage of the remainder of the bill.[11]

At the heart of the UMT story was the longtime friendship and mutual respect of Palmer and Wadsworth. Throughout the campaign, Palmer provided the strategic rationale behind UMT, and Wadsworth orchestrated the political drive to achieve its enactment. But one particular event cemented their relationship and characterized the bond they shared for the remainder of their lives. That event can best be characterized as creation of "the Washington imperative." When Palmer discovered George Washington's *Sentiments of a Peace Establishment* in the Library of Congress, he argued that it was incontrovertible evidence that the campaign for UMT was simply the fulfillment of Washington's original design for American military policy. Palmer's interpretation delighted Wadsworth. His own relative, Congressman Jeremiah Wadsworth of Hartford, Connecticut, was Washington's commissary-general during the Revolutionary War. After the war, Jeremiah Wadsworth reported a bill from the Committee on Military Affairs that attempted to enact the reforms that Palmer was arguing were at the heart of Washington's military policy. As it turned out, amendments altered the bill so much that even its original sponsor, Jeremiah Wadsworth, eventually voted against it. Even so, the Washington imperative allowed Palmer to argue that UMT was simply the fulfillment of George Washington's original design, while at the same time it allowed Wadsworth to argue that he was simply attempting to enact the reforms that his forebear had so presciently attempted in 1790. As a result, the fates of the two men were welded into one common purpose from that moment on.[12]

Little attention was paid to military manpower policy throughout the interwar period. There was one exception to this general rule. Palmer was one of the earliest and most consistent proponents of UMT in America. In fact, he was both a prophet and a heretic within the army. He was a prophet because he had an evangelical zeal regarding UMT that he consistently preached throughout both army and government circles. He was a heretic because much of his philosophy regarding military manpower policy flew in the face of professional army dogma. Palmer spent most of the interwar period crystallizing his views on military manpower policy and promulgating them through his writings. Palmer was the intellectual heavyweight of the army. He had published numerous books, and most viewed him as an expert on military organization and history. He had direct access to the army chief of staff, and his views were taken seriously. His career had been long and varied. Although he wrote several books, his final and most complete work, *America in Arms,* distilled his decades of thinking with regards to military manpower policy. With it, Palmer intended to influence the debate over UMT that was heating up. The book also provided insight into Palmer's life and experiences and why he was able to exert such influence throughout the initial phases of the army's campaign for UMT.[13]

Understanding the US Army's campaign for UMT following World War II requires an understanding of Palmer's background and his early work on UMT. It also requires an appreciation of his philosophical views on military manpower policy and the context that hindered the acceptance of those views during World War I and the interwar period. That context had changed during World War II and in the immediate postwar period and allowed a widespread acceptance of Palmer's basic views throughout the senior leadership of the army by the end of his career. Palmer's core philosophy derived from his interpretation of the military policy of George Washington. He focused heavily on Washington's admonition to maintain a "respectably defensive posture." He also maintained a distinction between different types of military organization and their likelihood to either provoke or prevent war. He reasoned, "If war is a phase of human politics it is plain that there can be a war-provocative as well as a peace-conservative type of military organization." Palmer argued that preparedness was the best deterrent of war. Not only did preparedness help to prevent the human losses of warfare, but it also avoided what were in his eyes the unnecessary and vast costs of war. As he alleged, "Unreadiness for war has been the principal cause of all of our great national debts." Palmer maintained that adequate preparedness would prevent wars and as a result save countless lives and money.[14]

In *America in Arms,* Palmer's purpose was simple. First, he claimed that Washington's principal military policy was compulsory military training in time of peace. After establishing his premise, he explained, "how and why [Washington] was unable to persuade his countrymen to accept it; how their rejection of his advice affected their subsequent history; and finally how, after a century and a half, their descendants have at last been impelled to return to his guidance." Palmer based his work on a treatise on military policy that Washington wrote in 1783 entitled *Sentiments on a Peace Establishment.* Palmer argued that this document laid out four different premises clearly demonstrating Washington's preferred military organization for America. First, it argued for a small regular force. Second, it sought to create a well-organized militia. Third, it outlined the necessity of producing arsenals to equip the forces. Fourth, it proposed military academies to instruct the officers of those forces. Palmer claimed that it was Washington's intent to have a standing army that was no larger than necessary. Palmer acknowledged that a standing army was necessary, but only for those tasks that a citizen reserve could not accomplish. These included garrisoning bases, meeting sudden emergencies, and training the citizen reserve. He explained, "although [Washington] relied upon citizen soldiers for the general defense, he found that some professional soldiers were necessary. He therefore proposed enough professionals to do those things that manifestly could not be done by citizen soldiers. He wanted enough professional soldiers for these special purposes but no more. This was the crux of his military policy."[15]

Palmer argued that much of the misunderstanding about Washington's views regarding citizen soldiers emanated from the distinction between an ill-organized militia and an organized one. As Palmer clarified, "The explanation of this paradox is to be found in the fact that Washington had two kinds of militia in mind: one, the *ill-organized* militia that actually existed throughout the American states; the other a *well-organized* militia such as that of Switzerland which he praised." Palmer described the evolution of the militia starting all the way back with the *fyrd* established by Alfred the Great and followed its development through all of America's wars. Palmer professed that the main obstacle keeping America from achieving Washington's goal of a well-organized militia was a lack of training in peacetime. As Palmer noted, "There was nothing in the militia organization itself to produce either trained soldiers or trained leaders."[16]

Palmer blamed the failure of Washington's intended military policy on one factor, namely, the concept of an expansible standing army that emerged in December 1820 when John C. Calhoun, secretary of war, submitted his plan to Congress. That concept of an expansible standing army reached official orthodoxy later when Upton's *The Military Policy of the United States* was published. Palmer crystalized the difference clearly. He wrote sarcastically, "It will be seen that there was one marked difference between the 'old army's' military policy and Washington's. He wanted as many professional officers and soldiers as were strictly necessary—*and no more.* We disciples of Calhoun and Scott and Sherman wanted just as many as we could persuade Congress to give us. And we were perfectly sincere about it. We had been bred in the doctrine that citizen soldiers are worthless and that only professional soldiers are worth their salt."[17]

This institutional disdain throughout much of the regular army for citizen soldiers effectively stifled most efforts at organizing and training citizen soldiers in peacetime from 1820 until World War II. As Palmer reasoned, "On the basis of the facts so presented Upton's doctrine as to the military organization was accepted as the orthodox statement of the proper military policy for the United States." Following World War I, a younger generation of army officers softened on their commitment to Upton's expansible standing army and looked with hopeful favor on the ability of citizen soldiers to fight given the proper training. It was up to the younger army officers—men such as Palmer—to find another way. Palmer recalled, "I came away with another idea. If American citizen armies, extemporized after the outbreak of war, could do as well as Washington's Continentals and as well as the citizen armies of Grant and Lee, what might they not do if organized and trained in time of peace? This then should be the basis of our war expansion. Instead of expanding a standing army we should simply mobilize a preexisting citizen army and give it further training after mobilization."[18]

Palmer also held interesting sociological views on a citizen army. He believed that a citizen army based on universal military training in peacetime was a truly American army. Palmer insisted that the more emphasis that a society placed on professional military forces, the more access to advancement within the military became limited to only professional soldiers. He contended, "There will always be a place for professional soldiers such as Grant and Lee, Sherman and Stonewall Jackson and Pershing, but the door must not be closed to civic leaders with native military talent such as Washington and Greene, Andrew Jackson and John A. Logan. This is one of the essential foundations of the modern democratic state." Palmer deemed that if America relied on citizen soldiers to fight its major wars, but then mustered them out of the army as soon as the fighting ended, then it followed the same pattern as autocratic regimes such as Germany and Japan. If, on the other hand, America allowed citizen soldiers to advance up the ranks of the military based on merit, it could achieve a truly democratic military establishment.[19]

Palmer also believed that such a system was more effective militarily. By opening up advancement to a larger pool of citizen soldiers rather than just to career professional soldiers, more high-quality military leaders would surface and strengthen the American military establishment. As he reasoned, "It is one of the essential elements of maximum military might. While we wisely cherish the military leadership in our limited pool of professional officers, it would be folly to disregard the latent leadership in that vastly larger pool that comprises every able-bodied American citizen. We must draw from that larger pool if we are to develop the full military might of an unregimented modern democracy."[20]

On November 13, 1941, George C. Marshall, army chief of staff, recalled Palmer to active duty to serve as his primary staff officer on postwar military manpower policy and principal advocate of UMT. Palmer arrived in Washington, DC, and settled into a private office in the Library of Congress that he referred to as "my work shop."[21] Less than a month later, the Japanese attacked Pearl Harbor, and the attention of most army officers understandably shifted overseas.

Throughout 1942, Palmer quietly and diligently laid the groundwork for the US Army's campaign for UMT after World War II. He consulted with the National Guard Executive Committee on tentative plans for a reorganization of the National Guard. He worked with John H. Hilldring, assistant chief of staff, G-1 (Personnel), regarding postwar manpower issues. Throughout the year, he refined his ideas regarding postwar army organization. As he indicated to Marshall, "I am making some exploratory studies relating to future military policy that may be useful when you get through licking the Axis." Palmer further analyzed the previous efforts for UMT associated with the National Defense Act of 1920. He confided to Marshall that "The War Department's approach to Congress in those days gives some fine examples of 'How *not* to do it.'"[22]

Palmer helped establish the Postwar Planning Board on June 24, 1942. The board consisted of Palmer and seven members of the general staff, including the assistant chiefs of staff, G-1 and G-3 (Operations). Almost immediately, the board members found it difficult to conduct both wartime and postwar planning concurrently. As a result, they requested that Idwal H. Edwards, assistant chief of staff, G-3, create a new advisory body to steer "advance work on all problems relating to demobilization and postwar organization . . . as soon as practicable by a carefully selected group of officers free to give their entire time to them." The appeal spurred the formation of the Special Planning Division (SPD) led by William F. Tompkins. Palmer immediately and officially became its key advisor. His hopes for UMT were high. As he confessed to Marshall, "As you know, I am not a very prayerful man, but each day I find myself praying for our cause and for your great part in it."[23]

Palmer's recall to active duty set the stage for the beginning of the US Army's campaign for UMT after World War II. By early 1943 there was a prophet proselytizing throughout the War Department, convincing senior army officers of the merits of UMT and converting them into disciples. He had witnessed firsthand the Plattsburg Movement and had been a central figure in the failed effort to establish UMT in the National Defense Act of 1920. During the interwar period, he had created a body of literature that in effect overturned the previously dominant philosophy of Emory Upton and fostered increased acceptance of citizen soldiers by professional officers. Palmer had outlined the philosophical rationale behind UMT — both militarily and sociologically. His extensive contacts, both in the War Department and in Congress, had sown seeds in fertile soil. UMT was beginning to take root.

3   The Basis for All Plans

[Marshall's] directive, it was learned tonight, has just been issued as basic
policy for all officers planning the permanent post-war Army organization.
—*New York Times*

As a matter of fact, I have talked with the Secretary of War and with General
Marshall about these things several times. Also, I have spent considerable
periods of time with the members of a committee of the General Staff charged
with the duty of planning the future. All of these men are basing their plans
upon a system of universal military training.
—James W. Wadsworth

ven with Palmer's growing influence and continuous activity advocating UMT throughout the interwar period, he
achieved little in the way of actual results prior to World
War II. Without acceptance from the senior leadership of the
army, his views would have little impact. He would simply be
a prophet wandering in the desert. Palmer's longtime friendship with Marshall allowed Palmer's views access to the army's inner
sanctum. The two generals had been friends for over thirty-five years,
ever since Captain Palmer was president and Lieutenant Marshall was
secretary of the Service Schools Branch of the Infantry Association at
Fort Leavenworth. Their wives, Maude Palmer and Katherine Marshall,
were also close friends.[1]

Once Marshall recalled Palmer to active duty, a small group of officers began planning for the postwar era. As a result, 1943 marked
the beginning of official calls from the War Department for UMT after
World War II. Throughout the spring and summer of 1943, senior War
Department officials made public appeals urging UMT. In his address
to the Maryland Historical Society on March 9, Robert P. Patterson, undersecretary of war, formally called for a system of UMT following the
war. Representative Andrew J. May of Kentucky, chairman of the House
Committee on Military Affairs, announced on August 31 that he planned
to pursue legislative enactment of UMT. On January 14, 1944, Frank
Knox, secretary of the navy, formally advocated UMT in an address to
the Greater Cleveland Council of the Boy Scouts of America. On May
23, 1944, Brig. Gen. Walter L. Weible, director of military training in the
War Department, vigorously urged UMT. Palmer was ecstatic. A consen-

sus for UMT was beginning to take shape within the War Department. General agreement was not enough, though. What was needed was a mandate.[2]

Palmer set out to ensure that Marshall issued one. On August 3, 1944, he wrote Marshall. In the memorandum, he analyzed the failure of the National Defense Act of 1920 and attributed it primarily to aversion among senior army officers for citizen soldiers. Palmer noted the preference of senior army officers of the World War I era for a large professional standing army instead, and he contended that this collective mindset made it impossible back in 1920 to secure UMT or even more limited reforms such as a federalized National Guard. To Palmer, the solution was official direction. He called for a War Department circular signed by the chief of staff and approved by the secretary of war that would place UMT at the foundation of all army postwar planning. He argued that such a policy mandate would unify senior army officers' thought and overcome the internal objections that had paralyzed army reform after World War I and killed any chances of passing UMT then. As Palmer pleaded, "It therefore seems to me that all organizational plans should rest upon a general statement of policy fixing the proper place of the 'citizen' or reserve forces in our military system. Such a statement of policy, if approved by the Secretary of War and published for guidance of all concerned will tend to narrow down many divergent views on army organization." But Palmer went further than just seeking a narrowing down of views. He urged a policy statement that would create "the fundamental policy to be followed, without deviation, by all persons concerned in the preparation of plans for a post-war military establishment." He argued that such a policy mandate would become the basis for all plans and ensure a consistent approach by senior army planners.[3]

The rest of August saw a flurry of activity. On August 17, Henry L. Stimson, secretary of war, issued a call for UMT following the war. The following day, President Roosevelt put his own spin on the introduction of UMT. He indicated that his initial preference was for a youth training program similar to the old Civilian Conservation Corps (CCC) of the 1930s rather than a purely military training program. Although the President would remain opaque on UMT throughout the war until his death, his shifting of its rationale to a broader social program would foreshadow a similar role for later politicians more interested in UMT. On August 23, prominent civilians interested in preparedness measures, led by Archibald G. Thacher and with official War Department sanction, formed the Citizens Committee for Universal Military Training of Young Men. Stimson praised the committee's stated purpose: "to inform public opinion and to secure nationwide support in favor of the promotion of useful citizenship and the unity and security of the United States through a Federal system of universal military training." The formation of the committee launched a joint partnership between government officials, mostly in the army, and private civilians in campaigning for UMT.[4]

Palmer's memorandum succeeded. On August 25, 1944, Marshall signed War Department Circular No. 347, which made UMT the primary goal of the army's postwar military establishment. As Marshall informed his planners, "It is also assumed, for purposes of planning, that the Congress will enact (as the essential foundation of an effective national military organization), that every able-bodied young American shall be trained to defend his country; and that for a reasonable period after his training (unless he volunteers for services in the regular establishment of the armed forces) he shall be incorporated in a reserve all, or any necessary part of which, shall be subject to active military duty in the event of an emergency requiring reinforcement of the Regular Army." By issuing Circular No. 347, Marshall explicitly recognized UMT as the stated policy of the War Department and the primary strategic outlook of the US Army. Even though the general's circular contained four separate sections, Section III, entitled "Military Establishment," outlined the general principles of national military policy to govern the preparation of postwar plans. In it, Marshall made UMT the foundation of army postwar planning.[5]

Marshall listed four major advantages of a postwar military establishment based on UMT. First, such a system would not concentrate military leadership into a special and separate officer class. Second, the participation of all citizens in military training would serve to better inform public opinion regarding military policy. Third, a UMT-based military establishment would reduce the costs of the standing army to a minimum. Fourth, the system fit well with American democratic traditions due to its reliance on a small standing army and full civic participation in defense.[6]

Besides publicly announcing the expectation within the War Department that Congress would enact UMT "as the essential foundation of an effective national military organization," Marshall discussed military organization more specifically. He presented two types of military organizations, the "standing army type" and the "professional peace establishment (no larger than necessary to meet normal peacetime requirements) to be reinforced in time of emergency by organized units drawn from a citizen army reserve, effectively organized for this purpose in time of peace." He left no uncertainty about which type of military organization was appropriate for a democracy.[7]

Marshall characterized the "standing army type" of military organization as one that employed American citizens simply to fill the lower ranks of the military establishment. He criticized such a system in which "the function of the common citizen is ordinarily to be a private soldier or, at most, a noncommissioned officer in war. Reserve officers are drawn from the better educated classes but are generally employed in the lower grades and in subordinate capacities." Marshall was clear what the result of such a system would be. He contended that "under this system, leadership in war and the control of military preparations and policy in peacetime are concentrated largely and necessarily in a special class or caste of professional soldiers." The characterization was distinct. This type of military organization was better suited to authoritarian regimes and was less appropriate for democracies like America. As Marshall concluded, "This is the system of Germany and Japan." The reason such a system was not well suited to a democracy was simple. According to Marshall, "Under such a system only the brawn of a people is prepared for war, there being no adequate provision for developing the latent military leadership and genius of the people as a whole. It therefore has no place among the institutions of a modern democratic state based upon the conception of government by the people."[8]

In stark contrast to the problems inherent in the "standing army type" of organization, Marshall lauded the "citizen army reserve" and argued that such an approach held two distinct advantages over the standing army model that made it better suited to American democracy. The first was that it provided increased opportunities for leadership. As he boasted, "Its leadership is not exclusively concentrated in a professional soldier class. All citizen soldiers after their initial training are encouraged to develop their capacity for leadership to such an extent as may be consistent with their abilities, their tastes, and their civil obligations." No longer would citizen soldiers simply provide enlisted manpower to be led by the officers of the professional army during war. Instead, as members of the citizen army reserve they would be able to gain promotion based on ability and lead other citizen soldiers if conflict should emerge.[9]

The second advantage of the citizen army reserve was that it better educated the American populace about military issues. According to Marshall, "As a great majority of the leaders of the war army are included in the civil population in time of peace, an intelligent and widespread public opinion is provided as the basis for the determination of all public questions relating to military affairs." Marshall and Palmer argued that the universal nature of the proposed plan would better integrate American society with the American military and provide a common framework through which public discourse on military matters could be enhanced.[10]

As the heat of August slowly gave way to the cool, crisp air of September, senior army leaders publicly and privately announced that UMT was now the foundation of their postwar policy. Less than one week after signing Circular No. 347, Marshall publicly articulated his views on the postwar army. He revealed that a large professional army was not his preference. Instead, he sought UMT. He called for a postwar American Army that consisted of the smallest possible professional army backed up by trained citizen reserves. Marshall argued that a large standing army had "no place among the institutions of a modern democratic State." He communicated to reporters that Circular No. 347 would serve as "basic policy for all officers planning the permanent postwar Army organization." Following the issuance of such a mandate by Marshall, all army planners went about their respective tasks with the understanding that UMT was now the basis for a postwar army. Shortly after Marshall signed Circular No. 347 and issued it throughout the War Department, Palmer sent a confidential letter to Clifton A. Woodrum (D-VA), a key UMT supporter in the House of Representatives, outlining "the background and origin of the circular." Palmer revealed his behind-the-scenes role in pursuing such a policy mandate. He sought to provide Woodrum with some context on War Department policy, but he also urged Woodrum to "please keep my connection with this subject confidential. . . . So far as the War Department circular is concerned, it should be attributed solely to General Marshall."[11]

In addition to Marshall's reinforcing his policy with public statements, other key participants in the campaign for UMT also noticed the shift in the War Department. Wadsworth disclosed to his colleague Walt Horan, representative for the 5th District of Washington, that UMT was now official War Department policy. As he divulged to Horan,

> General Marshall's public statement to the effect that a large stand-ing professional Army will not do for this country and that we must always rely upon citizen soldiers, properly trained, has made it clear that the War Department does not intend to urge the maintenance of a vast professional establishment. As a matter of fact, I have talked with the Secretary of War and with General Marshall about these things several times. Also, I have spent considerable periods of time with the members of a committee of the General Staff charged with the duty of planning the future. All of these men are basing their plans upon a system of universal military training.[12]

Palmer immediately promulgated the significance of Marshall's cir-cular to a broader audience. He confided to Marshall, "Now that there is an official pronouncement of our national military policy, I think I can serve the cause best by writing one or two magazine articles" ar-ticulating to the general public Marshall's ardent support of UMT and its newfound status as official policy. The editors of the *Reader's Digest* wanted to publish Palmer's article, but he chose the *Saturday Evening Post* instead to attain "wide circulation." He considered the article "the most important and timely paper that I have ever written" and with it publicized the fact that the War Department now officially based its postwar policy on UMT.[13]

Palmer's theoretical conceptions of UMT could have been just a plan. As a result of his intellectual reputation, extensive publications, and close friendship with Marshall, they became *the* plan. Palmer's secret memorandum to Marshall distilled his views on military man-power and laid the basis for Circular No. 347. Marshall had issued a mandate throughout the army, and his acceptance of Palmer's views and his promulgation of them throughout the War Department con-verted the philosophical views of Palmer into official army orthodoxy. As a result, Marshall lifted UMT from a possible army policy for the postwar era to the army policy. His mandate in effect wagered all the army's chips on a bet that was anything but certain. Now that UMT was the plan, it was up to army leaders to explain the rationale behind it to the American public.

4   Target No. 1: USA

Our geographical position can no longer be considered as a protection. The development of long-range bombers, and of amphibious operations, has given a new character to warfare. If in the future we are attacked by a powerful enemy, or group of enemies, we may be sure that we will not be given the time to mobilize our industries and to extemporize an army from the untrained youth of the nation. If we wish to protect our nation and our democratic way of life, we must have a state of military preparedness which will enable us to take effective military action in the shortest possible time. This means that the youth of the nation must have had the great part of its military training before mobilization.

—Henry L. Stimson

If there is a World War III, any nation or alliance which hopes to topple Britain, China, France, Russia, and the United States can be counted on to read the lessons of World War I and World War II. Outstanding among those lessons will be: Hit the United States first, and as hard as possible. Do not give American producing power and war-willingness a chance to build up muscle for two or three years behind a protective screen of other fighting nations.

—*Collier's*

During the summer of 1944, Palmer sought to convert his philosophical ideas into concrete policy for the War Department. Marshall agreed and issued a clarion call to arms in the campaign for UMT. It was one thing to convince career army officers in the War Department of the need for UMT. Persuading the American public was something quite different. From the summer until the fall of 1944, military authorities introduced the American public to the strategic rationale behind UMT. Senior army leaders promulgated two principles as the basis for their postwar policy. First, they maintained that the strategic landscape had changed. The traditional reliance on geography and allies to protect America from attack was no longer realistic in the postwar era. Second, they argued that UMT was the answer. UMT would, for the first time in American history, create a trained General Reserve, a pool of manpower ready at a moment's notice. The creation of this General Reserve would shorten mobilization and thereby address the postwar strategic landscape. It would be with increasing focus that army leaders would fixate on UMT as the panacea for their problems.

Army leaders argued that the strategic landscape was different for several reasons. First, two widely recognized strategic factors that had kept America safe from devastation in the past no longer seemed fail-safe. These were America's geographic position and America's reliance on allies to fight the initial phases of conflict. There was growing concern among military planners that neither of these factors was as likely to prevent future attack as they had been in the past. Maj. Gen. Julian L. Schley, a highly regarded retired US Army officer, forcefully questioned the past assumptions that geography and allies would provide America the same safety shield behind which the American military could pre-pare for combat over a time period of months or even years. Although such assumptions had proven accurate in the past, Schley argued they "would be expecting too much of Providence" in the future. America's allies lay in smoldering ruins, and military technology was quickly shrinking the protection offered by vast oceans. Schley warned, "the world has been growing smaller at an ever increasing rate" and implied that the protection previously offered by geography was no longer the same bastion that it had previously been. Schley questioned reliance on geography and allies for future national security and instead urged novel approaches to the underlying issue of preparedness.[1]

Schley was not alone. Undersecretary of War Robert P. Patterson artic-ulated similar changes during an address at Norwich University in Ver-mont on August 6, 1944. The address was symbolic, as Norwich was the first university in America to weave military training into its curriculum as an integral fiber. Patterson contended that the time to prepare and mobilize in any future conflict would be greatly truncated, as advances in technology, especially aviation, would result in less geographic iso-lation. He advocated UMT as an appropriate solution, cautioning, "the bulwark of our security must rest on well-trained and equipped forces of a strength to command the respect of unfriendly nations. In my opinion we cannot maintain those forces and that necessary strength except by a system of universal military training for our youth." Others concurred. Palmer had already highlighted the role of air power in transforming the strategic landscape. He argued that the increased capabilities of modern air power eliminated a nation's ability to protect lines of communica-tions using a navy exclusively, as had traditionally been the case.[2]

Secretary of War Henry L. Stimson articulated his understanding of the postwar security environment to Archibald G. Thacher, a staunch preparedness advocate and confidant. Stimson confided, "The terrible lessons of this war should convince every thoughtful American that reasonable military preparedness is the only means by which the peace and security of the nation can be maintained." He characterized the postwar environment as quite dangerous, claiming, "The development of long-range bombers, and of amphibious operations, have given a new character to warfare." To Stimson, the rapid advances in military technology meant that American defense planners had much less time to respond to attack. As Stimson described a potential future attack, he warned, "We may be sure that we will not be given the time to mobilize our industries and to extemporize an army from the untrained youth of the nation." Stimson's conclusion was clear. He held that "our geographical position can no longer be considered as a protection." Stimson did not keep his views to himself. With his approval, Thacher ensured they were published quickly and disseminated widely.[3]

During the summer of 1944, leading American military authorities highlighted a growing sense of insecurity as they witnessed the speed and devastation of warfare that was being waged across the globe and contemplated the impact of it on the postwar environment. It seemed as though there were no limits to the increase in lethality that warfare was undergoing. Such drastic changes resulted in a dilemma for leaders attempting to defend against them.

By the fall of 1944, senior leaders within the army settled on UMT as the appropriate response to such changed strategic conditions. They decided that the only effective UMT program would have to be one year long and continuous in nature. By setting these two criteria rigidly, senior army leaders initially maintained that they only wanted a UMT program that would be effective militarily. It seemed at first that any watered-down version would be worse than nothing at all. On November 16, Maj. Gen. Ray E. Porter, director of Special Planning Division (SPD), informed the National Defense Committee of the American Legion that the one continuous year was a must. Porter outlined the steadfast position of the War Department and the reasons for it. As Porter informed them, "Effective preparation for combat must constitute the basis of our training schedules." The desire of senior army leaders to base any UMT plan directly on their own mobilization calculations meant that one continuous year of training was the only logical solution. As Porter stated, "Today we say with that complete assurance which is only possible after long testing and successful achievement that our Mobilization Training Program for new units is the only thoroughly sound program for Universal Military Training and that the time required for its completion is the absolutely minimum time in which units can be adequately trained for combat. The total time required to complete satisfactorily the five phases of training under our Mobilization Training Program for new units is fifty-two (52) weeks."[4]

Three weeks later, the General Staff formalized their postwar military insecurity and made mobilization and by extension UMT the solution to their angst. The assistant chief of staff, G-3, announced, "We now have two theme sentences for an appropriate presentation to the American people." The first sentence highlighted the military insecurity that drove postwar planning. It declared, "America will probably be the initial objective of the aggressors in any next war and the first engagements of that war will quite possibly be fought in our own homeland." The prospect of war coming to America was frightening indeed. In response, the General Staff had a solution: UMT. The second sentence contended, "Universal Military Training is absolutely essential in any practicable plan that can be considered adequate to insure the future security of our Nation." The General Staff also remained adamant that UMT would only prove useful if it were designed to improve mobilization. Idwal H. Edwards, assistant chief of staff, G-3, claimed such a requirement would take a year, based on the MTP. He warned, "We know that if we devote less time to the training of men who are to constitute units ready for combat, we shall be guilty of sending those men to battle without an average chance of survival and success."[5]

A better explanation for the army's insistence on one continuous year came less than two weeks later when Brig. Gen. Joseph S. Bradley, chief of the War Department Training Group, distilled army views in a planning document entitled "A Year with the Army."[6] Bradley spelled out the reasoning behind the army's requirement that the training be a full year, why it should be continuous, and why the army did not want it to be conducted on college campuses. He contended that the training had to be one year because it was unit training as opposed to replacement training. He maintained that all five contemplated training phases—individual, specialist, small unit, large unit, and combined arms exercises—had to be conducted in order for the training to be effective militarily. Second, Bradley insisted that the training had to be continuous, because processing trainees into and out of the program only once would lead to less interruption and maximize efficiency.

Finally, he maintained that the training should not take place at colleges for several reasons. Logistically, colleges lacked the large training facilities and the diverse training aids required—especially for live-fire, maneuver, and combined arms training. In addition, Bradley asserted that the training should be separate from colleges to ensure that ROTC would finally be improved to focus on officer training as opposed to basic military training. As he boasted, "With Universal Military Training completed prior to the enrollment of students in college, we shall be able for the first time to raise the Reserve Officers Training Corps courses to a real university level. Basic subjects will be eliminated. The more advanced and theoretical military subjects will be adequately presented. The graduates of the Reserve Officers Training Corps will then constitute a more competent group of junior leaders than ever have been available to the reserve components of our Army." Bradley asserted that carrying out UMT on college campuses would hurt the goals of military preparedness and educational development alike. He insisted that putting the two pursuits—military training and civilian education—under one program would inevitably lead to one of them dominating the other. To Bradley, whichever pursuit won the contest, the overall result would be negative for both. Each of them would be distracted from their primary goal due to the requirements of their secondary mission.[7]

Such military insecurity was not only evident among military thinkers. A more dramatic rendition of the same basic concerns appeared in popular magazines such as *Collier's*. In apocalyptic prose, the article entitled "Target No. 1: USA" warned, "If there is a World War III, any nation or alliance which hopes to topple Britain, China, France, Russia, and the United States can be counted on to read the lessons of World War I and World War II. Outstanding among those lessons will be: Hit the United States first, and as hard as possible. Do not give American producing power and war-willingness a chance to build up muscle for two or three years behind a protective screen of other fighting nations."[8] Insecurity regarding the military position of the United States was excellent tinder for those seeking to ignite a fire of public support for building up preparedness measures, chief among them UMT.

Perhaps the most compelling and nuanced explanation of the mobilization plan under UMT was presented to the Committee on Military

Affairs by Maj. Gen. Ray E. Porter, director, Special Planning Division. He had served for over a year as assistant chief of staff, G-3, for the largest army corps in 1940. His corps was the only one composed entirely of National Guard units, making him a recognized authority on the National Guard. Porter had also served as chief of staff of the 38th Infantry Division and as assistant division commander of the 34th Infantry Division. His impressive war record made him a formidable expert on both military training and the National Guard.

Porter painted a vivid picture of the mobilization benefits under UMT. He claimed that the National Guard could not be combat effective in a future war "without approximately a year of additional training after the Guard is called into Federal service." Porter highlighted three reasons why not. First, he revealed that "the guardsman receives less than three months of actual training during an enlistment of three years." Sensing that some opponents of UMT might simply recommend increasing the training requirement for the National Guard as the solution, Porter identified the problem with doing so. He reasoned that increasing the training requirement would certainly cause National Guard units to lose the "busier men." As a result, the National Guard "would lose a priceless asset—its superior personnel." Second, Porter indicated that the National Guard had an organizational "inadequacy of training facilities." He contended that National Guard training facilities were not large enough, lacked adequate firing ranges, and did not have the appropriate training aids to complete a comprehensive training program at their own facilities. Third, he maintained that National Guard units presented an inherent "impracticability of providing combined training." The limitation to Porter was one of geographical separation. As he asserted, "the unavoidable isolation of National Guard units from units of other arms and services precludes this absolutely essential combined training."[9]

Porter related the problem directly to the lack of a General Reserve. Without one, the United States would always face manpower problems during mobilization. As Porter explained,

> We have always conceived of the Regular Army and National Guard as forces which in event of war could be rapidly expanded to a material extent without loss of efficiency. However, such a concept has never been practical of execution, since there has never been a General Reserve of trained manpower from which to draw the personnel

required to effect the expansion. Quite to the contrary, in past wars it has been necessary to delay repeatedly the readiness of the Regular Army and National Guard by withdrawing from those components their best trained men to provide trainer personnel and cadres for the newly activated reserve units composed exclusively of wholly untrained inductees. In any future war such a practice may prove disastrous.[10]

Porter argued that with UMT, the United States would have an effective General Reserve for the first time in its history. Porter insisted that UMT would produce a pool of trained manpower that would in turn create a General Reserve. An effective General Reserve would serve three functions: It would provide trained manpower to fill out and activate the Organized Reserves units, it would provide the trained manpower to expand both the Regular Army and the National Guard in an emergency, and it would provide a pool of trained replacements for early casualties incurred in war.

Porter articulated two additional benefits of UMT to mobilization plans. First, he claimed that UMT would correct the training deficiencies of the National Guard. As he declared, UMT would "provide well-trained personnel from which the National Guard and the fully manned and equipped organizations of the Organized Reserves would recruit their enlisted personnel."[11] In doing so, UMT would relieve the National Guard of providing the bulk of training to its personnel. Eased of this burden, the National Guard units could simply provide refresher training to maintain and refine skills. To military professionals such as Porter, the result would be ideal, because it would marry the limited training resources of the National Guard—time, facilities, and equipment—with a more limited training mission. The National Guard would no longer have to hone completely raw recruits. With UMT enacted, they could instead polish recruits who had already received a year of basic military training.

Porter also asserted that, in addition to having a positive impact on the National Guard, UMT would elevate the effectiveness of existing officer programs. He maintained that UMT would "provide realistic and effective fundamental military training for Reserve Officers Training Corps students and other officer candidates prior to their entering officer training."[12] The result would be two distinct benefits to officer candidates. First, all officer candidates—including those from ROTC, OCS, and the service academies—would be required to participate in UMT. As a result, all future officers, both within the regular forces and within the reserves, would have to serve a year of basic military training as enlisted men. Porter believed that these officers would then have a better understanding of their men and a higher capacity for leadership. Second, Porter claimed that UMT, in addition to providing officer candidates some perspective on their future troops, would allow more advanced study at officer venues. All the officer candidates would have completed a year of military training and would not need to start with the basics upon arrival at their officer training program. They could focus their energies on learning how to lead men in combat rather than learning how to right face or salute.

Porter also presented an interesting notion. He discussed the relationship of UMT to civil defense. Porter argued that the older men most removed from their training as well as those accepted to UMT but physically unqualified for service could use their training in an enhanced civil defense role. As Porter envisioned, "Graduates of Universal Military Training who had passed military age would, in themselves, provide an invaluable nucleus about which to organize the defense of a community or an industrial center. If the Congress provides for the induction of men not physically fit for military service, it is our plan to give such men intensive training in all phases of civilian defense."[13]

Porter's conception of the civil defense benefits of UMT for physically disqualified trainees foreshadowed what would become an important question. During World War II, roughly one out of every three draftees was rejected from military service for physical or mental deficiencies. As a result of this experience, army planners would have to address how their UMT plan would handle individuals who were physically disqualified from actual military service. Some, such as Porter, saw military uses for such individuals. Others wanted to avoid the issue altogether by training only those fit for traditional military service. The debate would continue until more concrete plans for UMT could be formed.

From the summer until the fall of 1944, leading army authorities highlighted the strategic rationale behind their plans for UMT. They argued that America was vulnerable in ways previously unimaginable. Traditional inherent defenses of geographic position and reliance on allies no longer afforded the same protection. Their solution was UMT. Only through the creation of a General Reserve could the United States mobilize in the manner required in a potential future conflict. Anything else would be risking the safety of the United States. A traditional lengthy mobilization would take far too long given the probable speed with which conflict would come. Now that they had laid their strategic foundation, army leaders began marketing UMT nationwide.

5   Preaching the Gospel

Last summer War Department Circular 347, 1944, outlined the position of
the War Department on the question of Universal Military Training. The
Secretary of War and the Chief of Staff consider it a project secondary only to
winning the war. We have had public relations officers and service command
representatives in here orienting them, so that they could "preach the gospel"
before the public.
—Walter L. Weible

You recall that, when Nehemiah was rebuilding the walls of Jerusalem, his
adversaries conspired against the builders saying "they shall not know,
neither see till we come into the midst of them and slay them and cause the
work to cease." So it may be with us in the years of our building. Our one hope
of completing the structure of peace will be that, like the Jews of old, "the
builders every one had his sword girded by his side."
—Harold W. Kent

By the fall of 1944, senior army leaders revealed a general
sense of insecurity regarding the defense of the United
States. They had publicized the rationale for UMT to the
American public using foreboding language. As their anxi-
ety regarding the postwar security environment increased,
so too did their calls for UMT. It became the salve for their
fears of vulnerability in the postwar era. As a result, the senior leadership
of the army embarked on a serious and sustained marketing effort to
convince the American public and Congress of the merits of UMT. The
job of promoting UMT fell primarily to John J. McCloy, under secretary
of war. Some background on McCloy is important. In World War I, Mc-
Cloy served as captain of field artillery with the American Expeditionary
Force (AEF), and after the war he worked in the legal firm of Cravath,
de Gersdorff, Swaine & Wood of New York City. He participated directly
in the Plattsburg Movement and was a true believer in UMT. McCloy's
assistant in the UMT campaign was Maj. Gen. Walter L. Weible, director
of Military Training.[1]

The campaign began with speed and vigor. The first step for Mc-
Cloy and Weible was to publicize UMT. In order to do so, they took the
campaign to the airwaves. They launched the opening salvo on September 12, 1944. On that evening from the famous Shoreham Hotel in
Washington, DC, two well-known proponents of UMT made their case

Under Secretary of War John J. McCloy, February 19, 1945.
(Courtesy George C. Marshall Foundation, Lexington, Virginia)

vigorously on a radio broadcast that reached the nation. The *American Forum of the Air,* as it was called, had been broadcasting weekly radio shows on important topics for more than sixteen years. The broadcast that night highlighted to the nation the rationale for UMT. James W. Wadsworth, Republican congressman from New York, and Warren H. Atherton, national commander of the American Legion, both presented a strong case for UMT. In opposition, Norman Thomas, socialist candidate for president, and Dr. Broadus Mitchell, chairman of the Committee against Postwar Conscription of the Postwar World Council, and acting chairman of the council, spotlighted what they saw as serious problems with such a plan. The moderator put the issue to the nation and the participants succinctly: "Once the world is at peace, what kind of an Army should America have? General Marshall, our Chief of Staff, last week proposed to Congress a small professional Army, supplemented by a large civilian reserve. The General would base this reserve on universal training for every able-bodied young American. Who would serve, for how long, at what age—these are among the questions left for Congress, and the people, to answer.

The basic issue is 'SHOULD WE HAVE UNIVERSAL MILITARY TRAINING IN PEACETIME?'"[2]

The ensuing debate was lively and contentious. Wadsworth presented the standard War Department rationale for UMT. This included the basic preparedness arguments based on mobilization and readiness. Atherton presented a more individual justification of UMT well suited to the leader of a veterans' organization. Atherton insisted that if America was going to rely on citizen soldiers during wartime—few contested this claim—it was the responsibility of American military leaders to ensure their safety through adequate training. As he put it, "In every war, the seven of them this nation has had to fight, we have relied upon the common citizen. We have asked him to go out and die without training; to spread his limbs and his blood all over the battlefields without giving him an equal chance with the enemy he has had to fight. We are still for reliance upon that citizen, but we are for giving him an equal chance to prepare himself."[3] Atherton's case was a pragmatic one based on the responsibilities of American military leaders to provide adequate training—especially for citizen soldiers who were not volunteers but instead draftees.

The course of the debate soon departed from the details and benefits of the proposal to the criticisms of it. Norman Thomas argued that UMT would lead to an arms race benefiting no one. He cautioned, "In short, what I think you are proposing is a competitive armament, because if we go in for it every nation will." Thomas reasoned that the resulting arms race would be more expensive and more comprehensive than the officials in the War Department admitted. As he feared, in addition to the basic program to train American youth, "we will also have to have the most modern arms and a very large standing force to train them and to take care of military experimentation." In the eyes of a doubting Thomas, UMT would be only the beginning. It would by its very nature necessitate higher expenditures on arms for the trainees and larger numbers of officers and noncommissioned officers of the Regular Army to train them. In addition, Thomas cautioned that UMT would also be disruptive of the emerging world order. He warned that UMT would only serve to antagonize the partners that the United States would need in order to secure the postwar peace. He declared, "I do know that what you gentlemen are proposing is a race in arms, in armament, not primarily with the defeated enemy, who will be disarmed, but with our present allies." To Thomas, the only logical target of such a vast military preparedness measure was the Soviet Union. America's most recent enemies Germany, Japan, and Italy—not to mention American allies Britain and France—were in ruins with no chance of resurgence for years to come. Thomas presented what would become a major criticism of UMT, namely, "Who are we arming against?" Overall, Thomas characterized UMT as "the American reversal of the American position" by essentially claiming that it overturned the American tradition against conscription, a tradition that had drawn many immigrants to its shores.[4]

Mitchell presented a different but no less scathing line of criticism. His attack on UMT was two-pronged. First, he presented the dichotomy between preparing for war and preparing for peace. Instead of preparedness measures such as UMT, Mitchell pressed for more international cooperation: "It seems to me that unless we have learned that we must not accept a fatalistic attitude but must consciously concert means of preventing war by excellent international and national institutions, then we have nothing to look forward to but a dreary prospect of recurrent slaughter." He highlighted the optimism that many Americans held for the prospects of a true and lasting peace through the nascent United Nations organization.[5]

Mitchell did not base his critique solely on internationalism. He also indicated important domestic criticisms of UMT. When addressing Wadsworth's characterization of UMT as "a school of democracy," Mitchell reminded the audience of the flaws with such a view. As he vented, "May I remind you that we are now fighting a war for democracy with a Jim

Crow army; that we are segregating Negroes from other American citizens; that our Negro citizens are not admitted to some branches of our service at all; particularly the Navy has been reluctant to allow full rights to Negroes in combat duty. One has never thought of an army as a place to teach democracy; rather that is the business of our excellent school system."[6] Overall, the initial national debate on UMT left the War Department's marketing efforts in limbo. Certainly the radio broadcast had garnered much needed publicity for the plan. But the contentious debate had also revealed weaknesses in the plan that Thomas and Mitchell exploited successfully. What McCloy and Weible desperately needed was more clarity in their presentation and more high-level support in their campaign.

McCloy was up to the task. At the end of November, he participated in the University of Chicago Round Table. The National Broadcasting Company transmitted the event on November 26. The subject matter was similar to that of the earlier presentation and asked the same fundamental question: "Should We Have Universal Military Training in Peacetime?" In addition to McCloy, participants included Robert M. Hutchins, Chancellor of the University of Chicago, and Floyd Reeves. McCloy's appearance was significant for two reasons. First, his position gave official War Department sanction to the UMT publicity crusade. It clearly illustrated to the public that senior War Department officials wanted this program and were willing to campaign for it. Second, McCloy attacked the line of reasoning that UMT would hurt the US position in international negotiations regarding a United Nations organization. He informed the audience, "Of course, the developments which are now taking place in world organization are going to have a very important effect upon the condition of the world as we find it after this war. But I submit that it would be very foolish of us to disarm now in the hope that, some time in the future, the world organization might be of sufficient vigor and effectiveness to enable us to do away with universal military training or some system of national security entirely."[7]

After the traditional back and forth of debate, Hutchins summed up the overall theme of the debate for listeners across the country. All three participants agreed that "this subject is of first importance and requires extensive discussion." The main disagreement that resulted from the debate was not whether the issue was important, but rather when the issue should be decided. McCloy felt that action should be taken immediately in order to make an international organization more effective. Hutchins and Reeves disagreed and felt that "action should be postponed until the shape of the international organization is clear." During the debate, McCloy successfully presented his case. He articulated a clearer and more reasoned explanation than Wadsworth and Atherton achieved in the earlier debate. He was also able to overcome the objection that many cited regarding waiting for the United Nations to mature before taking any action.[8]

While McCloy personally launched an offensive on the airwaves, he also increased the involvement of other War Department personnel in the publicity campaign. On November 28, McCloy tasked the director of the Bureau of Public Relations (BPR) within the War Department with providing "complete coverage of all publicity relating to Universal Military Training originating in agencies other than the War Department and that such coverage and the analyses thereof be made available to this office weekly."[9]

One critical component of the War Department's marketing effort was to manufacture citizen interest in the subject. McCloy and Weible hoped that doing so would generate appeals to Congress for UMT from people outside the War Department. If done properly, McCloy and Weible could remove themselves from direct appeals to Congress and instead point to the support for UMT from citizens' groups. They could thereby reduce the risk of generating negative publicity for the War Department. The origins of this effort were fascinating. The story began with one Lt. Col. Jay Cooke, an infantry officer, who was set to retire from active duty on November 29, 1944. McCloy pegged Cooke to be the point man for the War Department's efforts to run a citizen group to advocate UMT. When Cooke's retirement ran into complications, McCloy stepped in directly to expedite the transition. As Weible wrote to Army Surgeon General Norman T. Kirk,

> The Assistant Secretary of War, Mr. McCloy, is very anxious to have Colonel Cooke separated from the service, either by retirement or discharge, in order that he may undertake certain duties important to the War Department. It appears from this telegram that there is much confusion on the subject. It was intended that Colonel Cooke's case would be disposed of by Valley Forge Hospital in the Third Service Command, and I have contacted General Hayes, Commanding

General of the Third Service Command, in order to expedite the matter.

It is requested that you take all possible steps from your office to, also, expedite this matter, as it has now dragged along for about a month. Would you kindly inform me as to what steps can be taken to expedite Colonel Cooke's separation from the service.

Such high-level attention yielded speedy results. Cooke appeared before the retiring board at Valley Forge General Hospital the same day and was recommended for retirement. A process that had dragged on for almost a month came to a conclusion within two short days.[10]

Now that Cooke was officially separated from active duty, he commenced setting up the civilian apparatus necessary to promote UMT from outside the War Department. He maintained weekly communication with Weible to strategize on the promotion of UMT. Within two weeks, Cooke informed Weible "I am starting in as of today on the work of the Citizens Committee and, for awhile at least, will be in New York a good part of the time." Cooke also requested priority status for both transportation and gasoline in executing his activities. In response, Weible immediately sent a handwritten memo to his primary assistant, Lt. Col. Harold W. Kent, ordering him to solve Cooke's transportation problems so that Cooke could focus on promoting UMT. Cooke first surveyed views of education leaders regarding UMT in hopes of both converting the nonbelievers and identifying the apostates. Within two days, Cooke met with Thomas S. Gates, president of the University of Pennsylvania, and "found him to be 100% in favor of UMT and ready to do anything to help." More important, Cooke garnered information from Gates concerning some highly influential foes of UMT. As Cooke recalled, Gates said that "in his opinion both Conant of Harvard and Dodds of Princeton would reverse their present stand (against) *if the President would declare that UMT was necessary for national security.* That one I'll leave to you, but I do believe that the theme of 'national security' is the most telling argument of all."[11]

After meeting with key education leaders in December, Cooke congregated with leading religious leaders in January. In recounting a Friday night meeting between himself, Archibald G. Thacher, chairman of the board for the Citizens Committee, and Archbishop O'Hara, Cooke relayed to Weible that the main opposition to UMT by leaders of the Catholic church derived from the perceived impact of the program on social mores. Cooke recalled, "We found that the main opposition to U.M.T. as voiced by the Archbishop, was based on the present handling of sex hygiene education in the Army and Navy, and the issue—sometimes forced—of contraceptives to men going on pass or furlough." Cooke declared that the "true cause for the opposition of the Catholic hierarchy" was the issue of birth control. Archbishop O'Hara complained to Cooke that current War Department figures for venereal disease were approximately forty-six out of one thousand soldiers, an unacceptably high rate that indicated a social laxness on the part of the army. Recalling that in his infantry division one out of one thousand was considered by the officers to be a high affliction ratio, Cooke doubted the accuracy of the archbishop's data. He suggested that Weible provide the "correct Army and Navy figures" to the archbishop. Cooke's overall recommendation was "that a definition of policy as regards to the handling of the sex hygiene situation among post-war trainees might improve the situation with the Catholic church. The only way that I can think of to crystallize the post-war plan would be to have a meeting of minds between the Chief of Chaplains, the Surgeon General and training sections of the War and Navy Departments." Weible immediately scribbled a handwritten memo to Kent to obtain the information on venereal disease cases.[12]

Cooke continued to operate at a feverish pace throughout February. He worked closely with Keith Morgan, the chief of the Management Branch, Industrial Relations Division, War Department, on a thirty-minute movie portrayal of the proposed UMT program. Morgan had traveled extensively giving presentations of army programs to both industry and labor leaders. In many ways, Morgan filled the official War Department role that corresponded to Cooke's unofficial role outside of the War Department. Morgan wanted to base the movie on the brochure entitled *The War Department's Views on Universal Military Training,* that was being composed. The ultimate goal of the movie was to "show the value of such training to parents and to the youngsters themselves." Morgan felt that if the movie were done properly and exhibited widely, then "many will say, 'I wish I could take a year off and get that experience.'"[13]

In addition to collaborating with Weible on marketing UMT, Cooke solidified his organization throughout February. By the end of the month, the Citizens Committee was formally incorporated with a clear mission. As the certificate of Incorporation and bylaws stated, "The purpose for which it is to be formed is: To assure the Security of the United States by promoting a sound military policy based upon the democratic obligation of all male citizens of a free State to be trained in arms to defend their country."[14] By the end of February, Cooke presided over a special-interest group that sought to influence military policy by advocating military preparedness and by sponsoring UMT legislation.

At the same time, Cooke turned his attention towards the publishing arena. Attacks on UMT were beginning to surface that if unanswered could prove fatal. On February 19, Weible informed Cooke of an opportunity to exploit on the editorial battlefield. Weible had learned that *Life* was interested in publishing a piece on UMT. There were two possible writers for the article, a Mr. Butterfield, whose "article would probably be favorable," and a Mr. Chamberlain, whose article "promised to be unfavorable." Weible felt strongly that if Mr. Butterfield's article were published first, then "Mr. [Henry R.] Luce would thereupon decide not to publish the other article and might thereby determine that the policy of his magazine would be generally favorable to the proposal." Weible implored Cooke to take action. He felt that Cooke could influence Luce and as a result secure a victory in the battle for public opinion. As Weible reminded Cooke, "This is an important medium in forming opinion and active, positive support of our principles will be a genuine help."[15]

The next day, Weible warned Cooke about another possible problem. It involved the Fifteenth Annual Debate Handbook. Weible suspected that a pamphlet by Sterling E. Edmonds, distributed by a group known as The Jeffersonians, based in Saint Louis, Missouri, might be included in the debate handbook. He feared that the inclusion of the pamphlet in the handbook would be a blow to his cause. As he relayed to Cooke, "The pamphlet is a strong statement of opposition to our proposal for Universal Military Training." Weible suggested that Cooke obtain a copy of the pamphlet and "see if there is some action which you can initiate that might serve to counteract the influence which this material may obtain."[16]

A little more than a week later, a significant opponent of UMT prepared to unleash another editorial broadside. Weible had obtained an advance proof of Hanson W. Baldwin's article for *Harper's* that promised to be published shortly. Baldwin was longtime military correspondent for the *New York Times* and one of the most influential American military commentators of the era. He was a Baltimore native, a 1924 graduate of the US Naval Academy, author of eighteen books and a plethora of articles, and winner of the Pulitzer Prize in 1943 for his compelling series about Guadalcanal. His views on military issues were respected and taken seriously. Any criticism he launched at UMT would have a direct impact. On March 2, Weible sent the proof to Cooke with specific instructions. Weible considered Baldwin's piece "a document with possible serious implications" and bemoaned his feeling that "Baldwin has never been too fond of the Army and is himself an Annapolis graduate." Weible's marching orders to Cooke were clear: Launch a counterattack—now! As Weible urged, "I think you ought to seek the immediate assistance of some outstanding writer and see if an article can't be handled by *Harper's* in the next issue. This requires action because their final deadline date is probably close at hand." Weible suggested Fletcher Pratt as a possible writer, "inasmuch as he has supported Universal Military Training and is himself a retired officer from the Navy."[17]

Throughout the remainder of March, Cooke turned his attention to solidifying his organization and recruiting personnel to fill out its structure. Weible coordinated visits for Cooke to all of the commanding generals of the Service Commands. Weible indicated that their responses promised that Cooke would receive "a cordial welcome," since he came with the explicit approval of the War Department. In addition, Weible passed along the names of certain individuals whom he felt would be effective in Cooke's organization.[18]

In addition to Cooke's efforts, Weible also increased his own publicity efforts. He contacted semiofficial army journals and encouraged them to provide ample coverage for the War Department's views on UMT. Weible wrote to fifteen of the editors of leading army journals requesting that they begin "stressing in the future issues of your publication, either editorially or through featured articles, the subject of Universal Military Training. I would like to urge strongly that you use your considered judgment in making an emphatic affirmative approach to this matter. Any assistance that you can render in informing your readers of this subject will be deeply appreciated."[19]

In addition to using trade publications to cement internal army support for UMT, Weible also wanted BPR to keep close tabs on resistance to the campaign. He tasked BPR to keep him informed of individuals, publications, and institutions "opposed to the program" and mandated that these updates occur "at not less than weekly intervals." The reason for Weible's interest in this information was simple. He wanted to know who opposed UMT so that War Department officials could contact them and plead their case. As one memo reported, "It is planned to utilize this report as a basis of contacting those parties opposed to the program, for the purpose of endeavoring to persuade them to change their opinions." Interestingly, War Department officials would not contact them directly. Army officers would merely gather the intelligence on the opposition, analyze it, and then pass it on to civilian groups such as the Citizens Committee, who would then contact the opponents. In this way, McCloy, Weible, and others working for them hoped to insulate the War Department from charges of impropriety. As the memorandum relayed, "In general, such contacts will be made by the American Legion, the Citizens' committee, and by other individuals who have expressed themselves as in favor of the program." Weible also wanted BPR to update him on any opponents of UMT who changed their position as a result of this tactic.[20]

Cooke's feverish pace began paying dividends by April. On April 4, Cooke sent a letter to seventeen hundred newspapers throughout the country. In it he declared the formation of the Citizens Committee for Military Training of Young Men, Inc. This nonprofit organization incorporated in New York was "the outgrowth of a small group which played a leading part in organizing the Plattsburg Camps of 1915 and 1916, the War Camps of 1917 and the adoption of the Selective Service System in 1940. It is now directly interested in the subject of a military training program, both Army and Navy, for young men at about eighteen years of age, to begin after this war is over and the Nation comes face to face with the realities of the future in maintaining peace and avoiding war."[21]

Cooke's purpose was twofold. First, he sought to provide momentum to the campaign for UMT by having a citizens' group specifically dedicated to its principles. As he revealed, he wanted "to inspire interest in our proposition." In addition, he desired to test the waters. He sought to identify more clearly friends and foes. Cooke aspired "to obtain reactions from the newspapers in the various sections" and wholly expected to "get some interesting answers." Cooke intended the letter as a shot across the bow in which newspaper organizations would reveal their positions. As a result, the committee would know who its friends were and who its foes were. The overall result was that by April 1945, McCloy,

Weible, and their subordinates had joined forces with a separate civilian organization headed by a veteran whom they had handpicked. Together, these two groups could now promote UMT. McCloy and Weible felt confident that such a move would prevent the outward appearance of being directly involved in propagandizing for a specific military policy. For a while, the ruse would work.[22]

In mid-April, restrictions on advocating UMT were lifted. Almost immediately, Kent contacted BPR to ensure that they communicated the lifting of publicity restrictions throughout the War Department in their *Liaison Bulletin.* Kent reiterated Weible's message that "Reference is made to the Continental Liaison Bulletin No. 33, dated 20 Jan 45, paragraph 1, on UMT. Restrictions have been lifted on War Department personnel in connection with UMT effective 13 April 1945. Requests for Army personnel as speakers or writers on this subject may be filled in accordance with existing policies and regulations of the War Department Bureau of Public Relations."[23]

Once Cooke began the work of the Citizens Committee, other civilians interested in preparedness increased their involvement. One such ardent advocate was Archibald G. Thacher. Thacher had a long history advocating preparedness measures and was intimately involved in the push for the 1940 draft bill. As chairman of the board for the Citizens Committee, Thacher helped Weible immensely, most notably in preparing for the upcoming congressional hearings on UMT before the Woodrum committee. Thacher suggested that Weible obtain the testimony of opponents of UMT during the 1916 and 1920 debates and use their testimony to discredit the opposition and buttress their own case. As Thacher remembered, "My recollection is that at that time numbers of such opponents very unwisely committed themselves to certain positive statements or predictions to the effect that either the United States was invulnerable or would not become involved in another war; or that, if attacked, we would have plenty of time to prepare, etc." As a lawyer, Thacher approached the campaign for UMT as a trial. He felt that "the preparation of a few questions to be put to witnesses of this type, if and when they appear before the Woodrum Committee would, I believe, be of great value, and, to use a legal trial phrase, should 'destroy such witnesses.'" Thacher convinced Weible. Weible responded that his "suggestion as to the use of previous testimony of opponents strikes me as possessing much merit." As a result of Thacher's suggestion, Weible obtained extensive information on previous testimony of opponents of UMT for representatives of both the Citizens Committee and the War Department to use in the upcoming congressional hearings.[24]

For the rest of the summer, Weible's office coordinated efforts to have the BPR produce a short film explaining the strategic rationale behind UMT and advocating its adoption. Early efforts were met with resistance by BPR personnel. Looming over the issue of production of a film was the fear of impropriety. On April 10, A. D. Surles, the director of BPR, informed Weible that his office had "temporarily, at least, been forced to remove this [UMT] film from the production schedule." Surles explained his reversal by stating that "the question of the possible propriety of the utilization of public funds for a project of this nature" was a driving factor in his decision.[25]

McCloy and Weible succeeded in advancing their case. Even so, one recurrent problem kept rearing its head. Opponents repeatedly argued that War Department officials were calling for a drastic measure without even spelling out the specifics of their plans for UMT beyond some vague generalities. It soon became clear that War Department personnel would have to settle the details of the UMT plan if they hoped to maintain the momentum of their marketing campaign. Army planners had to crystallize their own plans for UMT as well as ensure a consistent approach with the Navy Department, which was traditionally less enthusiastic about UMT but willing to follow the army's lead nonetheless. Throughout the spring of 1945, military planners within both departments worked feverishly on accomplishing just that. Their labors produced results in May with the publication of a joint planning document entitled *The War and Navy Departments' Views on Universal Military Training*. As soon as the brochure came off the presses, army leaders began circulating it widely. With *Views* in their hands, they were able to summarize both the strategic rationale underpinning UMT and specifics of the War Department proposal.[26]

Army leaders used the brochure to fortify the argument that the nature of modern warfare had changed dramatically. By reinforcing the claim that geographic position no longer afforded America adequate protection, army leaders highlighted the "new character to warfare" that included long-range bombers and successful amphibious operations against defended objectives. They recalled that in both previous world wars, America's enemies attacked her allies first, allowing the United

States precious time to mobilize. As they warned, "The next time an aggressor will not make the same mistake. He will attack us first."[27]

Army planners argued that the result of these altered conditions was significantly less time to mobilize in a future war: "In order to protect our nation and our democratic way of life, we must have a state of military preparedness which will enable us to take effective military action in the shortest possible time." To army planners, the most logical solution was doing much of the preparation ahead of time: "This means that the youth of the nation must have had the greater part of its military training before mobilization." This meant UMT.[28]

Army leaders next used *Views* to outline their planned UMT program. To their credit, most army planners within the War Department were interested in UMT for military reasons, not societal ones. Their underlying goal was to increase military readiness. They spelled out what would happen to trainees after their year of training. Trainees would graduate into an inactive reserve status and thus be ready for recall if Congress declared a national emergency. They explained, "After completing the prescribed year of training, each trainee should become a member of the Army's enlisted Reserve Corps or of the US Naval Reserve, remaining in this status for five years."[29]

Army leaders next addressed several key objections to the plan that were being raised. The first objection was that UMT did not need to be adopted immediately, especially before the war was over. Army leaders took issue with this objection in *Views.* They stated that "so vital to the over-all scheme of our military organization is the presence or absence of a system of Universal Military Training that, without a Congressional decision with regard to such a program, no broad design for the over-all postwar military defense of this nation and its interests can be perfected."[30]

Army leaders also answered critics who argued that there was not a compelling need for UMT. Many critics pointed to the fact that the roughly twelve million men who had served in World War II were well trained and would constitute a ready reserve for the immediate future. Critics argued that a far-reaching program such as UMT was unnecessary in the face of such trained manpower reserves. Advocates of UMT within the War Department felt differently. They contended that relying on World War II veterans for trained manpower was inherently unjust. As they chided, "It would be manifestly unfair to place this great responsibility twice upon the shoulders of the present generation of fighting men." In addition, regardless of the fairness of relying on World War II veterans for a ready reserve in case of war, army planners saw such a tactic as shortsighted. Doing so would only guarantee American security for five years at most and would simply prolong efforts to ensure adequate preparedness. Army leaders went further than just addressing the veteran issue. They made a broad appeal for universality in any program enacted. The military planners felt that "the success of such a program depends in large measure on the equality of obligation to serve." As such, they outlined only five specific exemptions to the proposed UMT plan. Of these five, only three were really exemptions, as the other two gave credit for military service already rendered. They included exemptions for family members of foreign diplomatic personnel, "persons having bona fide religious scruples against non-combatant participation in warfare," and "persons physically or mentally unfit and those rejected for cause." Army leaders followed the exemptions clause with an interesting paragraph on the "moral standards" of UMT. Comparing UMT to the "present Selective Service law," they argued that the War Department should have the final say on the acceptance of trainees to the program. They reasoned, "Security requires the right to reject persons suspected of espionage or disloyalty, and the good order and discipline of the services requires the right to reject certain types of moral offenders." They left unclear exactly what characterized a "moral offender" in the eyes of the War Department.[31]

Army leaders hoped that *Views* would also overcome another objection critics often lobbed at UMT: the impact of UMT on the nascent United Nations organization. Critics of UMT argued that embarking on a peacetime training program such as UMT while at the same time participating in the meeting at San Francisco would send the wrong signals to the international community. It would show no faith in international solutions to security. Army leaders disagreed. They made two distinct points affirming the usefulness of UMT with regards to international cooperation.

First, they argued that UMT would buttress the position of US delegates "at the Peace Table." While noting that "our realistically-minded principal allies have indicated no intention of abandoning their programs of Universal Military Service" because of fear that it might "risk failure of retaining the security of existence for which we are all fighting," they argued that "adopting Universal Military Training at the present time will demonstrate the earnestness of our intention effectively to participate in the maintenance of a peaceful world order."[32]

Second, army leaders argued that in addition to strengthening the case of US diplomacy in the short term, UMT would also bolster the international position of the United States in the long term. In other words, UMT had value as a deterrent. They argued, "It would enhance the chances of perfecting an international peace organization." The logic was simple. UMT would "serve notice to the world that this country will never again be unprepared." Army planners remained undecided on the long-term prospects of international cooperation and basically took a wait-and-see approach. As they cautioned, "Until the effectiveness of such an international peace organization is proven, Universal Military Training will provide prudent insurance against the risks of its failure."[33]

Army leaders closed *Views* with an interesting point. They advocated UMT as the critical component of the War Department's postwar plan. As they discussed the comprehensive plan for postwar national security, which included UMT, scientific and technological development, industrial mobilization, and an improved intelligence service, they argued that "trained manpower, however, is the keystone around which all other components must be built. The most modern weapons are useless in the hands of persons untrained in their use." Even while placing UMT in such a vaunted position, the authors explicitly refused to accept a training program that was geared towards any political or social purpose. Army planners wanted a UMT program that was based on improving military effectiveness, period. Anything else would be worse than nothing. They warned, "War is not a game nor is it an activity in which 'second best' is very useful. Our military requirements may be defined very simply; they are that we be prepared to fight and win a war at the least possible cost of time, money and, above all, the lives of our men. It would be better for the American people to have no military training program at all than to have one which would, through inadequate training, build a sense of false security and one certain to result in disaster when put to the test."[34]

Producing such a detailed planning document as *Views* was no easy task. Doing so crystallized some important specifics about the War Department plan for UMT. One of the details that came into greater focus in May was the estimated cost of UMT. The War Department had their own estimates, which were rooted in a specific historical context. War Department planners were startled by the astronomical costs of World War II compared to any military endeavors in American history. For example, George J. Richards, Budget Division director, compiled a report that tracked war expenditures by fiscal years. Richards reported "Total Budgetary Expenditures (excluding Government Corporations)" for two distinct periods of time. The first period was from 1789 until July 1, 1940. During that period of 151 years, Richards estimated, expenditures totaled $173 billion. During the second period of less than five years—July 1, 1940, until May 5, 1945—expenditures were $300 billion. To War Department planners grappling with the daunting task of formulating postwar military policy, such figures made an indelible impression regarding the massive scope that the American military machine had reached at remarkable speed.[35]

Richards analyzed in further detail the costs of each specific war that the American military had fought. Even though he conceded that perfectly reliable figures were unavailable, his estimates were the most comprehensive available at the time detailing the cost of warfare in American history. Richards presented two clear lessons. First, he illustrated the unprecedented nature of World War II in terms of costs. Second, he demonstrated the general trend that war was getting exponentially more expensive with each conflict. He estimated that the Revolutionary War had cost approximately $70 million, the War of 1812 approximately $134 million, the Mexican War approximately $166 million, the Civil War approximately $15 billion, the War with Spain approximately $2 billion, and World War I approximately $42 billion. Richards pointed out that these figures paled in comparison to his estimated cost of World War II at $300 billion.[36]

Richards clearly demonstrated the staggering costs of World War II compared to the costs of other wars. More important, the implication of Richards's work was that any future war would be even more expensive than World War II, perhaps astronomically so. When presented with Richards's numbers, many in the War Department began to see UMT as a logical alternative to a large—and thereby expensive—permanent military establishment. Throughout 1945 there was general agreement within the War Department that UMT would cost approximately $1.75 billion per year to operate. This was no small amount, but UMT advocates in the War Department touted this figure as a good insurance policy against the high cost of future war. As William F. Tompkins explained to Weible, "Compared to the direct and indirect cost of war the peacetime expenditures of the nation on its military establishment are relatively insignificant, and . . . , considering the enormous increase in the cost of waging modern war, an expenditure of a few billion dollars annually on the peacetime Armed Forces is not out of line with the pre–World War I relationship of peace to war costs." The costs of UMT relative to war were therefore reasonable.[37]

In late August, Porter contacted BPR about the film issue. BPR had produced a film entitled *War Comes to America.* Porter and Weible, along with Cooke and Thacher of the Citizens Committee and the leadership of the American Legion, all felt that a wider distribution of the film would be helpful for their cause. Porter pleaded with A. D. Surles: "These representatives state that this picture can be of substantial assistance to them in their attempt to develop in the American people an understanding of the need for a program of universal military training." Porter tasked BPR with providing six copies of the film to each service command and to the military district of Washington so that representatives outside of the War Department would have better access to the material to use in their own marketing efforts.[38]

In November, Porter contacted the acting director of BPR after Surles had left. He again pleaded for a UMT film and wanted to ensure that BPR produced a film that was "'informational' and not 'argumentative.'" Porter contended that the film should simply illustrate UMT by following a trainee through the proposed program. He suspected that if it was "skillfully done," it would "do much, as a most important by-product, to sell universal military training."[39]

A major marketing blitz occurred in September. *Annals of the American Academy of Political and Social Science* dedicated its entire issue to UMT. Senior military leaders jumped at the opportunity to present publicly their case for UMT. McCloy outlined the sociological context that he saw as a primary weakness plaguing effective national security planning in a democracy such as America. He lamented that Americans had a short attention span, claiming that Americans were able to focus on national security requirements diligently during times of national emergency, but as soon as peace resumed, they lost all concern for preparedness. McCloy complained that "the historic American policy of military weakness between wars and military improvisation to fight them have been dangerous and costly in American lives and wealth. In the past, it has been our habit to prepare for war after war began." One should analyze McCloy's assertion in the context of the interwar period. Many War Department planners grappling with the monumental challenges of both waging World War II and preparing for the postwar period evidenced frustration at the lack of national security planning that had taken place in the interwar period. As McCloy reasoned, "The interval between World War I and World War II provides a clear moral lesson to us. It is that a people must inherit its sense of security from the generation that has seen that security jeopardized." He sought to ensure that major changes to ensure America's future national security—specifically UMT—were implemented as soon as possible to prevent the public from losing interest in defense issues as it had done after World War I. If proponents of UMT such as McCloy were to make their case, they had to go beyond just articulating reasons why preparedness after World War II was more important than in the past. They also had to make the case why UMT was essential to ensure America's national security.[40]

In making a passionate case, McCloy reiterated the strategic arguments for the program. First, he highlighted time—or lack thereof—as the main strategic factor in a future conflict. As he warned, "We would be foolish indeed, with the development of weapons and the diminution of spaces, if we again assumed that we will have a measurable period of time in which to prepare while other nations hold the line." He indicated three strategic factors that weighed heavily upon the minds of national security planners in the immediate postwar era. First, technology had improved rapidly, and the future development of weapons technology seemed limitless. World War II had introduced powerful military technologies such as strategic airpower, missiles, and nuclear weapons. All of these advances had one thing in common—they shrank the globe. This "diminution of spaces," as McCloy termed it, was especially relevant to the United States, which had traditionally relied upon geographic isolation between two major oceans for its security. No longer were the Atlantic and Pacific such cozy security blankets. Second, he was arguing that our enemies, whoever they might turn out to be, were not foolish. The pattern of both World War I and World War II was clear. The United States had sat on the sidelines during the early portions of both conflicts in order to mobilize its economy and manpower for a decisive contribution in the later portions. Hoping that future enemies would allow the

United States the same opportunity in the future was unrealistic to Mc-Cloy. As he cautioned, "That the United States is the logical No. 1 target in any large next conflict is so clear it must be assumed that our future enemies, whoever they may be, will attack us vigorously at the outset." These two factors, technological developments and enemy adaptation, were the prime reasons that time was now such a critical factor. McCloy reasoned that the new weapons of war could reach farther and attack faster than anything previously imagined, and there were no longer any viable allies to stand behind while America mobilized her potential military power: "Hence the factor of time must dominate every calculation in our national defense. It is this time factor that prompts the War and Navy Departments to recommend that the postwar military organization must rest, *inter alia,* upon a system of universal military training whereby the youth of the nation will constitute a reservoir of trained military manpower from which a balanced force can be speedily mobilized in the event of an emergency to meet any threat to our national security."[41]

In addition to reiterating the strategic rationale for UMT, McCloy also presented the specifics of how the department intended to implement the plan. McCloy described two major options that American military planners had immediately following World War II. The first was to maintain a large standing army capable of action immediately upon attack. Since time was no longer a strategic buffer, such a force had to be large enough not only to take care of the mundane tasks of the occupation and maintenance of military bases at home and abroad, but also to be immediately capable of repelling attacks. The implications were obvious. With America's newfound position as a world leader, such a force would have to be massive compared to the historical trends in American military manpower. The alternative to McCloy was a small professional military "no larger than necessary to meet normal peacetime requirements" augmented by a "citizen army reserve." McCloy held nothing back in promoting UMT as the preferred option. He declared, "As between these two types, the Armed Services unhesitatingly prefer the second."[42]

What is most interesting about this preference for a small professional military augmented by a trained citizenry is the reason why military planners such as McCloy clung to it. The more obvious but less intriguing reason was its supposed reduction of costs. Theoretically, a large standing army was more expensive than a small professional military augmented with a trained citizenry. Training many men, then equipping them, then stationing them continually costs much more than training many men, keeping some of them, and then sending the rest back into civilian life to be called upon when needed. Beyond cost, though, a less obvious reason why McCloy argued so forcefully for UMT had to do with socioeconomic class. Any system that maintained a large standing army allowed and perhaps even necessitated formation of a separate and powerful military officer class. Such a problem cut two ways. On one hand, a large standing army clustered national security policy in the hands of a limited number of lifetime military officers. On the other hand, it also closed the ladder of opportunity to many citizens who had fought so valiantly as draftees but would be released the moment the draft expired. As McCloy reasoned, "First, it involves great cost. Second, it tends to concentrate leadership in war and control of military preparations and policy in peace in a professional and bureaucratic-minded military class. Third, it does not adequately provide for developing or giving play to the latent leadership and genius of the people as a whole."[43]

Interestingly, senior military officers involved with UMT echoed McCloy's concerns regarding a powerful military officer class. Maj. Gen. William F. Tompkins also argued forcefully for UMT and warned about the dangers of an officer class. Tompkins maintained that "the dangers to a free people in the necessary development of a powerful officer caste to lead such professional armies generation after generation are obvious. It is therefore, the deliberate policy of the War Department to advocate principal dependence for our national security upon the citizen soldier in arms." In some ways, McCloy and Tompkins were setting up a straw man and knocking him down with their preferred option of UMT. They continually presented the dilemma as an either-or scenario with only two viable options. It is interesting that voluntary methods were dismissed out of hand. Tompkins argued that "the consistent practical failure of the 'volunteer' system in our past history is proof enough of its inability to meet the needs of the national defense; but in addition, it should be reflected that a volunteer system violates the very principle of democracy, in that the few are saddled with the responsibility of sacrificing to defend the many." Both McCloy and Tompkins targeted the traditional American fear of large standing armies by insinuating that the UMT option would eliminate the need for such a massive force.[44]

In addition to presenting the benefits of UMT, McCloy also detailed

the specifics of the War Department plan. He praised its universal nature: "The training should be truly universal. It should be applied impartially so that no young man capable of contributing to national defense
will be exempted." McCloy had a fine line to walk. On one hand he had
to ensure that UMT would not allow physically fit young men to be exempted from training because of personal connections, wealth, or occupation. Such a system would be viewed as unfair, undemocratic, and
perhaps un-American. On the other hand, he also had to guarantee that
UMT would not exclude young men with minor physical ailments. Since
one rationale for UMT was to promote democratic opportunity for all, it
had to be extended as widely as possible. As he wrote, "The system must
be universal for all in that age group because the American people will
not look with favor upon a system which exempts boys who are physically and mentally qualified, nor will they tolerate a plan that bars boys
that are prepared to accept the benefits and responsibilities of training,
but who are disqualified because of a punctured eardrum or flat feet."
Such an approach to the universal principle would be problematic later
as the War Department attempted to devise plans for UMT that could
be implemented.[45]

McCloy also clung tenaciously to the tenet that the training should
be for "one continuous year." The issue of length of training was controversial, and McCloy was aware of objections from various segments
of the population over the proposed year of continuous training. Other
proposals had been presented for shorter training, perhaps six months,
or for twelve months of training broken into several installments, such
as four consecutive summers. One of the reasons for discord was the
experience with training during World War II. Revelations that servicemen deploying into combat operations during the later phases of World
War II had received much shorter periods of training were producing
two outcomes. Shortened training lengths were decried as irresponsible
and akin to sending young soldiers off to be slaughtered. But shortened
training lengths also raised the criticism that the training envisioned
by UMT supporters could be accomplished in much less time than one
full year. The first objection actually strengthened the case for UMT. The
second, however, presented a stronger criticism of the proposed plan.
Even so, McCloy held steadfastly to the plan for one continuous year.[46]

In doing so, he drew a sharp distinction between unit training and replacement training. Unit training involved training the entire unit from

scratch to be employed en masse as an indivisible piece. Such training was critical to any mobilization policy by which whole units would have to be formed and applied during a transition from peace to war. Replacement training involved training individual soldiers to be added to existing units to replace casualties suffered during war. The new soldiers were expected to be strengthened by the veterans around them who already had not only extensive training but also, more important, experience. McCloy reminded the public that UMT had to be based on a unit training philosophy, whereas the shorter training times used during the war were all for replacement training. As he emphasized, "At the outset, it should be made clear that the Army training program upon which the proposed year of universal military training is modeled is that for developing units. Replacement training is quite different. Replacements in time of war have to be trained in less time. . . . Unit training is a far longer process—the task of a full year."[47]

McCloy saw two direct benefits in such a position. First, it effectively deflected criticism of current War Department training practices by explaining the rationale behind it, replacement training. He maintained that the War Department was not irresponsible in its training methods because it could effectively train an individual replacement soldier in a short period of time. Second, it also solidified the outlines of the UMT program by cementing the "one continuous year" philosophy and articulating the unit training philosophy it rested upon. McCloy asserted that the end result of a UMT program based on unit training was that "the nation will be assured that the units of the armed forces will be ready for combat within weeks, rather than months or years, after mobilization."[48]

McCloy also explained how many young men UMT would impact. He pegged the potential number of inductees at 1,133,000 per year, which was a theoretical maximum estimate. Tompkins held the actual number at 800,000 per year. This total would be allocated 600,000 for the army and 200,000 for the navy. Other studies confirmed Tompkins's number. One economic study estimated that somewhere between 750,000 and 800,000 young men would go through the training every year from 1946 until 1955. Since the War Department proposal for UMT envisioned a five-year reserve status, the reserve forces would stabilize at about 4,620,000 men. This reserve force would complement the active forces, which most War Department planners estimated at 1,000,000 men.[49]

In addition to the cost estimates that Richards had arrived at in the spring, others added more specific estimates of cost during September. Rainer Schickele, principal agricultural economist at the US Department of Agriculture, studied the issue in an attempt to define clearly the costs associated with such an ambitious project. Schickele, a widely published authority on economics and political science, had previously held positions at the Social Science Research Council, the Brookings Institution, George Washington University, and Iowa State College. He warned, "Any policy of so broad a scope as the proposal of universal compulsory military training is bound to have a considerable impact upon the nation's economy." Schickele sought "to describe this impact and evaluate the economic costs involved in this projected program." He maintained that the US military establishment following World War II would have to be larger than it had ever been previously, and therefore UMT would not reduce the cost of the military establishment but rather increase it.[50]

Schickele figured that the cost of UMT would be roughly one billion dollars per year. He based that figure on compensation of $360 a year for each trainee along with an annual cost of food, clothing, lodging, and equipment of $1,000 per trainee for 770,000 trainees per year. He warned that because there was some uncertainty about the pay rate of trainees, the cost of UMT could be as high as $1.3 billion per year. However, he reminded the public that UMT would not obviate the need for the professional army. Army leaders already estimated that they would need approximately 1,000,000 men in the active forces following World War II. The cost of those active forces would be staggering. The average cost per active serviceman was calculated to be $4,000 per year. This brought the estimated cost of the professional personnel of the armed forces to $4 billion per year. The total direct cost of the entire armed forces, assuming a regular military establishment of 1,000,000 men and 770,000 trainees per year, then stood at $5.3 billion per year.[51]

Unlike Richards, Schickele did not view the total cost of UMT solely as the dollars that the federal government would spend on the program each year. He also maintained that there would be an "opportunity cost" associated with UMT, because the young men who were training for one year would be removed from the economy. Schickele broke the problem down into two parts. First, he calculated the opportunity cost of the total manpower resources employed by the postwar military establishment, arriving at $2.8 billion per year for the professional military personnel and $1.9 billion per year for the UMT personnel. Next, he calculated the opportunity cost of the total industrial resources employed by the postwar military establishment: $2.5 billion per year for the professional military personnel and $550 million per year for the UMT personnel. By combining the total manpower costs and industrial resources, Schickele argued that the total opportunity cost of the postwar military establishment stood at roughly $5.3 billion per year for the professional military personnel and $2.5 billion per year for the UMT personnel.[52]

Schickele's analysis clearly showed that UMT would cost about $1.3 billion per year in direct costs and might divert as much as $2.5 billion per year away from the national economy. These numbers were more comprehensive than those presented by Richards but did not seem unreachable to an economist such as Schickele. Schickele presented the issue of UMT as a strategic problem, not an economic one. He conceded, "Universal military training would not bankrupt the economy of the United States. The main issue is rather whether it really is the most effective means of bolstering our defense, or whether an equivalent amount of resources might not be employed in a different way to greater advantage."[53]

Beginning in the fall of 1944 and continuing throughout 1945, proponents of UMT in the War Department began a campaign to market UMT nationwide. They went on the airwaves to outline the rationale for UMT. They handpicked one of their own to lead the efforts of a special-interest group dedicated to achieving UMT. They solidified the specifics of the War Department's plan and disseminated those views in a joint planning document. They detailed the estimated cost of UMT with precision and clarity. And they published widely in the hopes of convincing the American public of the merits of UMT. By preaching the "gospel," McCloy, Porter, Weible, and others in the War Department undoubtedly converted many to their cause. They also stirred up opposition throughout various segments of American society.

6   A Pig in a Poke

Congress is mulling over legislation on the subject of universal military training. Propaganda agencies representing hundreds of civic, labor, religious, industrial and veterans' organizations are spending heavy money trying to influence people on both sides of the fence. College students debate the issue in classrooms. Bar flies have come to blows over it.
—*Yank*

Oodles of young foot soldiers, half trained and half spoiled, is not the answer.
—Edwin C. Johnson

Defense is the scarecrow sought to be erected in our minds.
—Roscoe S. Conkling

At the same time that senior army leaders within the War Department marketed their plan for UMT, opponents attempted to stall their progress and prevent UMT from becoming a reality. The opposition was actually several different groups, each opposing UMT on specific grounds. The groups included pacifists, labor leaders, clergy, and military personnel with strategic reservations about the actual effectiveness of UMT. The first opposition group to play a role was pacifists.

In mid-November 1944, members of leading pacifist organizations converged on Washington, DC, to attend the Pacifist Conference. The conference was held on Thursday, November 16, beginning at two in the afternoon and lasted until one in the afternoon of Friday, November 17. Interestingly enough, War Department personnel kept detailed shorthand minutes of the meeting. These documents reveal that the author was not personally familiar with all the pacifist leaders and their positions but was keenly intent on tracking the main personalities and their arguments against UMT. These minutes were not published by the Pacifist Conference but instead were taken hastily during the meeting by a proponent of UMT and then given to the War Department. The majority of the members of pacifist groups in attendance were staunchly opposed to UMT, but there was less consensus among labor groups in attendance. For example, Tucker P. Smith, a committed pacifist who was active as the secretary of the Committee on Militarism in Education, onetime officer of the Fellowship of Reconciliation, the League for Industrial Democracy, and the War Resisters League, among other organizations, revealed that labor leader William Green was "uncertain of how the AF of L will go. The professional staff of the AF of L is opposed to peacetime conscription and Green believes they will not come out in favor of it." Another pacifist, Mr. Newton joined in the discussion of labor group sentiment towards the early plans for UMT. Newton stated that "the CIO is now divided 50–50, but may be expected to come out against it. *If* the CIO does come out as a whole in favor of conscription, there are some sections which might come out against it." Labor opposition had not solidified at this early juncture. Perhaps the most interesting fact was the revelation that leading pacifists at the meeting directly revealed their strategy for resisting the push for UMT. Pacifist leader Evan Thomas summarized his plan succinctly. He "proposed the tactic of studied confusion in promoting complete opposition through 'exemption' which he would extend so widely that the whole system would collapse." Thomas campaigned forcefully for exemptions to participation in UMT—for example, a conscientious objector exclusion—and for continually adding others to any that were obtained. In doing so, Thomas hoped to water down the UMT plan to the point of uselessness and therefore one that could be more easily defeated.[1]

One week later, on November 24, the distilled version of these shorthand notes appeared on McCloy's desk. The memorandum labeled certain individuals as the leaders of the pacifist opposition to UMT. As the memorandum spelled out for McCloy, "Fred Libby, Dorothy Detzer, Tucker Smith, Coe, Barnes, Sayre, and Villard are among the leaders of the pacifist movement." The memorandum highlighted Fred Libby as the most dangerous opponent. It warned, "Libby is the most influential, gathers in the most money, prints the most literature. He is opposed to almost any measure for preparedness, and maintains his sanctity by avoiding any traceable relationship with the more radical groups."[2]

The memorandum also detailed tactics of pacifist leaders as perceived by War Department personnel. The memorandum argued that "the policy of the pacifist groups appears to be: First, to seek delay; second, to high-pressure Congressmen individually; third, to defeat the measure outright before it is brought to a vote; fourth, to use restriction of the period of service to ninety days; fifth, to emasculate the measure through insertion of a conscientious objector clause." It is important to note that the first tactic, "to seek delay," was gaining traction and achieving success. One of the main reasons for this accomplishment had to do with servicemen themselves. As the memorandum observed, "It will be noted from the papers attached that a basic argument for delay centers around the plea that men serving in the armed forces should have opportunity to express their views. This was a potent argument that influenced the action of the National Catholic Welfare Conference and is repeatedly expressed by the Journal of the N.E.A."[3]

Such analysis illustrated the views of proponents of UMT in the War Department during the fall of 1944 regarding the overall estimation of the pacifist movement as an opponent in the campaign to promote UMT. McCloy's staff viewed the pacifist opposition as small but effective: "The pacifist groups are small numerically, but have been most potent in other years in arousing fears against militarism. The veteran organizations' approval of universal training is taken for granted and is discounted by the public. Their influence is limited. Support of universal military training should originate with purely citizen groups. Legion members could be utilized for that purpose."[4]

More important, McCloy's staff urged an active approach to counter the pacifist opposition. The memorandum suggested, "It would be a mistake to discount the influence of the pacifists group, yet it is doubtful if they are as strong today as their voice would indicate. Their arguments and tactics can be met and overcome, but it will take planning and able direction." It was this "planning and able direction" that McCloy, Weible, and their staffs sought to establish in the War Department's marketing of UMT.[5]

By early 1945, McCloy, Weible, and their staffs shifted focus from pacifist opposition to organized labor. American labor leaders were a critical audience for the marketing efforts of the War Department. With their help, the leadership of the War Department might secure approval of UMT. Without their help—or worse yet, in the face of their outright opposition—securing approval of UMT would be an uphill battle. One of the first activities McCloy and Weible embarked upon to counter opposition was planning and holding "off-the-record" meetings with what they termed "National Phase Groups." The War Department defined these groups specifically as labor, industry, agriculture, education, religion, and women's interest. The first and most important group McCloy and Weible targeted was labor. The goal for the meeting with labor leaders was simple. As Howard C. Petersen, McCloy's executive assistant, wrote to his boss, "The main objective of the meeting should be to impress on the labor leaders the absolute necessity from the standpoint of national security of having Universal Military Training and, equally important, that the War and Navy Departments will exert every possible effort to obtain legislation for this."[6]

Petersen distilled five major points that McCloy should articulate to labor leaders during the meeting. First, McCloy should emphasize that there was "complete agreement" between the army and the navy as to the fundamental need for UMT. Second, McCloy should insist that a viable UMT program demanded, "one year's continuous training." Third, McCloy should demand that the proposed program would "take in all physically qualified males, but no females, with no exceptions or substitute forms of training." Fourth, McCloy should stress that UMT was "a training program and not a service program." Finally, McCloy should reiterate that the War Department wanted UMT as a "*military training program, conducted solely for military purposes and not as a grand scheme to educate young Americans.*" Petersen also suggested a tacit threat to labor leaders if they failed to support UMT. He urged, "It would be helpful if the Secretary could, in a very subtle way, call attention to the responsibilities which must rest in the hands of the leaders of organized labor if they oppose what the constituted military authorities unanimously agree is essential for the security of the nation."[7]

Senior representatives of the War Department held their meeting with American labor leaders on November 10, 1944. War Department attendees included Secretary of War Henry L. Stimson; Under Secretary of War John J. McCloy; Army Chief of Staff George C. Marshall; Howard C. Petersen, executive assistant to the under secretary of war; John M. Palmer, special advisor to the army chief of staff; Wilton B. Persons, chief of the Legislative and Liaison Division; Secretary of the Navy James V. Forrestal; Chief of Naval Operations Ernest J. King; and Randall Jacobs, UMT representative for the navy. In attendance were also two key members of Congress, Representatives James W. Wadsworth (R-NY) and Clifton A. Woodrum (D-VA), both members of the House Select Committee on Postwar Military Policy. The labor leaders present included William Green, American Federation of Labor (AFL); Philip Murray, Congress of Industrial Organizations (CIO); A. Johnson, Brotherhood of Locomotive Engineers; H. W. Fraser, Order of Railroad Conductors of America; T. C. Cashen, Switchmen's Union of North America; A. F. Whitney, Brotherhood of Railroad Trainmen;

and D. B. Robertson, Brotherhood of Locomotive Firemen and En-ginemen.[8]

Army leaders viewed this initial meeting as a success. In fact, some within the War Department felt that the labor leaders were prepared to help promote UMT. Lt. Col. A. H. Raskin, chief of the Labor Branch, In-dustrial Services Division, distilled for Weible what he felt were the "two prevailing points of view among labor leaders toward universal military training." He perceived a split among labor leaders that he felt UMT ad-vocates could use to their advantage. As Raskin explained to Weible,

> The predominant view is one of suspicion toward the entire project based on a fear that the Army will misuse the year of training to implant a spirit of reaction, militarism and hatred for labor among the youths who undergo training. The second attitude, which is held by William Green, president of the AFL; James B. Carey, secretary-treasurer of the CIO; and a number of other important labor leaders, is one of being for universal military training as a necessary measure for safe-guarding our national future but of being afraid to speak out publicly in favor of it because the people down the line have shown no readi-ness to follow an advocacy of this proposal.[9]

The significance of this perceived split was that War Department leaders felt that they could use it to secure the support of at least a por-tion of the major labor leaders of the country. Raskin continued, "Once a receptiveness to the idea of universal military training is created at the top, we can utilize the assistance of Mr. Green, Mr. Carey and others in presenting speeches and articles about universal military training to la-bor gatherings and labor publications." Raskin's optimism was not with-out cause. He cited a specific example of support for UMT within labor circles. Optimistically he relayed to Weible, "Lester M. Hunt, editor of the Teamster Journal, official organ of the largest single AFL publication, is a strong supporter of universal military training and was instrumental in having the executive council of the Eastern Labor Press Conference go down on record unanimously in support of a peacetime military training program." It was precisely this result that supporters of UMT hoped to accomplish with their meeting with labor leaders.[10]

Exactly two months later, on January 10, 1945, virtually the same cast of leaders reconvened in Washington for a second meeting between War Department leaders and American labor leaders. The optimism with which War Department leaders emerged from the first meeting slowly faded as labor leaders began to voice serious reservations about a plan that would put every eighteen-year-old American male through a year of military training. Even though this meeting, like the one in November, was off the record, War Department staff documented the main points of contention that labor leaders now voiced regarding UMT. Col. Douglas Parmentier, chief of the News Division, highlighted three specific issues that labor leaders raised behind closed doors. First, he recalled that labor leaders suspected that UMT would be an unfair infringement on them if no corresponding sacrifice were made by industry. Labor leaders argued that having a large trained reserve would do no good if industry were not providing the materiel necessary to equip this citizen army. As Parmentier reported, "A really important thing and unanimously agreed to was that a comprehensive plan for keeping industry ready for instant mobilization for military production was essential as concurrent planning with military training." Parmentier recalled that several labor leaders present at the January meeting, in addition to wanting to ensure equity between labor and industry, also "expressed the idea that a greatly enlarged national guard would result, which would be an instrument used against labor in industrial disputes by State governors." Finally, Parmentier recalled that labor leaders were wary of a UMT program run entirely by the War Department and "stressed desirability of having initial selection of trainee completely in hands of civilian local boards."[11]

The next day, Col. Dillon Anderson crystallized the meeting with the labor leaders. Anderson claimed that the labor leaders present viewed UMT as an imposition on their sovereignty. He commented, "Labor's thinking as disclosed in the conference may be characterized as a variation, in three themes, on the elementary instinct of self-preservation—of the union, of the union members and of the country in which they exist." Regarding self-preservation of the country, he reiterated labor leaders' articulation that the current plans for UMT would give industry an unfair advantage over labor and therefore any plans for UMT should also consider compelling industrial mobilization as well as coercing the training of manpower. With regard to the effects of UMT on union members, Anderson recalled that the labor leaders complained that the proposed plan would interrupt apprenticeship in the various trades and thereby be a handicap for the professional development of union members. Most important, he recounted the apprehension of labor leaders that the UMT plan would directly affect the labor unions themselves: "To the labor leader, survival of organized labor is closely akin to self-preservation. By far the majority of questions reflected apprehension on this third subject. Labor leaders fear the use of the Army or the National Guard or the Militia to break strikes, and those in attendance expressed this fear frankly."[12]

One interesting dynamic that emerged from the second meeting with labor leaders was the assertion by Carey of the CIO that the army was a conservative—perhaps reactionary—organization led by a caste of Southern gentlemen. Even though Brig. Gen. W. W. Irvine, acting assistant chief of staff, G-3, recalled that "it was so obvious that he was misinformed that no one made a reply," Irvine immediately set out to disprove Carey. Irvine recalled, "As a matter of interest, I asked the AGO to give me a list of the number of Regular Army officers by state of birth. I then had determined the number of officers each state should have based on the ratio of state to national population. . . . Considering the twelve states generally classified as southern, the number of Regular Army officers are about 25% of the total and 20 less than their proportionate number based on population."[13]

The early opposition to UMT on the part of pacifist groups and labor leaders meant that McCloy, Weible, and their staffs had to identify more clearly the enemies of their plan. As a result, their offices began compiling information on individuals that they perceived opposed UMT. One manifestation of this effort was an official study on opponents of UMT. The title of the study was "Summary of Study of Personnel in the Overhead of Organizations Devoted to International Peace and in Some Respect Opposed to Universal Military Training." The study tracked members of organizations opposed to UMT in two distinct but related ways. First, it listed the organizations themselves and categorized each by how many leading members also had active memberships in other organizations opposed to UMT. The second part of the study shifted the emphasis from organizations to individuals. It listed individuals ranked from most involved in opposition to least involved. The ranking was based on the number of organizations that the individuals were active in. As the study explained, "They are listed not in alphabetical order but rather by the frequency rate of organizations to which they belong. It may be assumed then that in the upper ten names on the list in part two will be found the individuals of greatest influence, ingenuity, and ability in opposition to Universal Military Training." The top ten opponents of UMT, according to this study, with their corresponding number of opposition group memberships, were A. J. Muste (7), A. Philip Randolph (7), Allan Knight Chalmers (6), Oswald Garrison Villard (6), John Haynes Holmes (5), B. F. McLaurin (4), Victor Reuther (4), George S. Counts (3), Henry Hitt Crane (3), and Dorothy Detzer (3). It is interesting that Thurgood Marshall was listed on this study because of his involvement with the ACLU and NAACP, as both organizations opposed UMT.[14]

One of the most fascinating aspects of the opposition to UMT and its impact on the US Army's campaign was religion. Not only did the concept of UMT spark both resistance and support among various religious groups, but it also produced a reaction within the War Department to mobilize religious assets in order to counter opposition. This effort started in January 1945. On January 17, McCloy wrote to Gen. Douglas MacArthur, who was then serving as commander in chief of the Southwest Pacific area and was still actively engaged in planning and executing combat operations. McCloy sought the transfer of Russell C. Stroup to begin work on UMT immediately. As McCloy explained to MacArthur:

> As you are probably aware, the question of Universal Military Training in the postwar period will probably be the subject of hearings before Congressional Committees within the next several months. Part of the opposition to the subject consists of organized religious groups such as the Federal Churches of Christ of America. We have been attempting to combat the opposition of such groups by all means at our disposal. For the purpose of attempting to change the opinions of the religious groups, we need a Chaplain who has been commissioned from civilian life since 1940, has had overseas service, who believes in Universal Military Training, and who is a good writer and speaker. I am told that you have such an officer, namely, Chaplain (Captain) Russell C. Stroup, 0–4911090, in the First Infantry, of the Sixth Division, which is part of your command. I should very much like to obtain the services of this Chaplain to assist in informing the public, particularly the religious groups, of the plans for Universal Military Training.[15]

MacArthur immediately agreed, and within a short period of time Stroup was in Washington managing the War Department's efforts to counter religious opposition to UMT. Stroup embarked on his task with earnestness. On February 22, he outlined his planned crusade for Weible. He envisioned using chaplains "for promoting the cause of UMT among the church groups of the country," with the broader purpose of "presenting the UMT program to the general public." His plan also entailed more direct activity. He tasked chaplains with "attending the various church conferences" during the spring of 1945, with the intent of actively participating in the "discussion of UMT which is certain to come before the conferences for action in the form of resolutions." In addition to influencing the conferences, Stroup requested the distribution of articles by "selected chaplains and ministers" to the religious publications of all the major denominations. Some of these chaplains were still on active duty, whereas others were recently retired. Stroup prompted Weible to call for help. In response, Weible requested assistance from William R. Arnold, army chief of chaplains, to know whether the "prospect that Chaplains in the military service, upon returning to their civilian charges and duties, will have any constructive effect upon the attitude of their respective churches toward this matter." To this end, Weible tasked Arnold with providing a list of a dozen recently retired chaplains to work with the American Legion in their efforts on UMT.[16]

However, Stroup did not only want to send out chaplains to the denominations. He also envisioned bringing religious allies to Washington. Weible's office compiled a list of church leaders "who might be called upon for testimony before the committees of Congress holding hearings on the Bills dealing with UMT." Weible was highly interested in the positions that these church leaders took on UMT. He wanted to ensure that his office compiled a list of church leaders that were supportive of UMT. As Stroup reported, "We are now checking on the men whose names were submitted to make certain that they are in favor of UMT." The implicit assumption was that they would be taken off the list if their support waned.[17]

Stroup's second task was to complete a more detailed study of the position of religious groups relative to UMT. He produced a report entitled "A Survey of the Position of the Churches Relative to UMT." In it, he provided the basic assessment of religious resistance to UMT and thus suggested some strategies to overcome religious objections. Stroup made several basic assumptions. First, he assumed that religion did not mark a serious obstacle to UMT. As he clarified, "It is a fairly safe generalization that the more vocal church agencies and individuals are not always the most representative. The probability is that on this as on other subjects the opinion of the lay members of the church at least does not differ greatly from that of the public at large." Stroup indicated the dangers of not actively marketing the positive religious features of UMT. He warned, "There is always the possibility, however, that unless those favorable to UMT can reach church members through the church press or meetings and conferences they may be unduly influenced by a one sided presentation of a vital issue."[18]

Stroup attached to the survey an appendix entitled "Suggestions for Service Command and Supervisory Chaplains." In it he suggested that commands seek out those chaplains "who are in favor of UMT." Once commands identified those chaplains, he urged that they involve them in marketing UMT. He advised, "It is hoped that every encouragement will be given them to express their views on this matter from the platform and in the press provided that they are informed and provided further that they emphasize as far as possible the moral and spiritual aspects of the subject since it is on these points that they may speak with the greatest authority." Stroup also suggested, "It is particularly desirable that these men should appear before church and civic groups such as church brotherhoods, women's organizations, young peoples' societies, P.T.A., Kiwanis, Rotary, etc. It is also desirable that they should gain a place for their opinions in church publications. This might be done most effectively in answering such adverse articles as may appear by letters to the editor. No such article should be permitted to go unanswered." Stroup expected these chaplains to reach out to civilian religious leaders in their community to help influence public opinion regarding UMT. He hoped that "in personal contacts and through informal gatherings with their ministerial associates in civilian communities they may help to mould church opinion and perhaps persuade such civilians to make pronouncements upon UMT for which they can provide them with information and source material."[19]

Stroup closed his benediction with a disclaimer that the War Department did not want the appearance of putting pressure upon chaplains to promote UMT. As he advertised, "All such activities must be purely voluntary." He then tasked the chaplains with the responsibility of "protecting the War Department from any adverse reaction that might come from the slightest suggestion that the chaplains were being used unwillingly to support UMT or that the Chaplain Corps had become a propaganda agency for the War Department." Stroup did not want fear of impropriety to limit action by the chaplains, though. He urged them that "on the other hand, we feel that in fairness to the general public the experience of the chaplains and their informed opinion should be made available." In context, Stroup's disclaimer was a clear attempt to create the perception of propriety. The documents clearly suggest that his view of voluntary meant that supporters of UMT in the War Department should seek out the chaplains who favored their proposal and employ them in a voluntary fashion. The clear implication lingered that those chaplains who did not support UMT should simply remain on the sidelines.[20]

Stroup articulated the type of religious argument that might help overcome opposition among religious groups: "There is no valid reason why a year of military training should not strengthen rather than weaken the character of the trainee who comes from a Christian home and there is reason to hope that hundreds of thousands of others might find in that year of contact with Christian ministers and priests a religious faith which otherwise they might never have known. It is important that this side of the picture should be forcefully presented to the parents of men affected by the program."[21] Such an evangelical tone would reverberate throughout the efforts of War Department personnel to overcome religious opposition to UMT.

Stroup transitioned from the general religious aspects of UMT to specific ones. He compiled and updated a detailed list of major denominations and the number of members that each claimed. He also met with key religious leaders both to get their opinions and to attempt to overcome their religious objections. He met with Father Tanner of the National Catholic Welfare Conference in order to ascertain the attitude of the Roman Catholic Church toward UMT. The feedback was not what Stroup wanted to hear. As he relayed to Weible, "Throughout the interview, however, Father Tanner left no doubt that he believed that no individual or organization could favor UMT and remain in accord with the policy of the Church." Undeterred, Stroup went on to meet with the National Jewish Welfare Board.[22]

Emerging from these individual conferences, Stroup recommended to Weible a new stratagem. He suggested that they convince religious opposition groups that instead of constituting an "evil effect," the UMT program would actually improve the morals of the young men involved.

He proposed, "It would seem that the best way to answer arguments as to the evil effect of UMT on the character of our youth would be to present a positive program containing challenging provisions for the development through I&E, Special Service, the Chaplain Corps, etc. of the moral and spiritual side of the trainees' personality."[23] Weible liked the idea. As a result, he and Stroup hunted for a mechanism with which to overcome religious opposition by promoting the religious benefits of UMT.

The first such opportunity came to Weible's attention on April 26. Joseph R. Koch, an army colonel, chaplain to the Fourth Army, relayed that his command had just completed the first Meet the Chaplain program in San Antonio, Texas, on the tenth of that month. Held in the auditorium of the Scottish Rite Temple, fifty-five chaplains coordinated the event, and over two thousand people attended. Its success led to similar Meet the Chaplain events in such far-flung locations as Los Angeles and Muskogee, Oklahoma. The program originated with a letter from the mother of a young soldier in the Fourth Army who wrote, "Too bad we mothers do not have the opportunity of meeting chaplains—there is much we could discuss; it would be of benefit to us as well as our sons and daughters in the service." Koch immediately saw the possibilities of the program in much larger terms. As he excitedly relayed to Weible, the program held promise for "education of the citizenry" regarding UMT. As Koch envisioned, the Meet the Chaplain program could assure the public that "when Universal Military Training becomes a matter for public discussion, that the religious and moral needs of our youth will be emphasized and served, then I believe the opposition of Churches and churchmen and people will become insignificant, and the support of the Churches in general will be had."[24]

Weible wasted no time in expanding the program throughout other commands. Less than two weeks later, on May 10, he wrote to Maj. Gen. Sherman Miles, commanding general, First Service Command, headquartered in Boston, Massachusetts, lauding the program as an excellent pulpit from which chaplains could advocate UMT. He explained, "The interest of this office in the program grows out of our feeling that a better understanding by the public of these activities of the army would help parents to view with increased favor the proposed program of universal military training for all young men in the postwar period."[25]

Stroup's aggressive efforts started running into resistance. In particular, key religious leaders began to question the appropriateness of the active role that Stroup, Weible, McCloy, and others within the War Department were engaging in to promote UMT. One such religious leader was Franklin C. Fry, president of the United Lutheran Church in America. Fry initiated his protest with Weible. He wrote a forceful complaint on May 11 and in it claimed that "the United Lutheran Church in America is unanimously and emphatically on record requesting the United States Government to delay its decision concerning Universal Peacetime Conscription until at least one year after the completion of the present war. I hope to be present at the hearings in Washington in early June and to present this view as vigorously as I can."[26]

More important, Fry claimed that the efforts of War Department officials in overcoming the opposition of religious groups had become inappropriate: "My zeal in that conviction is increased by the apparent indication in your letter that the armed forces are openly propagandizing for the adoption of such a measure. In my judgment there is a high degree of impropriety about such activity." Weible naturally shared Fry's protest with Stroup and implored him to take action. Stroup then contacted Fry in an effort to convert him to the cause. Fry responded just as negatively to Stroup's overtures as he had to Weible's. Fry denied Stroup's request to meet with him to educate him on the positive religious features of the UMT program. In addition, he outlined his displeasure with Stroup's request, emphatically declaring, "I shall be happy indeed to counsel with you concerning the religious aspects of Universal Military Conscription if and when it has been adopted by the Congress. Meanwhile I shall exert myself fully to see to it that you will be relieved of this burden. After all, I am confident that the religious aspects of such a program could not be settled in advance in detail, unless of course the War Department were framing such a bill for the Congress' action."[27]

Stroup was taken aback. He replied that he was "distressed" by Fry's accusations, "not because your charge of 'impropriety' effects me personally but because it casts an unwarranted suspicion on the good faith of the War Department." However, Stroup did not give up. He continued to preach the religious merits of UMT to Fry. He counseled, "For this reason I hasten to disabuse your mind of a misapprehension which I feel certain you would not hold if you were acquainted with all the facts." It was these facts that Stroup was so committed to presenting.[28]

In response to repeated religious opposition to UMT, Weible and

Stroup embarked on a campaign to address the specific religious issues brought up by opponents of UMT. One of the main religious critiques was the impact it might have on the morality of America's youth. Opponents often charged that UMT would erode the morality of American youth by removing them from their homes and churches and marshaling them into camps surrounded by temptation and vice. To counter such charges, Harold W. Kent, Weible's right-hand man on UMT, wrote an article on the religious implications of UMT that was published in *Christian Advocate* in June 1945. In it Kent attempted to overcome the perception that UMT might weaken the moral fiber of young men. He implored religious leaders to view UMT not as a religious problem, but rather as an evangelical opportunity to strengthen the morality of American youth and, more important, to reach nonbelievers. Kent sermonized,

> Indeed, while this is not the purpose of military training, I can see how, properly accepted by our churches, such a program might offer to our Christian forces an unparalleled opportunity to reach the youth of America. Let us remember that more than half of our young men are wholly outside the influence of any church. What a missionary challenge this represents! For years we have recognized the failure of our churches to reach our youth, our men, our un-churched. Here, gathered together each year in training camps we would have the young manhood of America. Have the churches the vision to accept the challenge and give the best we have in ministers and materials or enlarge the horizon, perspective and Christian idealism of the men from Christian homes and to bring the faith of our fathers to "those who have never known?"[29]

Kent's evangelical prose won converts. Ernesta Barlow, vice president of the Citizens Committee for Military Training of Young Men, praised it. She confessed to Kent that she "was delighted with your epistle to the Methodists" and planned to use similar rhetoric in her own efforts to convert nonbelievers. Brig. Gen. Luther Miller, acting chief of chaplains, was ecstatic about the opportunity. He exclaimed, "I like to consider the whole question of universal military training in terms of the opportunity presented to the spiritual forces of America by such a program. Can anyone doubt the magnitude of the opportunity? Under the plan approximately a million young men of 18 would be gathered together each year from all sections of the country and all walks of life forming a great potential congregation. Here we would have literally the young manhood of America available to the ministry of our religious communions."[30]

To Miller, the implications were obvious. He argued that, done properly, UMT would present an evangelical opportunity of vast portent. As he described optimistically, "Given the right sort of chaplains, backed by the resources of the government and the cooperation of the churches of America there is no reason why this should not become the greatest opportunity for the extension of religion that we have ever known."[31]

Initial opposition to the campaign for UMT did not come solely from pacifists, labor unions, and religious groups. One of the most ardent early critics was a longtime army officer, Lt. Col. Roscoe S. Conkling. Conkling had served as a judge advocate general in the US Army during World War I. He eventually became the primary organizer and first director of the draft in New York City in World War I. He had also served as deputy attorney general of the State of New York, and he had remained in the army in World War II. In the spring of 1945, he authored *The Case against Compulsory Peacetime Military Training,* and the Postwar World Council published the brochure in New York on March 24, 1945. Conkling's attack was direct, vociferous, and personal. He asserted that War Department officials used UMT as a propaganda tool to achieve their own ends and inflated the threat to the United States in the postwar world in order to secure the approval of UMT as the solution. He claimed that War Department officials used these "attacks by some conjured-up spectre which constantly and covetously stalks the American nation" to argue for an expanded defense posture in postwar America. He warned, "*Defense* is the scarecrow sought to be erected in our minds." He centered his attack on the militarism that UMT would produce in America.[32]

Even though attacking UMT for promoting militarism was nothing new, Conkling's critique was unique for several reasons. First, he censured the military establishment itself. He made the debate personal and had the military experience and clout to do so. According to him, the main drivers behind the campaign for UMT were noncombat staff officers who had much to gain from the proposed enlargement of the defense establishment:

The most feverishly patriotic planners of *defense* through universal compulsory military service are not in Congress but wear the habil-

iments of high ranking army and navy officers of the regular establishments, or have been recently commissioned from civil life as so
called "specialists" and rapidly promoted during their three or four
years of service, or have become reserve officers since the last war
via the correspondence school and vacation camp routine with its
paper advancements, and ordered to "active" duty within the past
few years; who sit at desks in comfortably appointed offices, receive
thousands of dollars annually for their services—more than less often the recipients of much larger incomes than allowed the regulars
as army or navy peacetime pay or than the civil occupations of the
"specialists" or the reservists yielded—not $50 a month, K rations and
G.I. uniforms to become sweat or blood-soaked or even to be hastily
buried in.[33]

Conkling contended that if the main drivers of the campaign for UMT
were staff officers within the War Department and not Congress or the
executive branch, one would have to question their motives. And he felt
certain they had ulterior ones. The first was that UMT would enlarge the
defense establishment enough to ensure their retention in it even after
the war. He charged, "That is militarism; one side of it; the easy side!
And it is among this grouping of our 'unarmed forces' that the prospect
of universal military service is so attractive and so worth insisting upon
for the good of the nation, and, incidentally, for the possibility that they
themselves will be retained in a new military structure and avoid going
back home, minus the striking and labeling uniform, to work at the pro-
saic old job where superiority must be demonstrated by merit and in free
fields open to all competitors."[34]

Conkling further alleged that an enlarged defense establishment
would also enhance the prospects of advancement within the system
for many of these officers. He contended that "unadulterated patriotism
is not the *sole* reason for the present ballyhoo campaign for compulsory
peacetime military training. Higher and higher permanent rank is the
ever gnawing ambition of the professional army and navy officer from
the beginnings of his service, and attainment is practically assured by
greater and greater masses of soldiers and sailors." To Conkling, the ultimate safeguard against such self-interested policy was ensuring civilian
control of military policy. He argued persuasively that civilians should
be formulating military policy in a democracy, and the military should

be focusing on the best way to execute such policy. He cautioned, "True to our proved theories we must keep our self-interested military minded groups under the absolute control of our civilian population, which policy has successfully prevailed since the first days of the Republic."[35]

Conkling also directly attacked the methods that War Department officials employed in their campaign for UMT. He censured their drive for UMT prior to the end of the war as ill timed. He wrote, "Probably the unfairest aspect of the effort to force compulsory military training upon us is the strategy of its proponents—somehow to get legislation for it quickly passed while we are in the midst of war enthusiasm—or hysteria." Conkling deemed that campaigning for UMT during war was premature, as every effort should go into winning the conflict. To him, anything else was suspect. He also attacked the direct involvement of War Department officials as the primary drivers of the campaign. In a letter to President Truman dated three days prior to the release of his publication, Conkling articulated the view that War Department officials were taking too active a role in promoting UMT. Conkling illuminated an off-the-record meeting that high-ranking members of the War Department, including Forrestal and Weible, had with the Citizens Committee. The meeting took place at the Waldorf Hotel in Washington, DC, at 12:30 on May 25, 1945. Aside from the humorous fact that Conkling lamented that the four-dollar-per-person charge, including gratuity, was outrageously high and a waste of taxpayer dollars, Conkling declared, "Vigorously do we protest this campaigning for peacetime legislation on government time, at government expense and outside their line of duty by high officials of the Army and Navy while our boys under their command are being killed and wounded every hour of the day." Conkling urged that army leaders should be executing policy, not attempting to make it, especially in times of war.[36]

Conkling's attack rested on a supreme confidence in American military might. The American military that Conkling had served in was a strong one in his eyes and had been repeatedly proven so to the world. As Conkling noted with pride, "America fights, how well our enemies twice within a quarter of a century and to their sorrow have learned, when it has to, or is dragged into war. But it is not a warrior nation and certainly, in its normal life, frowns dourly upon grandiose militaristic activity. Yet its doctrines and traditions have proved the most successful of all the nations of history." Such success was even more important to Conkling considering who America's adversaries had been. He made a persuasive case that most of the defeated nations in both World Wars had some form of compulsory military training while the victorious United States had not: "Isn't the complete answer to the proponents of Universal Military Service that America's five major foreign wars have been decisively won without it, the greatest of which were against nations prepared by years of the most exacting compulsory military training of their youths? Every nation we fight today and every nation we fought in 1917–18 had compulsory military training for its young men."[37]

Conkling condemned the campaign for UMT primarily based on militarism. Other army leaders, however, attacked the plan on practical grounds. Some military authorities attacked UMT because they deemed it ineffective at accomplishing its strategic goals. One such military leader was H. C. Holdridge, a retired army brigadier general who had graduated from West Point as part of the class of 1917 and had served almost thirty years in the army. During that time, he had graduated from the Command and General Staff School at Fort Leavenworth in 1938 and had retired honorably from the army in February 1944. Following his service, he became chairman of the Legislative Committee of the Veterans League of America. Holdridge opposed the UMT program on strategic grounds, his primary contention being that in focusing exclusively on UMT as the foundation for the postwar defense establishment, War Department officials failed to account for the massive changes in warfare that World War II had ushered in. He asserted that the army was committing the cardinal sin of war planning: planning for the last war instead of the next, and he contended that War Department officials had completely missed the importance of air power coming out of World War I and now missed the importance of atomic weapons coming out of World War II. He insisted that War Department officials were so far off track that they were not even close to a viable answer. He pleaded, "The army has looked in the back of the book, put its finger on the same old answer 'compulsory military training' and is trying to work the problem backward to force that answer to fit the problem of the atomic bomb. As a matter of fact, not only is that not the right answer, but the problem is no longer in the same old book."[38]

The curious fact was that Holdridge's conception of a possible future war was not completely dissimilar from the ideas of McCloy, Marshall, Weible, and Palmer. As Holdridge avowed, "Even the layman can grasp the fact that the next war—if there is a next war—will be sudden, short, and devastating. The army asks for a force comprising 'strength in being,' and 'immediately available.' The proposed program will give neither." Whereas senior army planners argued that the suddenness of a possible World War III meant that there would be little time for mobilization, and hence a trained citizen reserve was necessary, Holdridge maintained the opposite. He claimed that any force that was not "immediately available" would be useless to secure America. He made two specific strategic points regarding postwar planning. First, he contended that the lack of time to respond to an attack negated the strategic value of UMT. Holdridge reasoned that if American military planners did not have time to train the citizen reserves, then they also would not have time to retrain them. Second, he acknowledged the suddenness and devastation of a possible future war and its impact on actionable intelligence. He claimed that American military planners probably would not know who attacked the United States immediately after an attack and therefore would not be able to retaliate instantly. Holdridge advocated a much smaller defense establishment than previously imagined that focused on highly trained forces in being rather than a small professional army backed up by a moderately trained citizen reserve. Holdridge avoided too many specifics but did support MacArthur's estimate of one hundred thousand as the appropriate size of a postwar army with a much higher standard of training and specialization.[39]

In addition to criticizing the campaign for UMT on strategic grounds, Holdridge also condemned it for being a politicized movement. He maintained that the main drivers behind UMT—the army and the American Legion—were focusing more on which organization could seize control of UMT than on whether UMT was the right answer in the first place. In criticizing the Legion, Holdridge proclaimed, "Again the Legion is trying to force the wrong answer without having read the problem. The purpose of the Legion proposal is not to preserve the United States, but is a political move to preserve the National Guard and the Organized Reserves. It has become a race to see who shall run the new conscript army, the Regular Army, or the National Guard and the Organized Reserves backed by the power of the Legion. National defense is being kicked around like a football, by the 'ins' and the 'outs' who are struggling for supremacy."[40]

Holdridge reserved his greatest criticism for the army. Whereas he saw the leaders of the American Legion as attempting to maneuver that organization into a more favorable position in controlling the UMT structure, Holdridge perceived the army as purposely deflecting attention away from the strategic realities of UMT towards peripheral aspects of the program:

> Our army leaders are trying to sugar-coat the pill. They are trying to sell us a pig in a poke, by emphasizing the by-products in education, health, recreation, and discipline. This raises a basic conflict in attitudes which the army cannot resolve. The army is not, and cannot be, a benign, socially-conscious institution acting as god-father to our youth. *This is no youth movement.* Our youth can learn to clean their teeth, do 3rd grade arithmetic, or the meaning of true discipline, in our homes and in our schools. We do not need to turn the army into a reformatory for the standardization of military discipline. . . . An army has only one purpose—*to kill.* Its training program must be directed toward teaching how to kill, by the most effective and brutal means. Anything else is pure eye-wash.[41]

One final group that voiced opposition to UMT was education leaders. George F. Zook, president of the American Council on Education, took the lead in articulating the concerns of educators. The council represented more than sixty national and regional associations, fifty associate member organizations, and more than seven hundred institutional members, including universities, colleges, junior colleges, and city school systems. Zook aimed directly at the underlying rationale military planners gave for UMT. As he cautioned, "Defense involves much more than the military mobilization of manpower." He urged Congress to give thoughtful consideration to "alternate ways through which adequate defense can be maintained."[42]

Zook recommended that military planners take four actions before committing the country to UMT. First, he advocated that leaders seriously consider the Martin resolution "asking for an immediate international agreement eliminating compulsory military services from the policies and practices of all nations." Second, he urged that civilian leaders in either the legislative or the executive branch "appoint a National Commission to study every aspect of total defense and to make a report prior to any action on the question of compulsory military training." Third, he demanded that "definite quotas of minimum military needs to assure adequate national defense be determined" and pushed that these quotas be filled "by voluntary enlistment." Finally, he pleaded with military planners to focus more attention on international efforts for peace. He urged that American leaders "concentrate upon the fundamental and vital issue of world organization to preserve peace and security by strengthening the existing United Nations Organization."[43]

Zook closed his critique on UMT with an interesting assertion. He argued forcefully that civilian leaders should control military policy decisions in America during peacetime, although he conceded that during war, military authorities deserved special authority. As he reasoned, "During war when there was but one end to be gained—that of total victory on the battlefront—the military were the undisputed authorities as to the ways through which this end could be achieved." However, Zook quickly pointed out that peacetime was different. As he claimed, "In time of peace there are other values than military strategy, and in the weighing of such values, the civilian has equal responsibility with the military."[44]

As military planners such as McCloy, Marshall, Porter, and Weible marketed UMT, opposition arose. The resistance was multifaceted and composed of multiple groups. Pacifists, labor leaders, clergy, some military professionals, and educators all voiced serious opposition to UMT for various reasons. As opponents pointed out legitimate concerns, die-hard advocates shifted their rationale. Sometimes the shifts were subtle, but they were important, nonetheless. Those directly responsible for campaigning for UMT strayed from the mobilization basis that had underpinned their campaign. Other strange justifications for UMT began to be used, such as religious outreach. For every criticism War Department officials thought they overcame, they failed to realize that they were making UMT something much larger than just an improvement to mobilization. Instead, they were allowing UMT to become a much broader policy that would impact American society for better or for worse. In this manner, the War Department began losing control of its own campaign as others began to see potential value in UMT.

7   A Matter of Broad Policy

In that way, we would have a real democratic army, a real citizen army, which
could be continually trained in the ideals of a republican form of government.
—Harry S. Truman

For these and for other reasons your committee, therefore, recommends that
the Congress adopt, as a matter of broad policy, a system of universal military
training for the critical years ahead.
—Woodrum committee

The US Army's campaign for UMT became politicized in the summer of 1945. In essence, UMT promoters in the War Department such as McCloy, Marshall, Weible, and Palmer faced a dilemma. Their ultimate goal was to institute UMT in order to create a viable General Reserve to speed mobilization. To secure their goal, they needed to court politicians who could champion their cause and translate their proposal into a legislative reality. Doing so would risk surrendering some measure of control over the campaign. The political phase of the campaign for UMT began with congressional hearings during the summer of 1945 that would publicly explore issues of postwar military policy. Informally known as the Woodrum committee after its chairman, Clifton A. Woodrum (D-VA), the actual title of the committee was the Select Committee on Postwar Military Policy. The key individual responsible for the formation of the Woodrum committee was none other than James W. Wadsworth. Wadsworth submitted a resolution creating the committee which provided that Speaker of the House Samuel T. Rayburn appoint twenty-three representatives—seven from the House Committee on Military Affairs, seven from the House Committee on Naval Affairs, and nine who were not associated with either of those committees. The Woodrum committee's charter was to "investigate all matters relating to the post-war military requirements of the United States."[1]

The committee wasted little time in starting hearings. Committee members held an administrative meeting on April 14 and began holding formal hearings on April 24. The agenda of the Woodrum committee was an ambitious one. It included five main areas of focus: procurement and training of personnel, including UMT and ROTC; organization of the reserve components; unity of command; supply issues, including research and development, maintenance, and industrial mobilization; and "probable post-war missions of the armed forces."[2]

The most intriguing development of the Woodrum committee was to reveal Dwight D. Eisenhower's views on UMT. His stance would prove crucial in determining whether the senior leadership of the army would continue to campaign for UMT once Marshall left as army chief of staff. Eisenhower proved up to the task, writing Woodrum on June 2, 1945, to express his "general views on the universal military training program after the war." Eisenhower warned against the tempting notion that great technological advances negated the importance of mobilization in warfare. As he cautioned, "In spite of all technological advances, numbers (great strength in all arms, land, sea and air) are vitally important in war and America's approved military system must aim at the *rapid* development, after the beginning of any serious war, of the country's maximum potentialities in leadership, manpower, equipment, technique and industrial capacity." Eisenhower claimed that the solution was UMT. He had seen the performance of partially trained forces in Tunisia and contrasted their performance with that of the thoroughly trained forces he witnessed later in Italy and France. Eisenhower hoped UMT could avoid the loss of life and tactical ineffectiveness that the army first experienced in North Africa by creating a trained manpower reserve that could speed mobilization. As he advocated, "The great forces necessary in war must be produced through a citizen training system in time of peace; that is, with minimum sized professional nucleus and maximum capacity for training the national manpower."[3]

In addition to Congress, other government agencies, most notably the State Department, showed a growing interest in UMT. One of the major developments that paralleled the campaign for UMT was establishment of the United Nations. Much of the debate surrounding UMT hinged on the effect UMT would have on both the peace negotiations of World War II and the establishment of the United Nations. One leading advocate of UMT in the State Department was Joseph C. Grew, acting secretary of state. Grew attended the Women's Conference on UMT held April 26, 1945, and at that meeting outlined his experiences as a diplomat and how they influenced his thinking. He had been a diplomat in Germany preceding World War I and a diplomat in Japan preceding World War II. In both cases, he dealt directly with foreign military officers preparing for war who perceived that America's lack of preparedness signaled her determination not to act. These experiences had convinced him that military strength was a necessary deterrent to war. Grew claimed that UMT would provide just such a deterrent: "Those are my fundamental thoughts, as I have expressed them, and I believe and I'd like to say with all the force possible that from the point of view of our national interests in the world at large, this proposed plan for a year's military training is not only going to be a great asset, but in my opinion, it is absolutely essential for our future welfare, security and national life."[4]

By June it was clear that concern was being raised about the impact any potential UMT program would have on international peace agreements. Such a situation required close coordination between officials in the State Department and the War Department. Julius C. Holmes, assistant secretary of state, wrote to Weible to coordinate a rebuttal to criticism that UMT would hinder diplomatic efforts at both peace negotiations and the initial organization of the United Nations. After recalling that Grew had "stated the view of the [State] Department that Universal Military Training is a buttress for our effective participation in an International Security Organization" before the Woodrum committee, Holmes showed Weible a form letter from the secretary of state that would be sent to organizations concerned with the relationship between the Dumbarton Oaks proposals and UMT. The goal of such a letter was clear. It was to relieve any concern on the part of the recipients that "interest in the Dumbarton Oaks Proposals be compromised by the adoption now of post-war universal military training legislation." The letter was intended to provide "an expression of the views of the [State] Department on this subject."[5]

That "expression" was complete support of "General Marshall's conception of a national military institution" composed of a small professional standing army supported by a citizen army reserve. The State Department letter went further than merely advocating support of the War Department plan for UMT. It actually argued that other government departments should follow the advice of the War Department personnel on military policy and reasoned that implementation of UMT would not jeopardize the international discussions taking place. The letter stated,

The [State] Department's view is that we civilians should, therefore, accept the judgment of our highest military authority, that unless a universal military training system were to be in effect, there would not be available the reserve of trained men required to make both our military and our naval establishments adequate for meeting our obligations in an international security organization and for meeting any other possible future needs of providing for our national security. Until experience shall have proved that the international security organization will be able to preserve the peace of the world, and that we can enjoy our liberties and our way of life without having to defend them solely with an American army, navy, and air force, we cannot afford to risk our national security by not being prepared for any eventuality.[6]

An important shift took place during the summer of 1945. Earlier that spring, President Roosevelt passed away. Harry S. Truman assumed the office on April 12, 1945. Truman's unexpected ascendancy to the presidency marked a significant event in the campaign for UMT. Immediately upon assuming office, President Truman grappled with a myriad of issues ranging from the atomic bomb to demobilization to price controls. One of the issues he quickly addressed was UMT. Truman's background of service in the National Guard, his World War I experiences in the army, and his deep personal interest in military history demonstrated his individual attraction to military issues. UMT was no exception. Roosevelt had always been ambiguous towards UMT. On several occasions he discussed the issue with reporters but often left his support for the plan vague and clouded with generalities. He certainly never took an active role in pressing for action on the issue. Truman brought a different attitude to bear. He became truly interested in UMT and, often against the advice of his closest confidants, actively pushed for UMT. During the summer of 1945 Truman crafted his initial plan for UMT. It differed in notable ways from that of army leaders. First of all, his conception of UMT emphasized more strongly the aspect of universality. He wanted to lessen physical qualifications dramatically to include young men who would clearly not have qualified for military service by World War II standards. As he explained, "Every young man, including the so called 4F's—particularly those who have some slight eye defects, those with flat feet, those with dental shortcomings—would be required to attend. Only actual cripples not able to walk, not able to see, or those who are mentally deficient, would be excused."[7]

Army leaders had allowed some reduction of physical standards, but

President Harry S. Truman, ca. 1945.
(US Army Signal Corps, Courtesy Harry S. Truman Library)

always with an emphasis on the ability of the individual to possess some military utility as a reservist. Truman, on the other hand, envisioned a program that would take virtually every eighteen-year-old male, even ones who could not function as soldiers. His rationale for such wide inclusion was simple. He felt that many of the ailments that had ruled out wartime service were minor and could be surmounted. He commented,

"My honest opinion is that most minor physical defects could be overcome during a training period of this sort."[8] Truman saw UMT as an excellent opportunity to improve national health.

In addition to opening up military training to a much larger audience than army leaders contemplated, Truman's initial plan shifted UMT away from mobilization planning to the broader impact it could have on American society: "These young men could be taught discipline, be trained in association with other young men, and understand exactly what it means to make a contribution to his country which is necessary if it is to be maintained."[9] He portrayed UMT as a way to inculcate much-needed discipline in American youth, overcome sectional and class differences in youth from wide-ranging locations and backgrounds, and educate future generations of Americans on citizenship. Truman's ascendancy to the presidency marked a shift in emphasis of the campaign for UMT from mobilization to citizenship.

Truman also differed from army leaders' focus on creating a viable enlisted reserve by focusing on an improved officer reserve instead. Truman depicted UMT as an opportunity to democratize the leadership ranks of the army. Explaining the relationship of UMT to officer development, Truman exclaimed that "I would get the officers for this professional army from accredited schools, commission them after not less than a year of service in the ranks, and from special training camps after they had a complete understanding of what it means to be a private in the ranks." At the heart of Truman's rationale was his collective disdain for military "brass hats" or professional, career military officers. Truman planned to use UMT to convert both West Point and Annapolis from officer commissioning programs to graduate schools for senior military planners. As he detailed, he would "abolish the special schools for the training of officers, and use them for other purposes." Truman's rationale was simple. He saw UMT as one way to democratize the army and to avoid the creation of a military caste of officers able to dominate military policy. To Truman, one of the major benefits of UMT would be that all officers would be trainees first. As a result, they would become better leaders who were more attuned to the lives of the men they would lead. The result would be that "we would have a real democratic army, a real citizen army, which could be continually trained in the ideals of a republican form of government; and I believe we would have a successful backbone for defense which would be respected by the other nations with whom we have to do business, and which under no circumstances could be turned into a military machine for the personal aggrandizement of some dictator."[10]

On July 5, 1945, the members of the Woodrum committee submitted their final report to the House of Representatives. They recommended "that the Congress adopt, as a matter of broad policy, a system of universal military training for the critical years ahead." The committee went beyond merely articulating broad policy guidance, though. It also outlined seven specific characteristics of the type of UMT program that would be most advantageous for the United States to adopt. The committee recommended that UMT take account of the "conditions of modern warfare"; integrate "future technological developments"; "be universal and democratic"; conform with the structure of the National Defense Act of 1920; preserve the National Guard and Reserve components; "cause the least interference" with education and career development; and "provide for training of men only" and not military service. The significance of the Woodrum committee report was that it represented a congressional endorsement of UMT as a matter of broad policy. Such an endorsement would provide valuable ammunition for advocates of UMT pursuing its enactment.[11]

Another significant revelation of the Woodrum committee was the break between officials in the War Department and President Truman regarding UMT. Following the conclusion of the hearings, Wilton B. Persons, chief of the legislative and liaison division, indicated to Marshall that there was reason to believe that Truman's views on UMT differed from those War Department officials advocated. As he noted regretfully, "The President indicated that his thinking was not then in accord with War and Navy Department planning. Among the probable points of difference are (a) The continuous year of training, and (b) The nonmilitary aspects, i.e., educational and social welfare features."[12] Persons's intuition proved correct. Truman's views on UMT were actually quite different from those that McCloy, Marshall, Weible, and Palmer developed and marketed. Whereas those army leaders conceived UMT as a strategic response to postwar manpower requirements, Truman championed UMT for more wide-ranging reasons.

By early September, Truman made UMT the primary issue for discussion at his cabinet meetings. In those early sessions, Henry L. Stimson played a major role. He articulated a new shift in strategic emphasis for

President Truman and his cabinet, January 31, 1947.
(National Park Service, Abbie Rowe, Courtesy Harry S. Truman Library)

UMT. Whereas in the first two years of the campaign for UMT army leaders such as Porter, Weible, and Palmer routinely argued that UMT was
required to speed mobilization through the creation of a General Reserve, Stimson argued that UMT was required as a deterrent. As Stimson
explained, "Some of the gentlemen this afternoon have discussed this
subject of military training from the point of view of what it will do or
not do in regard to the defense of the country in wartime. I prefer to look
at it from another angle. I do not want war to come. I want to prevent
it from ever coming. And I want to look at this subject of training from
that standpoint."[13]

Stimson implored the cabinet to consider the difference in international perspective between the wartime and peacetime images of American youth around the globe. Aware of a view different from the positive

international image of courageous young American soldiers fighting for freedom in World War II, Stimson reminded the cabinet that "the picture which is painted of the American youth in peacetime is a very different picture. It is a picture painted by our movies and our newspapers and it is not a flattering one." Stimson argued that the international view of peacetime American youth was one of weakness. To staunch preparedness advocates like Stimson, weakness invited aggression. As he explained, "The people of other nations during those times have regularly got the impression of this nation as a frivolous, selfish, pleasure loving country which did not take the stern business of living in a rough international world seriously. Consequently they have habitually underestimated our patriotism and our ability to fight. Twice in my lifetime I have seen this happen." Stimson claimed that UMT would correct such negative impressions. He contended that the proposal would certainly convince other countries—friends and foes alike—that America was prepared to fulfill its commitments as a world leader. He explained,

> One of the main reasons why I favor universal military training is that I am sure that it will combat this dangerous misconception which the outside nations habitually form of us in peacetime. They will not only regard us as unprepared, which will be true, but they will also regard us as too irresponsible ever to take the trouble to prepare or to defend ourselves. They will form the same impression of our young men that our movies and our other peacetime expressions regularly give them. I believe that it will have a tremendous effect upon our surrounding neighbors, both friendly and unfriendly, in the outside world to know that America takes it duties of citizenship in the family of nations seriously enough to stand a year of training to perform the primary duty of citizens, namely to defend their country.[14]

Stimson's portrayal of UMT as being an effective deterrent convinced Truman, who with his advisors spent early September preparing a message to Congress on UMT. By September 13 they had a final draft that detailed Truman's thinking on the topic. Truman asserted that UMT was required to signal American resolve and as a result would be a deterrent to nations contemplating aggression against American interests. As he planned to tell Congress, "It is, therefore, of enormous importance that our neighbors in the world, friendly and unfriendly, now understand the true character of the American people. In the past three decades, we have twice hidden our giant strength under a veneer of internal interest and of apparent obliviousness to the world outside our own continent. And twice in that short time aggressor nations, misconceiving that latent strength, have sought to strike us down in bloody and premeditated wars." Truman maintained that UMT would prevent such misconceptions. As he explained, "A basic purpose of universal military training is to encourage the other world powers to believe that the United States not only desires, but is now ready to enforce its determination, to outlaw aggression." He formulated a call for UMT as an outgrowth of the new-found preeminence of the United States in the postwar era in which the proposal was both democratic and fiscally responsible. Discussing "the responsible burden of world leadership that victory has placed upon" America, he argued that "if we are to bear this responsibility, we must choose a way that is compatible with our democratic traditions and that is within the financial resources of our people." The solution to Truman was UMT: "That way lies in the adoption of a democratic and universal system of military training of our youth. Under such a system, every young American who is physically able would be called upon to give one year to his country." To add strength to his appeal to Congress urging enactment of UMT, Truman finished by citing the final report of the Woodrum committee recommending UMT and seconded the report's conclusions.[15]

President Truman's cabinet spent September reviewing his plan for UMT and providing their feedback. Most of his cabinet supported the general concept, although there was no shortage of disagreement over the preferable details. For example, Stimson already openly advocated UMT and had for years. Secretary of the Interior Harold L. Ickes supported UMT but focused on the democratization of military leadership that Truman had proposed. He declared to Truman that "this objective has my enthusiastic support. We hear too much about cliques made up of those who have graduated from the service schools." Not surprisingly, Ickes strongly supported Truman's plan to convert West Point and Annapolis to military graduate schools. Fred M. Vinson, secretary of the treasury, expressed to Truman his "firm belief that military training is necessary to strengthen this Nation and to maintain its effective vigilance" but also suggested broadening the scope of UMT "to develop disciplined and constructive thinking, as well as to reduce the illiteracy rate." Maj. Gen. Philip B. Fleming, administrator of the Federal Works

Agency, informed Truman that he was "thoroughly convinced that for many years to come we must have compulsory military training along the lines suggested" by Truman. Fleming also supported Truman's shift in emphasis to the social benefits of UMT. Fleming emphasized both the literacy and health advantages that the program might provide. Fleming suggested that illiteracy could "rather easily be eradicated in the course of compulsory military training of the type proposed" and that many physical defects could also "be eradicated during military training to the enhancement of the nation's health as a whole." The one notable exception in the cabinet was Henry A. Wallace, secretary of commerce, who disagreed with the basic premise of UMT, although he did endorse Truman's shift away from an exclusively military program to a broader social program.[16]

The most contentious feedback on Truman's plan for UMT came from the War Department. Secretary of War Robert P. Patterson distilled major differences between the War Department approach to UMT and Truman's own. On September 21, 1945, Patterson cautioned that he held two major areas of disagreement with the President. They were the demand by officials in the War Department that the primary function of UMT must remain military utility—hence a need to avoid mentioning vocational skills—and the requirement for one continuous year rather than a shorter period of training. Patterson informed Truman that his own conception of UMT differed in fundamental ways from the President's. The first difference was the length of training. Officials in the War Department had zealously and consistently advocated one continuous year. All of their planning for the past two years was based on that assumption. Truman's plan proposed four months of training. Patterson warned that without one continuous year, "the efficacy of the program would be prejudiced, if not destroyed." Patterson articulated other points of disagreement. He complained that Truman's focus on vocational training for those not physically qualified for military service would distract the program from its military mission: "The Department is concerned, however, lest this statement be construed to mean the development of a system of vocational education alien to the military mission of a program of universal military training." In addition, Patterson felt that Truman's plan might allow National Guard officers to be commissioned without going through UMT. He argued that they should go through UMT like everyone else. Patterson not surprisingly raised objections over Truman's proposed plan to convert West Point to a graduate school instead of basic officer training. Patterson reasoned, "It is further believed that a year of universal military training as a prerequisite would greatly enhance the undergraduate course at the Military Academy."[17]

Truman's personal advisors, Clark M. Clifford and George M. Elsey, spent all of September and most of October revising drafts of Truman's upcoming speech to Congress on UMT. As a result, Truman modified several of his initial plans for UMT to conform more closely to the War Department's proposal—or at least to avoid outright contention. For example, the issue of one continuous year continued to differentiate Truman and War Department officials. On October 15, Elsey confided that a key administration figure, Samuel I. Rosenman, was convinced that the army position of one continuous year made the most sense. He remembered, "On the question of 12 months solid, or in phases, Rosenman has been sold to the Army idea of a straight solid year. President is wavering." Since there was still no solid agreement between the two camps, Clifford suggested ambiguity to avoid controversy. As Elsey recalled, "Clifford suggests that President duck the issue to simply say there must be 12 months training. Let Congress decide in what form."[18]

On October 23, 1945, Truman addressed Congress specifically on UMT. He once again used the Woodrum committee's report to create the impression that the initiative for UMT rested squarely with Congress: "The importance of universal training has already been recognized by the Congress, and the Congress has wisely taken the initiative in this program." Truman specifically cited the Woodrum committee and discussed the fact that the committee had heard from a wide array of groups concerned with UMT. He declared, "After careful consideration the Committee has approved the broad policy of universal military training for the critical years ahead. I concur in that conclusion, and strongly urge the Congress to adopt it." In making his case for UMT, Truman clearly moved closer to the War Department's plan. He discussed the General Reserve as a rationale for UMT and also called for one full year of training followed by six years in the General Reserve—a clear concession from his earlier advocacy of four separate three-month periods of training. His conversion to the War Department policy was certainly not complete, though. In the remainder of his message he hammered home the social benefits of UMT. As he reasoned, UMT would substantially aid American society because "the period of training could well be used to

Harry S. Truman addresses a joint session of Congress
advocating a program for universal military training, October 23, 1945.
(Courtesy Harry S. Truman Library)

raise the physical standards of the nation's manpower, to lower its illiteracy rate, and to develop in our young men the ideals of responsible
American citizenship."[19]

In November, James F. Byrnes, secretary of state, publicly favored enactment of some form of UMT. He told members of Congress, "At the
outset of my remarks this morning, I should like to make clear that I
advocate adoption by the Congress of legislation establishing Universal
Military Training for all young men. I say this as a matter of personal
conviction. But I am none the less certain that our progress toward
reaching a sound basis for lasting peace through cooperation with other
nations depends squarely on this Government's willingness to remain a
strong military as well as moral force in the councils of the world."[20] Even
more striking was the reason why Byrnes held this position. In addition
to expressing "a matter of personal conviction," he also relayed to members of Congress that "the President and our military commanders hold
the position that only through the trained civilian reserve provided by

Universal Military Training for all young men can this nation safeguard its security. I do not consider myself a military expert, but as an American citizen I feel that the logic which has led them to this conclusion is unassailable."[21]

Byrnes addressed two specific issues that were becoming potential stumbling blocks for the army's UMT efforts: the impact of UMT during peace negotiations and the effect of UMT on the formation of an international peace organization. Byrnes countered the contention that increasing American military strength in the form of UMT would undermine the United Nations process. He forcefully emphasized:

> On the contrary, a strong military and naval establishment will go far to convince other nations that the United States is determined to carry out the obligations we have assumed as a member of the United Nations Organization. This is not a matter of opinion, but a fact which is implicit in the charter of this body which I had the honor to declare in force on October 24, 1945. We have accepted the responsibility, in common with other nations signatory to this charter, of working constructively for peace in the world—maintaining peace by force, if necessary. For this purpose we have obligated ourselves to furnish such troops, planes, vessels and material of war as may be required of us to join in discouraging or crushing an aggressor. Our share in such a cooperative venture might be small if the threat were minor. But in the event of a major crisis, our diplomacy could make itself felt only if the aggressor were convinced that the might of a trained America could be mobilized immediately if he were so foolhardy as to pursue his aims.[22]

The origins of such an influential argument for UMT were found in the lingering memories of the Munich Pact of 1938. Byrnes, along with many Americans—especially diplomatic and military leaders—saw in Munich an important lesson for the immediate postwar era. Their mantra became, "If you want peace, prepare for war." As Byrnes concluded, "The beginnings of the war just ended contain the clearest lessons for all peace-loving countries who feel that their appeals to reason and justice will be effective. There was only one appeal which could have stopped it. The certainty that the democracies could and would react instantly to any attack. The certainty that they were unable to react effectively determined Hitler and his General Staff that their gamble was well worth taking."[23] Such an attitude clearly revealed that preparedness measures such as UMT were being planted in what was highly fertile ground.

Other groups also attempted to exert influence over UMT. In June 1946 the American Legion presented their own plan for UMT that differed in significant ways from the army's. The Legion plan called for the creation of a National Security Training Corps (NSTC). It also called for a civilian commission of five people appointed by the President to oversee the implementation of training. There would be a civilian executive director as well as a civilian welfare board composed of between ten and twenty-four members to plan the nonmilitary aspects of the training. One significant difference between the army's proposal for UMT and the Legion's plan was that the Legion allowed two types of training. The Legion argued for military training for physically able trainees and "related" training for those not physically able to undergo military training. The related training would include "training for vocations, skills, or services of value to the military security of the nation."[24]

There were other key differences. The Legion plan envisioned four months of basic training followed by a variety of options. The choices included advanced military training in an armed service school or advanced vocational training in a college, both for thirty-six additional weeks. There was enlistment in the regular armed forces for two years or in the National Guard or the Organized Reserves for three years. Finally, there was the option to continue training in the NSTC for another thirty-six weeks.[25]

The conclusion of World War II had come suddenly. No less rapidly, the campaign for UMT underwent a significant shift with the end of the war. What had been a US Army campaign for more than two years experienced a political metamorphosis. The increased involvement of Congress and the unexpected ascendancy of Truman to the presidency marked a departure from the realm of purely military policy to broad national policy. As a result, the strategic rationale initially behind UMT began to blur. Army leaders did not abandon UMT but instead were joined by politicians whose views and goals were quite different. It was up to army leaders how they would react. What they decided to do was to conduct an experiment.

8   The Fort Knox Experiment

This unit is in effect, a training aid in the task of convincing the mass of the American people that UMT, as contemplated by the War Department, will be beneficial to the average American boy. Here critics may come and prove or disprove their criticisms. With a section of UMT materialized on the ground, nebulous generalities should give way to specific comments. We should be able to get the discussion on the value of UMT training out of the realm of hypothesis and bring it into the world of practical reality.
—John M. Devine

Congress, conscious of votes and mothers, would be hard to persuade. But the Army had a test-tube experiment in which U.M.T. was apparently working well. From its youngest recruits it had drawn a battalion, made them U.M.T. guinea pigs at Fort Knox.
—*Time*

If every one of the 140,000,000 people in America could visit this convincing experiment at Fort Knox I feel certain that they would endorse universal training.
—Karl T. Compton

As the year 1946 came to a close, the US Army's campaign for UMT shifted from Washington, DC, to Louisville, Kentucky. It also shifted from theory to reality. In theory, the army planned for UMT to last one year composed of two distinct phases. The first phase would last approximately six months and focus on individual training. The first nine weeks would concentrate on "the fundamentals of life as a soldier" and include topics such as personal hygiene, first aid, field sanitation, individual weapons, physical training, map reading, and cover and concealment. The following seventeen weeks would involve specialized training, during which "the trainee will become qualified in one or more of the hundreds of specialties required by a complex modern Army." The first six-month phase would culminate with the application of individual training, both basic and specialized, at the squad, platoon, and company levels.[1]

The second phase would also last roughly six months but center on unit training. For thirteen weeks "the trainee will learn the workings of a team within a team when his company builds with other companies into battalions, regiments, and finally divisions." This training would include coordination between different types of units such as infantry, artillery, and engineers. During the final eight weeks "the trainee will play his part, with his unit, in large-scale combined maneuvers. Here, in as near combat conditions as can be achieved in training, Air, Ground and Service elements will come together in simulated battle waged by two sides." In reality, the army limited its plan from the envisioned one year to just the first six-month phase dedicated to individual training. It did so because there were not yet multiple UMT units with which to conduct the unit training phase. However, the one-year plan remained the goal for the envisioned nationwide program.[2]

Before long, residents near post heard the cadence of young soldiers referring to themselves as the "Soldiers of the UMT":

> Marching along together
> Soldiers of the UMT
> Marching along together
> For people far and wide to see
> Guardians of the future
> Look to the morning sun
> Our basic training is Infantry
> But when the job is done
> We'll take our places in history
> With men behind the gun . . . Oh,
> Marching along together
> Soldiers of the UMT[3]

By October 31, Army Ground Forces (AGF) headquarters finalized a detailed plan to establish an army unit that would both experiment with the best ways to implement UMT and demonstrate the proposal's value to the American public, and it submitted the detailed plan to the War Department for approval. The AGF headquarters designated the unit the UMT Experimental Demonstration Unit and named Brig. Gen. John M. "Johnny" Devine its commanding officer. Devine was an up-and-coming star in the army who had commanded the Eighth Armored Division during the war. His new unit was a battalion "made up of five (5) composite companies in addition to the necessary Headquarters and Headquarters and Service Company." The unit would be segregated at the company level, as "one of the companies will be composed of Negro

John M. Devine instructs UMT Experimental Unit trainee.
(Courtesy Harry S. Truman Library)

personnel." Army officials chose Fort Knox, Kentucky, as the home for the experimental unit. As its name, Experimental Demonstration Unit for UMT, implied, the primary purpose of the unit was not necessarily military training. Instead, the unit was to demonstrate to the trainees, their parents, and the nation as a whole that UMT was a viable and positive program for national defense. As a result, the unit was no ordinary battalion. Whereas a normal battalion had a lieutenant colonel as commanding officer, the experimental unit had a brigadier general. In addition, the unit had a massive staff, heavy with public relations and special service personnel.[4]

The soldiers of the battalion were also intentionally different from those found in an average battalion. The men would all be young. In arrangements approved by Dwight D. Eisenhower, army chief of staff, there would be no one over twenty years of age and preferably no one over nineteen. The men selected would be a "cross section of the youth of the nation intellectually," as determined by representative score percentages on the Army General Classification Test (AGCT). The men would epitomize the country geographically, with every state represented in the battalion. Finally, all the trainees would be newly enlisted, with "none to have previous Army training."[5]

The War Department approved the AGF plan on November 13 but made one significant revision. Lt. Gen. C. P. Hall, director of organization and training, informed Maj. Gen. Jacob L. Devers, AGF commanding general, that "Negro personnel will not be included in this demonstration unit. The size of the unit will be reduced by deletion of the Negro company and such Negro personnel as are included in the Headquarters and Service Company." The reasoning behind such a decision was simple. The army planned for the nationwide UMT program to include segregation at the company level. In a restricted lecture, Devers confided that "Negro personnel will be organized in Negro units. These Negro units will not be consolidated at separate stations but will form component parts of the larger training units. The smallest Negro unit will be the company." The "larger training units" envisioned for this type of integration were divisions. Since the experimental unit was only a battalion, it was just too small to replicate the army's nationwide UMT plan. More important, the army hoped that the deletion of African American personnel from the experimental unit would avoid highlighting the contentious issue of race in what was meant to be a positive public relations effort. Such a move was transparent to many African American leaders. NAACP official Jesse O. Dedmon later quipped before Congress that "it can be noted that the experimental camp conducted by the Army at Fort Knox, Ky., did not include any Negroes. It is our information that this particular experiment on the part of the Army did not contemplate the full integration of Negroes, so in order to not create opposition on his part left him out of the picture." As before in the US Army's campaign for UMT after World War II, initial attempts to avoid a controversial social issue only brought it into greater focus later on.[6]

On December 26, Devers formally announced to the public that the army would activate an experimental UMT unit at Fort Knox, Kentucky. He informed the public that the army planned to place approximately six hundred regular army recruits into the unit with the unique twist that all members would be eighteen and nineteen years old. He explained that the intention was to create a model with which to convert UMT from theory into practice. As the *New York Times* reported, "They will be treated not as regular soldiers but as if they were members of the proposed UMT program."[7]

On January 4, 1947, the train carrying the first group of thirty-four "Umties" arrived at Fort Knox to more fanfare than usually accompanied recruits disembarking at a training depot. Paramount newsreelman H. Stewart Dailey filmed their influx, and General Devine greeted them

Jacob L. Devers visits with training cadre of the UMT Experimental Unit.
(Courtesy Harry S. Truman Library)

upon their arrival at the train platform. The first youngster off the train
was Pvt. Lester G. Whetzel of Derwood, Maryland. As the post newspaper
reported, Whetzel "will be the only man who can tell his grandchildren
of being the first UMT Trainee." The hopes of the army rested upon the
shoulders of these volunteers. Hailing primarily from the Northeast—
New York, New Jersey, and the New England states—the first group of
Umties would be joined by the rest of the unit as other young soldiers
continued to filter in over the next week. After being divided into the
various companies, getting assigned bunks, and receiving tours of the

extensive training area known as Father Divine's Heaven, the unit began its training course on January 13.[8]

By the end of January, army officials announced that a civilian advisory committee would be named to help in the unit's training. The thirty civilian leaders of the advisory committee would "make a study of the experimental unit and report its findings" to Devine and Devers. Composed of citizens of Louisville and Elizabethtown, "The committee was appointed by Governor Willis of Kentucky in cooperation with Mayor Taylor of Louisville. It includes subcommittees of specialists to study all aspects of our program except technical military instruction. There are subcommittees on health, religion, education, physical training, self-government, entertainment; and there is a parents' subcommittee interested in the general well-being of the trainees." Devine praised the committee highly, stating that "its members have rendered services beyond price. They have given us the civilian viewpoint on our program and have provided an example of cooperation between the civilian and the military which should set the standard for all communities in a National UMT Program."[9]

Gilbert P. Bailey, a staff writer of *New York Times Magazine* and former Marine Corps combat correspondent with the 4th Marine Division in the Pacific, visited the unit at Fort Knox in February. Bailey observed that the experimental unit was top-heavy with officers—especially staff officers: "They called in enough line officers and non-coms to staff an ordinary regiment and almost enough public relations and special service personnel for an entire Army Corps." The puritan environment surrounding the unit shocked Gilbert. He exclaimed, "There is no liquor—not even beer—no gambling, no standing in line at the PX or the mess hall, no overseas duty, and no MP chaperons at social functions." In addition to the moral strictures, other aspects of the unit stood out. Devine and his staff had noticeably improved the unit's facilities. As Bailey described them, "The first thing UMT did was to drop the notion that discipline means third-class living conditions for recruits. Barracks, redecorated for him, are cheerful and sumptuous—shining, cream-covered walls, floors sanded and varnished, a radio plug at each bunk, a reading and study room in each barracks and individual lockers for each man—even the occasional frill of a curtain on the windows."[10]

As the first six-month course at Fort Knox neared its close on June 30, Devine reported the details for Devers, outlining the unit's mission, the difficulties encountered in its activation, and the training philosophy of the unit during its first six months in existence. He noted, "The accompanying report is a recapitulation of the program with the conclusions that have been drawn from six months experience in its operation." He revealed three important facets of the Fort Knox experiment and its implications for the broader UMT program. First, he wanted the UMT experimental unit to serve primarily as a model to convert onlookers to the positive value of UMT rather than a training unit in the purely military sense. Devine and his staff paid detailed attention to the facilities at Fort Knox and their impact not only on the morale of the trainees, but also on the perceptions of the Umties, visitors, and other onlookers. Devine recalled that "in order to provide the service desired by the majority of the young men who would become members of the unit, a soda fountain, a snack bar, and a commercial type record player were installed, which immediately gave the Post Exchange the appearance and atmosphere of 'the corner drugstore.' Beer, objectionable magazines, and other items for which 18-year-olds have no use were eliminated from the stock. With its potted plants, varnished floors, uniform showcases and wall fixtures, soda fountain, and lounge, it was immediately apparent that it would become the 'Privates' Club.'"[11]

The focus on recreational facilities was no accident. Devine spent the majority of his first month at Fort Knox overseeing the complete overhaul of the designated UMT training area, paying particular attention to the recreational facilities. The reason was straightforward. He intended to avoid potentially embarrassing conduct infractions off base by providing the trainees an overabundance of recreational options on base to occupy their free time. As he revealed to Devers, "It was the intention from the beginning to provide more interesting recreation in the unit area than could be found in nearby civilian communities." Devine's drive led to a virtual cornucopia of recreational facilities for the Umties. There was an athletic section that operated a sports center which included pool tables, table tennis, parallel bars, a rowing machine, a trampoline, a boxing ring, and even an indoor golf driving range. Devine also established a permanent dance band, The UMT Highlighters, consisting of three trumpets, five saxophones, two trombones, a drummer, a piano player, and a bass violinist. During the first class of Umties at Fort Knox, "the band played 71 dances, 51 of which were for UMT personnel exclusively." There was also a tour group that chaperoned visits to local attractions such as Lincoln's birthplace and the Trappist monastery at Gethsemane Abbey. In addition, the area encompassing Fort Knox was (and is) a dry county, which made it even more difficult for UMT trainees to get in trouble off post.[12]

Devine also changed the traditional army approach that had dominated World War II training. He insisted on softening some of the harsher features of combat training that had become common in the army. In setting the standards that his training cadre would operate within, he gave the cadre three basic principles to guide them in carrying out their training of the Umties. First, he demanded that the cadre be cognizant of the young age of the trainees. He reminded them:

> This is UMT, and you are dealing with 18-year-old boys. If you are to be successful you must have faith in what you are doing. You must believe that the average 18-year-old American boy is essentially good; that he wants to do well; that he wants to be well thought of by his associates and by his superiors; that he is at least a little bit ambitious and wants to get ahead; and that if he gets the proper guidance and the proper leadership he will do his best to be a success in the unit. This basic statement must be accepted by the cadreman, and must determine his attitude and his manner in handling trainees.[13]

Devine also insisted that his training cadre alter their approach in correcting trainee behavior. As he instructed his cadre, "If a recruit does something wrong, tell him how to do it right instead of cussing him out for doing it wrong. That statement appears too simple to need saying, but nevertheless it means a complete reversal in attitude for some people." Devine urged the cadre that "you must correct every fault when you see it—but you do not have to be nasty about doing it."[14]

Devine closed his admonition to his training cadre by demanding that they approach their work as instructors rather than drill sergeants: "You must be impressed with the fact that you are an instructor, and the proper relationship between you and the recruit is the instructor-student relationship. You must raise your prestige to a higher level, conduct yourself with dignity, and maintain your self-respect."[15]

The third goal Devine set for his unit was to establish a program of moral instruction that would result in less criticism of the potential problems associated with the proposed national UMT program. He believed that "the moral and spiritual development of the trainees is considered a vital phase of their training. To limit the program to physical and mental improvement of the trainee produces an unbalanced program because a man's character has a third side, a moral one, which sets his personal standards of behavior and attitude toward his associates, his superiors, and his country." Devine instituted this moral program through an increased role for his chaplains. As he explained to Devers, "In UMT the chaplain is considered more than a silent member of the staff. He is directly responsible for the morals and behavior of the men. He is not a police officer nor a disciplinarian, but it is his duty to instruct the men, trainees and cadre, on proper morals and standards."[16]

Devine instituted two specific roles for the chaplains in his unit. The first was a series of lectures, entitled Citizenship and Morality, given by the chaplains to the trainees at Fort Knox. The chaplains lectured weekly to each of the UMT companies. Devine deemed that "this material is nonsectarian in nature and is based on the moral law. The theme throughout is a definition of the responsibilities of the citizen to and for his government." Some examples of these lectures were "The Meaning of Citizenship," "The Citizen and His State," "The Citizen and His Government," "The Citizen and His Religion," and "The Citizen and His Speech."[17]

Devine also charged his chaplains, in addition to teaching the Citizenship and Morality lectures, with administering the venereal disease (VD) control program. He reasoned: "Certainly the entire problem is basically one of morals. I have long believed that the films, posters, forced issue of prophylactics, and other measures in common use are as apt to increase the venereal rate as to reduce it. To the soldier of character and high moral standards, they are offensive; and to the morally weak, they are suggestive. Upon the Chaplains' recommendation, suggestive literature was eliminated from the PX newsstand and Service Club library, the posting of 'pin-up girls' was prohibited, and two lectures of Military Sanitation series were devoted to the subject of venereal disease."[18]

After the first cycle of Umties graduated in June, another group of approximately 660 young soldiers arrived at Fort Knox to begin their training cycle on July 1. The extension of the training unit beyond one cycle stemmed from its perceived success as a model for the nationwide UMT program. After implementing a UMT unit and letting it run a full cycle, Devine was confident that little change was needed to implement the nationwide program. As he boasted, "As a result of six months experience with training one or more platoons under each of the training schedules now contemplated for the training of all AGF units when the national UMT program is activated, it is believed that a few relatively minor changes should be made to improve the program." Devine made two minor changes to the program based on the first cycle. He lengthened the basic training portion from eight weeks to eleven weeks and eliminated the three weeks of small unit training to "permit a more even flow within the training cycle with a resultant increase of efficiency in the utilization of cadre personnel." Following these two minor changes, he considered the program ready for implementation on a nationwide scale.[19]

Devine hailed the success of the UMT experimental unit. He praised the recreational program by noting that "approximately 85 per cent of the trainee corps voluntarily remained on the post and participated in one or more activities of the special service program." Devine rejoiced in the reduction of obscenities as a result of the new training methods employed and the strict demerit system aimed at reducing their use. As he conveyed to Devers, "On the whole the use of obscene language within the UMT Trainee Corps has been curtailed, if not eliminated, to a remarkable degree. This has been done through thorough indoctrination in the standards desired and prompt and incessant awarding of demerits for the use of obscenity." Finally, Devine bragged to Devers that "the Chaplains' program has been, on the whole, successful from the moral standpoint; the VD rate has been held to one-fourth of that for white troops of this post, and there has been no wanton use of alcohol."[20]

It was not only senior Army leaders who hailed the UMT Experimental Unit as a success. People outside of the army also noticed the unit and its novel features. Even well-known critics of UMT such as Hanson W. Baldwin, military correspondent for the *New York Times,* praised the Fort Knox program for its new approach to military training. He argued that the first cycle had "aroused much enthusiasm within and without the Army and has been, to date, a definite success."[21]

The measure for determining the success of the UMT Experimental Unit was peculiar. It was based largely on the conduct and morale of the young soldiers rather than any actual military efficiency. The discipline system employed demerits and self-government in which trainees served as defense, prosecutor, and judge over all but the most serious cases. The demerit system heavily punished profanity and obscenity.

The post served no beer to trainees, and the civilian advisory committee worked with bartenders in Louisville to limit the availability of alcohol to the trainees. The results of such a strict code of conduct seemed impressive. Baldwin reported, "So far, some three men of the original 664 men in the battalion have been dismissed from the Army—one for stealing a car, one for theft in barracks and one for inaptitude; a few others in the original group have been dropped from the unit because of prolonged sickness. There have been twenty-five summary courts-martial in four months, and some thirty-nine trainee courts; cases of 'AWOL' are not serious, drunkenness is unknown, or virtually so, and there is little or no profanity. There has been one case of venereal disease in the outfit to date."[22]

Converts such as Baldwin attributed such "success" to the revolutionary training approach being implemented in the unit. Many of the harsher aspects of military training common at the time were honed and polished in the UMT unit. This was the result of its dual mission. On one hand, senior army officials intended the unit to provide a workable framework within which leaders could experiment with handling units made up exclusively of teenagers. But there was also another side to the unit. It was a public relations vehicle for the army. Army leaders anticipated that the unit would become a showcase of UMT's promise to the nation. And showcase the unit they did. In just the first six months of existence, many prominent visitors—both civilian and military— toured the unit. Distinguished civilian guests included members of the President's Advisory Commission on Universal Training such as Karl T. Compton, president of Massachusetts Institute of Technology; Samuel I. Rosenman, presidential speechwriter; Truman K. Gibson, former civilian aide to the secretary of war; and Daniel A. Poling, president and editor of *Christian Herald*. Other well-known civilian visitors included Simeon Willis, governor of Kentucky; Mrs. Arthur Woods, consultant to the secretary of war on universal training; Adelaide Stedman, prominent national lecturer; Wallace M. Davis, chairman of the Civilian Advisory Committee on Universal Training; Cdr. Barry Bingham, president of the *Courier Journal* and *Louisville Times;* and Parks Johnson and Warren Hull, directors of the *Vox Pop* radio program. Leading military figures who toured the unit included Robert P. Patterson, secretary of war; Jacob L. Devers, AGF commander; Wade H. Haislip, chairman of General Eisenhower's Advisory Committee on UMT; J. Lawton Collins, chief of public information; and Raymond S. McLain, liaison officer between the War Department and the President's Advisory Commission on Universal Training.[23] Significantly, these military leaders were some of the most noted and successful combat commanders during World War II. During the war Devers commanded the 6th Army Group; Haislip commanded the 85th Infantry Division, the XV Corps, and the 7th Army; Collins commanded the 25th Infantry Division and the VII Corps; and McLain commanded the 90th Infantry Division and the XIX Corps. The direct involvement of such preeminent army leaders underscored the importance of the UMT Experimental Unit.

In addition to using the Fort Knox experiment as a showcase to entertain prominent guests and educate them on the merits of the UMT program, senior army officials also created another public relations tool to communicate their message on UMT. On January 18 the unit launched the inaugural issue of a newspaper entitled the *UMT Pioneer*. It was a well-designed newspaper that articulated and disseminated the benefits of the army's program for UMT. Devine christened the inaugural issue by claiming, "Our paper has been aptly named the Pioneer, for we are all pioneers in what may prove to be an experiment of the utmost importance to our country." The articles in the *UMT Pioneer* spanned an array of topics large and small. The public relations staff intended to paint a positive image for UMT. They included pieces such as "President Truman on U.M.T.," "Comprehensive I and E Program Planned for Trainees, Cadre," and "Newly Renovated PX at Disposal of UMT Men." They also carried human interest stories such as "Sergeant Willis is Father of First Baby Born in UMT."[24]

Overall, the *UMT Pioneer* was not an average army post newspaper. It was more highly funded, better staffed, and especially sophisticated. There can be little doubt that the primary aim of the newspaper radiated outward from Fort Knox towards a larger audience. As Devine himself acknowledged in the *UMT Pioneer*, "It is our mission to demonstrate that military training, as proposed by the War Department, is beneficial to the youth of the nation, as well as necessary to the security of the country."[25] The fact that each Umtie was issued not one but two copies of every issue of the newspaper merely underscored the fact that dissemination was a goal.

The corollary to this public relations mission was that the experimental unit could not draw undue criticism. Converting critics would take a softened approach. Baldwin was pleasantly surprised that "there is no 'chewing off,' dressing down, or bawling out, with lurid profanity interspersed, if a man makes a mistake." The real issue was the soldiers' youth, the compulsion implied in a national UMT program, and the difficulties army leaders were encountering in convincing Congress to take action on UMT. Baldwin praised the unit's methods when he crowed, "They treat the boys like men, but they remember they are boys; there is much of the paternalistic system in the 'Umtie' unit." He regarded the methods of the experimental unit as innovative and praised them by writing, "The doubters are diminishing and the method of training of the Fort Knox experimental unit is winning friends and influencing people." Baldwin was impressed mainly with the method of training being used at Fort Knox rather than the potential of a nationwide UMT program. He observed that the experimental unit was designed specially and given many features that would be problematic for a national program of UMT. Noting that "there are no Negroes in the outfit, and the intellectual average is admittedly above that of the nation," Baldwin spotlighted that all of the boys were volunteers—unlike the proposed national UMT program—and many of them were seeking benefits from the GI Bill of Rights, making their morale much higher than could be expected in a national program. Finally, Baldwin remarked that an expanded program would also mean that the army could not handpick the best training cadre as they had with the small experimental unit.[26]

One of the criticisms of the UMT Experimental Unit was that it was not representative of the challenges that a nationwide program for UMT would encounter. All planning for the army UMT program envisioned a UMT division at each training station, yet the existing experimental unit was only a battalion. Army leaders sought additional proof that the training program employed in the experimental unit could be applied to larger units as well. In addition, the experimental unit used handpicked trainees and cadre as well as far superior facilities and programs than the average army unit. The overriding question for boosters and critics alike became whether the practices demonstrated in Devine's unit could be replicated in normal army divisions. Senior army leaders attempted to address such concerns by expanding the Fort Knox Experiment.

Devine's battalion was not the only unit at Fort Knox. In fact, the main unit at the base was the 3rd Armored Division. Commanding general Ray T. Maddocks instituted reforms in his division that applied the UMT philosophy and techniques Devine successfully used in his battalion. Maddocks publicized his efforts widely, claiming his purpose was "to show that a practical application of the methods, procedures, and policies of the Universal Military Training Experimental Unit is possible and feasible in the ordinary training unit with the average training cadre, such as exists in the 3d Armored Division at Fort Knox."[27]

Maddocks wasted no time addressing criticism of the Fort Knox experiment head-on. He declared,

> Much has been spoken and written about the methods, procedures, and policies of the Universal Military Training Experimental Unit at Fort Knox, Kentucky. Critics scoff at the marvelous results obtained by this unit, maintaining that they are dependent on carefully selected administrative and trainer cadre and trainees, on a ratio of cadre to trainees of one to one, and on funds and facilities not normally available to a Regular army unit. The fact is, however, the 3d Armored Division (Training) has been utilizing generally the same methods, procedures, and policies and accomplishing roughly the same results as the Universal Military Training Experimental Unit. This has been done with a normal administrative and trainer cadre and trainees, a normal ratio of cadre to trainees of approximately one to three point three, and the usual funds and facilities available to a Regular Army unit in a World War II cantonment area.[28]

Maddocks documented his attempts to implement the Fort Knox Experiment in his larger unit. He and his staff undertook an "intensive effort . . . to stamp out swearing and the use of obscene language of both cadre and trainees." In addition to trainee courts and the demerit system instituted at the experimental unit, Maddocks added a merit system that rewarded trainees in a positive manner for tasks done well. His program copied the basic outline of the experimental unit program to include the prohibition of beer, "even 3.2 beer," a sizable recreational program including a hobby shop and sports center, a troop information program, a civilian advisory committee, and a chaplain-led program focusing on citizenship and morality lectures with emphasis on VD rate reduction. Maddocks also instituted a novel approach that was not instituted at the experimental unit. In his division he tracked each company not primarily on their training proficiency but instead on their conduct. The best-behaved unit won. Maddocks explained,

We endeavor to show the men that they are part of a team. To bring out the fact that a team is no stronger than its weakest link and that recognition goes to those who deserve it, a monthly competition is held between companies on the number of absences without leave, venereal disease cases, military police reports, and courts-martial, and on proficiency in Division training tests. The unit with the best score is designated as the outstanding trainee company of the month. Awards are made, and you can be assured that in all companies, among both trainees and cadre, a keen competitive spirit exists.

Maddocks boasted that the 3rd Armored Division successfully demonstrated to the nation that a UMT program could be successfully instituted not only in a small unit with favorable circumstances but also in any normal army division. He concluded, "We are not only training soldiers but also developing better citizens."[29]

In many ways, the Fort Knox Experiment inverted the traditional army approach to UMT. A desire to improve mobilization through the creation of a General Reserve had been the strategic rationale behind their overall plans to institute UMT. Once those plans ran into resistance from critics, army leaders began to market their proposal in ways that subtly but significantly altered their ultimate ends. The campaign for UMT had begun as a way to make every citizen a soldier. As illustrated by the Fort Knox Experiment, army leaders were now trying to make every soldier a citizen. This process began with the UMT Experimental Unit but greatly expanded with the creation of a presidential advisory commission designed to study UMT in depth. The input from this hand-picked body of advisors gave presidential sanction to the campaign for UMT. In many ways, it caused a metamorphosis in the campaign for UMT that co-opted the US Army's primary role and supplanted it with involvement and direction from above.

9 A Program for National Security

I want you to be known as the President's Advisory Commission on Universal
Training. I want that word 'military' left out. The military phase is incidental to
what I have in mind.
—Harry S. Truman

After nearly 6 months of the most intensive study, the members of this
Commission have arrived at the unanimous conclusion that universal training
is an essential element in an integrated program of national security.
—President's Advisory Commission on Universal Training

Concurrently with the army's establishment of the UMT Experimental Unit at Fort Knox, Kentucky, President Truman prepared to name an advisory body to investigate UMT thoroughly and make specific recommendations to him on the matter. Secretary of War Robert P. Patterson submitted a plan for the advisory body on October 7, 1946, and recommended "that the Council be appointed as soon as possible and that it be asked to make its report by 1 February 1947." Patterson hoped that the commission's report would be a clarion call to action for a Congress that had proven hesitant to enact UMT even when called upon to do so. Patterson knew that the selection of the advisory body would be crucial. It had to be composed of civilians in order to avoid charges of militarism that were being levied at the army because of its marketing efforts. In addition, the members would have to represent significant segments of American society, in order, it was hoped, to overcome opposition from various quarters. As Patterson recommended to Truman, "It is particularly important that the three large religious groups be represented and that there be a Negro representative." Patterson suggested James B. Conant, president of Harvard University, as "an excellent choice" to serve as the body's chairman. Truman wanted the commission to be a who's who of personalities, with each member intended to represent a particular segment of society. For example, Maj. Gen. Harry H. Vaughan, military aide to the President, drafted letters of invitation that actually assigned each member to a specific interest group such as "International Affairs," "Education," "Religion," "Science," "Labor," "Industry," and "Minorities."[1]

On December 19, Truman publicly announced the creation of a com-

Harry S. Truman with the President's Advisory Commission on
Universal Training, May 29, 1947. (Courtesy Harry S. Truman Library)

mission to advise him regarding UMT. Nine members composed the
President's Advisory Commission on Universal Training. They were
chairman Karl T. Compton, prominent physicist and president of Massachusetts Institute of Technology (MIT); Joseph E. Davies, former ambassador to the Soviet Union and author of the popular book *Mission to
Moscow;* Harold W. Dodds, president of Princeton University; Truman K.
Gibson, Chicago attorney and previous civilian aide to the secretary of
war; Daniel A. Poling, president and editor of *Christian Herald;* Anna M.
Rosenberg, regional director of the War Manpower Commission; Samuel I. Rosenman, presidential speechwriter for both Roosevelt and Truman; Edmund A. Walsh, American Jesuit Catholic priest and founder of
Georgetown University School of Foreign Service; and Charles E. Wil-

Truman K. Gibson, civilian aide to the secretary of war, April 9, 1945.
(Courtesy National Archives and Records Administration)

son, chief executive officer of General Electric. Truman's selection of the commission immediately sparked criticism. Some claimed that his intention was to create "a rubber stamp Committee," more interested in advocating UMT than in impartially ascertaining whether UMT was truly required. In response to charges that the committee was not representative, Truman fired back and flatly retorted, "There will be no additions to the committee."[2]

The day following the announcement, Truman met with the members. He also informally provided his initial guidance to them. After greeting them, he took a moment to discuss his background and how it influenced his thinking on UMT. He revealed to them, "I have been interested in the physical development and the mental and moral development of young people ever since I was graduated from high school. I have been somewhat of a student of history, and I have discovered that great republics of the past always passed out when their peoples became prosperous and fat and lazy, and were not willing to assume their responsibilities."[3]

Truman then imparted to the members his own conception of UMT:

> I want our young people to be informed on what this Government is—what it stands for—its responsibilities. And I think the best way to do this is through a universal training program. I don't like to think of it as a universal military training program. I want it to be a universal training program, giving our young people a background in the disciplinary approach of getting along with one another, informing them of their physical make-up, and what it means to take care of this temple which God gave us. If we get that instilled into them, and then instill into them a responsibility which begins in the township, in the city ward, the first thing you know we will have sold our Republic to the coming generations as Madison and Hamilton and Jefferson sold it in the first place. . . . I want you to be known as the President's Advisory Commission on Universal Training. I want that word "military" left out. The military phase is incidental to what I have in mind.[4]

Following the initial meeting of December 20, Truman provided the commission the resources—both personnel and financial—necessary to carry out a large undertaking in a short time frame. On January 15, Truman requested that Arthur J. Altmeyer, commissioner for social security, "arrange to allow the President's Advisory Commission on Universal Training to have the services of Mr. Wilbur Cohen for the next few months. The Commission is very anxious to have him assigned to act as its Director of Research."[5]

The first task the commission carried out was to ascertain the military utility of UMT. Compton wrote to Truman "to obtain the most reliable information available with respect to any military necessity which may exist for a universal training program." Compton asked for the opinion of the "highest military authorities" on UMT and sought to determine "the extent to which they consider that a program for universal training is important from a military standpoint." Compton specifically desired input on UMT from the Joint Chiefs of Staff (JCS). Truman wrote back two weeks later, informing Compton that the military need for UMT was growing in relation to the increased pace of demobilization. He warned, "Peacetime reduction of armed forces and armaments will increase the problem by raising the percentage of personnel which must be absorbed and trained after an emergency occurs. The more we reduce our armed forces and our armaments the more it becomes imperative that we establish a system of universal training." Truman did not rely solely on his own reasoning. He also informed Compton that the JCS definitely saw UMT as a military requirement: "The Joint Chiefs of Staff are of the opinion that an adequate system of universal training is necessary to insure the future security of the United States." The commission met on sixteen different occasions totaling twenty-nine complete days and fifteen evenings. Over the course of their six months of inquiry, they consulted approximately two hundred experts from across the country.[6]

Several of the more exciting witnesses before the Compton commission deserve mention. One was William H. Hastie, governor of the US Virgin Islands, who appeared before the commission during the evening session on January 25, 1947. Hastie cautioned that UMT should be "the very last resort—if, and only if, it is determined that nothing else can suffice for our national security." After setting a high standard for the commission to meet in order to recommend UMT, Hastie followed up with his main point: "But assuming the possibility that the Commission should come to that conclusion, that some form of conscription or universal military training is essential, I think there are some 'musts' and 'must-nots' that deserve mention in connection with any such program." Hastie clearly signaled where the commission should start with crafting any UMT program. He urged them, "The first of those, as to which I feel very strongly, is that there should not, in training or in the organization of our forces, be a segregation of personnel, whether by race, origin, or section of the country from which the individual comes." Hastie articulated what he saw as the potential impact UMT would have on American society:

This Commission, I know, is considering very seriously the non-military implications that are involved in any form of universal military training, the effect of the program upon the future lives and character of the young men who may be subjected to the training; and in that connection, it seems to me important to consider that if the United States should subject the young manhood of this country to a period of living under racial segregation, not only with the approval, but pursuant to the mandate of the Government of the United States, it would be one of the most tragic and catastrophic things for the future attitude of our people that could be imagined.[7]

As Hastie ended his testimony, Compton challenged him to clarify his stance on segregation. Compton asked, "Governor Hastie, when you said you believed there should be no segregation, how far down the line would you carry that?" Hastie responded flatly, "I would carry it all the way down the line to the individual human being."[8]

Another influential witness before the commission was James Patton, president of the National Farmers Union. Patton directly informed the commission that his organization "will oppose, politically and in every way we can, universal peacetime conscription." To explain his organization's opposition, Patton presented to the commission the plight of a farmer from Iowa he had recently met. The farmer's concerns were simple. He asked Patton, "If we are going to continue to spend 15 to 30 billion dollars a year for national defense, how in the world are we going to distribute enough income for the people of our country and the peoples of the world to have an adequate standard of living and to eat up the goods we farmers produce?" Patton feared that UMT would preclude needed investment in domestic programs such as education and health care. He contended, "Free education, freedom of opportunity to think and have initiative, an adequate health program, a discipline which arises out of a concept of cooperating and working with each other, rather than a discipline by dictatorial approach, will in the long run create whatever flexibility and adjustability are necessary to give us that kind of a people and that kind of a defense or offense necessary to protect ourselves."[9] Patton's main critique was the opportunity cost involved with such a huge undertaking. He listed the numerous valuable domestic items that could be funded with the large sums of money contemplated for UMT. In addition, Patton criticized a training system run exclusively by the army and argued that such a setup would allow the government too much control over the independence of citizens, especially farmers.[10]

The commission obtained the views of leaders of women's organizations as well. During the afternoon session on February 21, they heard from Elizabeth Smart, executive secretary of the Women's Christian Temperance Union. From the outset, Smart made it clear that both she personally and her organization were fundamentally opposed to "any form of conscription in peacetime." She gave two basic reasons. First, she contended that the best path to peace was not through prepared-ness measures: "The setting up of large armaments has practically al-ways been the forerunner of war." In addition, she warned about the domestic dangers inherent in creating and maintaining large armies in democracies. She feared "that in the process of forming these standing armies, the liberties of the people are inevitably curbed and destroyed." Smart did not focus on these general differences between her views and those of the proponents of UMT. Both sides probably agreed that such views represented an irreconcilable difference of opinion. Instead, she developed a specific critique of UMT based on two areas she argued were important to women.[11]

The first was women's role in citizenship development. Smart argued forcefully that teaching citizenship was the role of women in the home and that UMT "would have a disastrous effect on the woman's job of raising good citizens." Smart believed that there was a direct link be-tween a woman's role and the government's role to teach citizenship. She considered the relationship a zero-sum equation. The more army leaders taught citizenship and morals, the less control women would have in that realm. Smart argued that women should be carrying out this important role, not army personnel. As she stressed, "We appreciate that you have the task and responsibility of deciding what is necessary for America from a military viewpoint. We speak from the home woman's viewpoint. Our task and our responsibility is the building of America from the cradle up. And we submit that your task can only begin where ours leaves off."[12]

The second specific critique that Smart presented concerned vice. Smart maintained that the combination of extreme youth and physical separation from home amounted to emotional dislocation and vulner-ability to vice for trainees. She railed against the commercial exploita-tion that often accompanied military camps, arguing that "the sources and focus of most of this exploitation is the tavern or honky-tonk." According to Smart, such a seedy location "attracted to itself a host of uniform-crazed teen-age girls who constituted a very substantial part of the disseminators of venereal disease to men in the armed services during the war. They were employed as bar-maids or encouraged in the taverns as decoys to induce free spending on the part of the soldiers and sailors whom they attracted to them." Compton fired back that the vice in normal cities often outweighed anything found near military camps.

As he described his recent visits to military camps, he informed Smart that "at the ones which I visited I found the surroundings, I should say, far more wholesome than any Saturday night on the streets of Boston." Smart retorted that there was a key difference between youth in large American cities and the prospects of trainees in UMT camps. As she put it, "It is true that there are those same conditions obtaining in our large cities. The point that I was making was, however, that when you take these boys away from their homes they are more susceptible to those in-fluences." The only system Smart was willing to advocate was a voluntary system that had appropriate safeguards in place to protect a woman's role in citizenship education and to prevent a young man's exposure to iniquity—especially commercialized vice. In closing, she described the potential of UMT in frightening terms. Smart declared, "You might do it once, and everything might be all right, and nobody's freedom would be threatened, but we have had some pretty awful lessons. We have seen how from small things these terrible monsters have evolved, and we are afraid of small things. We are afraid of breaking down that safeguard that we feel has kept us a free people."[13]

The members of the commission also investigated the impact of the atomic bomb on universal training. Some critics argued that the atomic age made mass armies obsolete and, hence, universal training anach-ronistic. Advocates countered that the mobilization potential inherent in a citizen army was not only relevant in the atomic age, but actually more so. In April, Bernard Brodie, senior specialist on national defense for the Legislative Reference Service, Library of Congress, presented the major views in the debate for the commission. Brodie highlighted his belief that UMT's chances of success rested squarely on its military util-ity. He presaged that, "whether democratic or not, there is no question that American public opinion will accept it, if at all, only as a result of proved necessity." From a strategic point of view, Brodie stressed that the atomic bomb had "become the fulcrum of all debate on the issue." Brodie lamented that the advocates of UMT failed to make a case for their prescription in the atomic age. As he informed the commission, "All the protagonists of conscription have to do is to point out *how* con-scription or 'universal training' fits into the scheme of total mobiliza-tion for atomic warfare. The rub comes simply in that they seem not to know. For that they can scarcely be blamed. As Lord John Russell said just a hundred years ago about the effect of a military invention of his own time (the steam warship): 'We are walking if not in danger at least in darkness.' Today the darkness is not only impenetrable but all embracing, and there is little question either about the danger."[14]

Brodie enumerated three major arguments pertaining to the atomic bomb. First, he explored the contention that "the wholesale character of the destruction likely to follow from reciprocal atomic bomb attacks will make large armies redundant if not useless." He presented a work by William L. Borden, entitled *There Will Be No Time,* as the ultimate "rejection of the idea that large ground forces can be of any utility whatsoever in a future war." In his book, Borden argued that "soldiers on both sides in World War II unknowingly danced to a tune called by science. Millions were lost because science produced the bomb after German defeat. Millions more were saved because the bomb arrived before Japan's D-Day. G.I. Joe, with his beard and muddy boots, is the symbol of an age gone past." Brodie concluded that Borden "undoubtedly exaggerates the vulnerability of an army in the field."[15]

Brodie described a second argument regarding the atomic bomb and universal training. He explained to the commission, "The idea that conscription may be necessary if the purpose is to train men for the kind of war which will characterize the atomic age represents a much more sophisticated attitude than that which we have just been examining." One proponent of this view was W. A. Gerhard. In an article in the *Infantry Journal,* Gerhard made two significant arguments about the atomic bomb. First, he contended that the atomic bomb extended the battlefield to its theoretical maximum and completely blurred the distinction between soldiers and citizens. He cautioned, "It is only this new bomb that has been able to extend effective fire power to the point of complete destruction of the enemy. It is interesting to note the shift of emphasis from the battlefield to the behind the lines area. It is not presumptuous to suppose that wars of the future will not know the distinction between 'homefront' and 'battlefield' for our increased fire power will make both identical. What then of the distinction between soldier and civilian in the future? Already in this war the distinction had no practical significance."[16]

The second argument Gerhard made was that atomic warfare would require total mobilization. He warned,

War is not an accident in life; it is as likely to occur as any human function, and we cannot, for our own safety, merely speculate upon a program of military preparedness. If we are to have conscription it must be of such a nature that it will really prepare us for the next war. It must be total conscription of all forces in the country for every force a country possesses will be called for if ever again we engage in war. Industry and applied science and organization of personnel and resources are the means of winning the wars of the future, and military training must mean training in these techniques.[17]

Brodie did not merely present the views of others to the commission. He was an emerging strategic expert on the atomic bomb himself and had his own unique views regarding the relationship between the atomic bomb and universal training. Brodie argued in his book *The Absolute Weapon* that large armies were still relevant in the atomic age. As he conceived it, "The forces which will carry on the war after a large-scale atomic bomb attack may be divided into three main categories according to their respective functions. The first category will comprise the force reserved for the retaliatory attacks with atomic bombs; the second will have the mission of invading and occupying enemy territory; and the third will have the purpose of resisting enemy invasion and of organizing relief for devastated areas."[18]

What was most stimulating about Brodie's conception of the relationship between the atomic bomb and universal training was that the atomic age necessitated two distinct armies. He reasoned, "In the past it was more or less the same army which was either on the offensive or the defensive, depending on its strength and on the current fortunes of war, but, for reasons which will presently be made clear, a much sharper distinction between offensive and defensive forces seems to be in prospect for the future." Brodie contended that the atomic age did not automatically invalidate large armies. Instead, he argued that the two-army requirement of the atomic age might be well suited to a small professional army and a larger citizen army: "It is obvious that the force set apart for invasion or counter-invasion purposes will have to be relatively small, completely professional, and trained to the uttermost. But there must also be a very large force ready to resist and defeat invasion by the enemy. Here is the place for the citizen army, though it too must be comprised of trained men. There will be no time for training once the atomic bomb is used."[19]

Other writers were even more forceful in their arguments that the atomic age would not invalidate mass armies. One such writer was Walter Lippman. He insisted vigorously that the advent of the atomic age necessitated armies for one main reason. Lippman contended that certain geographic or strategic areas would be inadvisable targets for atomic bombs. These included conquered cities of America's allies—especially in Western Europe. Since American leaders would not want to destroy these cities, some form of conventional force would have to be used in order to recapture them if conflict broke out.[20]

The commission also engaged critics who argued that UMT was not useful from a military perspective. No individual personified this position better than Hanson W. Baldwin, who appeared before the commission on April 12. Most Americans regarded him as an expert on military affairs. Baldwin maintained that there were two clear problems with UMT from a military perspective. First, he noted that UMT would require large numbers of training cadre and therefore could potentially drain army personnel. As he reasoned, "I think so much of the energies of the Army would be devoted to training, if you take a million men a year into the Army and Navy, that a disproportionate amount of their energy would be so directed."[21] Baldwin also asserted that UMT, in addition to requiring large numbers of training cadre, would be useless in a critical mission area for the army: occupation duties. Baldwin pointed out that the trainees by design would not serve in the military or be capable of being stationed abroad, so they would not be available for the pressing duties facing American military leaders around the globe.

Instead of UMT, Baldwin proposed a varied military approach that he claimed would be more useful. It included "ahead of all, intelligence." In addition, he recommended increased research and development, industrial mobilization planning, a strong air force, and instantly deployable army and navy units. The theme of Baldwin's approach was offense. As he cautioned, "I believe we are approaching the time when the only hope of a sure defense is a strong offense, a very strong offense." Baldwin's strategic vision of the postwar world did not hold UMT in high regard. He explained, "Civilian components, I think, come last on the list, largely because I think you have to have emphasis in this atomic age on some fighting forces that are instantly ready." When faced directly with ranking UMT's value relative to other strategic options, Baldwin did not pull any punches. He boldly stated, "I would put it low on the list. In fact, from its purely military point of view, I would put it perhaps at the bottom of the list." In the end, Baldwin felt that UMT was a tempting—but dangerous—mirage: "What I would fear most of all would be a mistaking of the shadow for the substance, the Maginot Line mentality," which he characterized as "a weak reed." Although Baldwin urged innovative strategic concepts such as reorienting the National Guard to a civil defense role, he clearly advocated a volunteer army that used forces in being with high levels of training. He contended that the civilian components were necessary but not very helpful in the changing conditions of the postwar era and therefore should not be the focus of postwar military planning.[22]

After hearing from a myriad of individuals both for and against UMT, the Compton commission published its report on May 29. In their letter of transmittal to Truman, the members acknowledged that both their final report and their recommendations were unanimous. Their conclusion was that "universal training is an essential element in an integrated program of national security intended to safeguard the United States and to enable us to fulfill our responsibilities to the cause of world peace and the success of the United Nations." Truman now had his prize. He had named an advisory board composed of distinguished civilian experts representing virtually every segment of American society. The commission had deliberated extensively, compiling a vast mountain of both facts and opinions. After careful study, the commission had unanimously recommended UMT just as he had himself earlier. Truman formally submitted the report to Congress on June 4 and wrote to Arthur H. Vandenberg, president pro tempore of the Senate, and Joseph W. Martin, speaker of the House, pressing for swift action on UMT based on the commission's report. He wrote, "I urge that the Congress give early consideration to the subject of universal training."[23]

Not everyone blindly accepted the report of the Compton commission. Barely a month after Truman submitted it to Congress, a group critical of the report published their own findings. The result was the Hutchins report, named after Robert M. Hutchins, chancellor of the University of Chicago and vociferous critic of UMT. The group contained other notable members, such as Edwin C. Johnson, Democratic senator from Colorado; Josephus Daniels, secretary of the navy during World War I; and James G. Patton, president of the National Farmers Union. The purpose of the report was simple. The members strongly argued that "the Report of the President's Commission on Universal Training

**"Take It—Or Leave It at Our Peril: Unanimous Recommendation for Universal Military Training by President's Advisory Commission."
(Cartoon by Clifford K. Berryman, June 3, 1947; Courtesy Center for Legislative Archives)**

should have very critical examination by the American people." The members saw the Hutchins report "as an aid in securing further public discussion and as an expression of our disagreement with the Commission's Report." The group intended to "describe numerous fallacies and shortcomings in the [Compton Commission's] Report, including the wastefulness and futility even from a strictly military point of view of the universal military training which the [Compton] Commission strongly recommends." Some of the group's major objections were "U.M.T. Would Not Strengthen the United Nations"; "U.M.T. Would Be Inadequate for Atomic Disasters"; "Growth of Militarism Would Be Encouraged" under

UMT; "The Cost Would Be 'Staggering'"; and UMT would represent "A Forerunner of Conscription of Labor and Women."[24]

The significance of the President's Advisory Commission on Universal Training was that for the first time a diverse group of well-known civilians rigorously studied UMT and unanimously endorsed its enactment. No longer were the calls for UMT coming strictly from army officers in uniform. The commission's actions and the publicity they generated provided momentum for the campaign for UMT as well as ammunition for supporters. Time would tell whether such an impact would be enough to turn the tide for UMT. There was another outcome of the commission, though. By openly shifting the emphasis towards broader social benefits, the commission's work unintentionally increased the social criticism of UMT. Now that the commission's work widened the discourse about UMT's impact on American society, the negative implications of UMT for American society also began to take center stage.

10   The Normal Way of Life

Men must be trained for the future in accordance with individual aptitudes,
abilities, and skills. Bombs in any future war will not come marked for white or
for colored.
—Truman K. Gibson

We are launching in the Negro and liberal press a nationwide expose of
the race-minded UMT clique. Their hysterical campaign for a jimcrow bill is
threatening every substantial gain won by Negroes. We call upon responsible
leaders and liberals in both parties to crack down on this new-style lynch
party which would surrender Negro boys to Mississippi Army officers without
legislative safeguards.
—A. Philip Randolph

The leadership of the NAACP had held serious reservations
regarding UMT for quite some time. There were two main
reasons. One was that those leaders considered UMT ineffective. They claimed that not only would UMT contribute
little to national security, but it would actually lessen security by promoting an international arms race. William H.
Hastie represented the NAACP before the Woodrum committee and
publicized the rationale for the group's opposition to UMT. His testimony was "authorized by the Board of Directors" of the NAACP and
represented their "formal resolution." Hastie remarked that the group
was not convinced of the need for such a drastic program and doubted
its ability to make America more secure. He contended that UMT was
"generally unsound in principle," and he warned that the prospects of
a future war were fearful, given the vast increase in the destructiveness
of war evidenced during World War II. Hastie claimed that UMT would
not alleviate the destructiveness of future war and that its only possible
value and justification would be as a deterrent of future war. However,
he flatly denied any such justification. As he pointed out, "It is our belief
that it would have no such effect." Instead of being a deterrent, UMT
would actually lead to an arms race. Hastie compared the prospect of
UMT in the postwar world to a Darwinian jungle in which each nation
proclaimed its own preparedness measures were defensive in character but interpreted other nations' preparedness measures as offensive.
Hastie urged, "In my judgment we must make up our minds that there

is no tolerable future in an international jungle in which each lion calls himself king of the beasts and keeps sharpening his claws to prove it. And it does not help for us to say we are a benevolent lion who sharpens his claws only for self-protection. Neither the other lions nor the less powerful beasts will be reassured."[1]

There was also an important domestic reason for opposition to UMT on the part of African American leaders such as Hastie, who feared the social impact on America. Hastie worried that passage of UMT "would permit the continuation of the present racial segregation and discrimination in the armed forces." To Hastie, a program of UMT that endorsed segregation would have severe consequences on American society. For one, opportunities for individual African Americans in the military would continue to be limited. The pattern of segregation in the military meant that the army limited African American personnel to the segregated units. Since fewer of those units existed, there was less variety in the types of units. The result was far fewer military occupational specialties open for African Americans. Hastie gave specific examples. He railed against the navy's traditional practice of forcing African Americans to be messmen. Hastie charged that the problem extended to the army as well. The only units available for African Americans in the Medical Corps were sanitary companies. In the peacetime Army Air Corps, the Air Transport Command allowed no African American pilots to fly. As a result, a segregated army made up of roughly 10 percent African Americans held a dim possibility of equality. Hastie reasoned, "It is no more possible to provide opportunities in the segregated 10 percent of the Army equal to those in the remaining 90 percent than it is possible to duplicate in a Jim Crow coach the many facilities of a deluxe passenger train."[2]

Hastie's conclusion was clear. He regretted the basic pattern of discrimination. Worse, he feared that UMT threatened to change military participation for African Americans from one of choice to one of compulsion. He asserted, "All of these are indicia of the basic pattern of discrimination which should be corrected in any event, and particularly if Negroes are to go into the peacetime Army and Navy by compulsion rather than consent."[3]

The more details about UMT that surfaced, the more African American leaders became concerned with its implications. They did not have to wonder what UMT might look like. Instead, they merely had to gaze upon the experimental unit at Fort Knox to gain a preview. And they did not like what they saw. As one NAACP report revealed, "One should note that in the War Department's experimental U.M.T. Camp at Fort Knox, Kentucky, no Negroes were included among the 600 trainees." When questioned on this point, General Devine "indicated that in such a small unit it would not be practical to bring in enough Negroes *to form a separate platoon!* In other words, Negroes would definitely be segregated into special units if Congress passes U.M.T."[4]

The issue of segregation and UMT went further than perpetuating the existing pattern of segregation in the armed forces. Since all army plans proposed training camps virtually exclusively in the South because of the better year-round training weather, the passage of UMT would overturn the dynamic that legal segregation existed as a uniquely southern phenomenon. By forcing young men from across the country to participate in training predominantly in the South, UMT would introduce segregation as the national status quo. As the report went on:

> One of the principal benefits claimed by the Commission for its program of Universal Military Training is that it would "contribute to the development of national unity" by "bringing together young men from all parts of the country to share a common experience." Can national unity be promoted by subjecting a million young men each year to federally sponsored jim crow? Boys who have grown up in communities where racial segregation is not practiced would be forced to accept the jim crow pattern which would prevail under the proposed program. For many white boys, this would mean learning to regard segregation as the normal way of life; for the Negro, it would mean permanently [enduring], as in World War II, the degrading experience of being treated as an inferior citizen by a government which conscripts him in the name of democracy.[5]

This general pattern of opposition to UMT based on racial concerns continued until 1947. At that point, the debate over UMT and its racial implications congealed into two opposing camps, each with its own approach to ensuring a positive social result and each claiming to represent the dominant African American response. The two African American leaders who personified the two camps held vastly different viewpoints and pursued diametrically opposed paths. The two men were Truman K. Gibson and A. Philip Randolph.

Truman Kella Gibson was an unlikely but effective reformer. He was

born in Atlanta, Georgia, on January 22, 1912. At the age of twenty he graduated with a BA degree from the University of Chicago, and three years
later he received his JD degree from the University of Chicago. From 1935
until 1940 he practiced law in Chicago, gaining acclaim as a rising young
African American lawyer and leader. Gibson's big break came in 1940,
when he accepted the post of executive director for the American Negro Exposition in Chicago. His handling of such a large-scale enterprise
brought him national attention. In 1940, Gibson became the assistant to
the civilian aide to the secretary of war regarding Negro affairs, serving
in that capacity until 1943. At that time he became civilian aide himself,
serving in that role until 1945. In 1946, Gibson became a member of the
President's Advisory Committee on Universal Training.[6] Gibson insisted
that UMT was an essential preparedness measure. He conceded that
safeguards should be created to avoid discrimination as the army enacted the program, but he maintained that full participation by African
Americans in military service and training was essential to changing the
system from the inside for the better.

Gibson's view of full participation with safeguards against discrimination and segregation was not the only one at the time. A. Philip Randolph, international president of the Brotherhood of Sleeping Car Por-
ters, AFL, held a more pessimistic view of UMT. During the late summer
of 1947, several friends contacted Randolph with the idea of organizing
a civil rights protest directed against UMT. One of them was Bill Worthy.
Worthy wrote Randolph on August 14 to run an idea past him, informing
Randolph that Worthy and John Swomley of the Fellowship of Reconciliation had discussed the current prospects of UMT. Worthy recalled,
"Not having been on the scene when Congress was winding up, I had not
realized, as I'm sure many others hadn't, that the War Dept. and other
conscription advocates made great strides during the last weeks of the
session." Worthy and Swomley feared that UMT was gaining momentum
in Congress: "Staunch Congressional opponents are quite pessimistic
about the possibility of defeating it in the next session in January, barring
some miracle." Swomley knew of one tactic that might work to prevent
UMT from becoming a reality. Worthy recalled, "The bill as reported out
by the House Armed Forces Committee provides for racial segregation
of trainees. John feels that if an amendment with teeth were inserted
barring absolutely all jimcrow in the training program—which would
mean admitting Negroes on an equal basis to all 48 National Guards

and to ROTC units for the last six months of the year's training—enough Southern congressmen and senators would join with opponents of all conscription to beat the entire bill."[7]

Having laid out their overall plan to Randolph, Worthy requested a favor of him. Both Worthy and Swomley "felt that the serious threat of a new form of *government-sponsored* segregation touching a whole generation of youth merits drastic action. I agreed to contact you to ascertain if, around the middle or end of October, you would be willing to call a meeting in New York of perhaps a dozen key Negro leaders to plan action in a crisis equally as grave as the 1941 job crisis."[8]

Randolph accepted Worthy's prodding. After meeting informally with six friends to discuss the threat embodied in the UMT bill "now before Congress," the group decided to act. As Randolph revealed, "A canvass of the serious situation facing Negroes if this undemocratic bill should pass" led to calling a formal meeting for Friday evening, October 10, at eight o'clock in the evening at Randolph's New York office. Randolph divulged that during the meeting they would consider organizing a committee "for militant *action* on this issue." Randolph urged Roy Wilkins of the NAACP to attend, giving two specific reasons. First, he criticized the fact that "Chairman Walter G. Andrews of the House Armed Forces Committee refused to allow even consideration of an anti-segregation amendment when he steamrolled the bill through his committee in July." In addition, Randolph feared that "with the War Department determined to rush passage of the bill in an atmosphere of international hysteria when Congress reconvenes, we already are very late in organizing for action."[9]

Randolph created the Committee against Jim Crow in Military Service and Training on October 10, 1947. At that meeting in his New York office at 217 West 125th Street, the members elected Grant Reynolds chairman of the committee. Reynolds was the former New York state commissioner of corrections and was a former army chaplain in the 366th Infantry during World War II. Reynolds had also run for Congress in the 22nd New York district in the 1946 midterm election. Even though Randolph was in San Francisco attending the AFL convention, the members elected him treasurer. Randolph and Reynolds spent the remainder of October sending out letters to African American leaders throughout the nation asking for their assistance in the campaign and articulating the specific amendments they sought to add to the UMT bill.

On October 30, Randolph and Reynolds presented to the legal commit-tee a series of five amendments the organization would seek in order to ensure proper protection of African Americans in any UMT program enacted. They sought "an amendment prohibiting all segregation and discrimination in the entire UMT program," to include both the first six months and all options for the second six months. They requested "an amendment barring all jimcrow in interstate travel for trainees in UMT uniform." They demanded "an amendment making attacks on, or lynch-ing of, a trainee in UMT uniform . . . a federal offense, with severe pen-alties." They called for "an amendment banning the poll tax in federal elections for any trainee otherwise eligible to vote." Finally, Randolph and Reynolds presented the fifth option as a possibility. They suggested that "the Legal Committee consider the advisability of an amendment barring UMT camps in the South, on the grounds that Negro trainees would be subjected to local indignities and white trainees (at least from the North) would be exposed to the rigid jimcrow pattern."[10]

On November 12, Randolph used his position as a national labor leader to publicize the campaign against UMT among the membership of his organization. He wrote to Brotherhood locals and women's aux-iliaries informing them of the formation of the Committee against Jim Crow and the "very urgent task before it: to see to it that no jimcrow bill for peacetime military conscription is passed by Congress." Randolph went further by crystallizing the dangers for African Americans that he foresaw in the possible implementation of UMT. As he warned the mem-bers of his organization, "The proposal to draft all young boys of 18 and to throw them into jimcrow army camps is the most dangerous threat to the progress of the Negro in many years." Randolph argued that the im-pact of UMT on African Americans would be dreadful. He exclaimed, "It would set back the Brotherhood and the entire trade union movement. It would set back the campaign for the FEPC and make segregation in jobs all the harder to break down. Since conscription is proposed as a *per-manent* law, it would impose jimcrow on each new generation of youth and poison their minds."[11]

The following week, Randolph launched a broadside at his rival, Gib-son. He reminded Gibson that the President's Commission on Universal Training recommended "that there be no racial or religious discrimina-tion in any peacetime conscription program" but that "the bill for uni-versal military training, H.R. 4278, now before Congress, fails even to mention discrimination or segregation." Randolph warned Gibson that the proposed UMT plan would almost ensure segregation would be the new national status quo. He advised, "Indeed, the provision for trainees to enter, as one alternative, the National Guard, following the initial six months in camps, is iron-clad proof that jimcrow would prevail. The National Guard in nearly all states and the District of Columbia is notorious for drawing the color line." Randolph pleaded with Gibson to take a more confrontational role regarding UMT: "Having been the sole Negro to serve on the President's Commission on Universal Training, you are in a position to exercise a great influence on the final disposition of the bill's racial aspects. May I respectfully urge, therefore, that you publicly insist that strong, unequivocal provisions against every form of segregation be inserted in the bill, or, if Congress and the Administration would not agree to this, that you repudiate the entire program of jimcrow conscription."[12]

On November 22, Randolph and Reynolds publicly launched their campaign. In his first press release for the committee, newly appointed executive secretary Charles J. Patterson described the crusade as "a campaign to insure inclusion of racial equality amendments in pending legislation for universal military training." Patterson was a disabled African American veteran from Fort Wayne, Indiana, who had received the Purple Heart and Silver Star medals. In addition to announcing their purpose, Patterson publicized the extensive membership, which included world heavyweight boxing champion Joe Louis as well as "118 Negro leaders in labor, church, education and political life." With such staunch backing, Randolph and his partners threatened to incite mass civil disobedience on the part of African Americans in order to protest UMT without a complete abolition of segregation in any UMT legislation before Congress.[13]

On Sunday, November 23, the *New York Times* published a story based on the release that incensed Randolph and Reynolds so much that they charged the paper with distortion of their movement. They complained to the editor:

Our release clearly stated that the emphasis of the Committee's program at this time would be the inclusion of racial equality amendments in pending legislation for universal military training. At no point in our release was there mention of a *current* campaign "aimed at gaining admission for Negroes into all branches of the Armed Forces without limitation or segregation," which was the wording that appeared in the *Times* story. The name of the Committee certainly indicates an interest in ending Jim Crow in the regular military establishment, but the crisis facing Negroes if universal military training should be adopted as H.R. 4278 now reads has forced the cross-section of Negro leadership who constitute this Committee to concentrate now on the UMT bill.[14]

In an effort to broaden their campaign, on December 10 Randolph and Reynolds requested a meeting with President Truman. They hoped that the President would grant them an audience "in the near future" to discuss "the prospect of jimcrow in pending legislation for universal military training." They emphasized that the proposed legislation "does not even mention the issue of racial discrimination and segregation." Randolph and Reynolds emphasized to Truman that "such a deficiency is all the more striking in view of the recommendations in this connection of both your Advisory Commission on Universal Training and your Committee on Civil Rights." Finally, Randolph and Reynolds reminded Truman that two members of his own civil rights committee, Sadie T. M. Alexander and Channing H. Tobias, were also active members of the Committee against Jim Crow. David K. Niles, administrative assistant to Truman, responded on December 17, conveying the message that Niles would "be glad to talk to a delegation at any time that is mutually convenient." Annoyed at the apparent dismissal by Truman, Randolph noted that the entire committee felt that the "prospective U.M.T. legislation is a grave threat to Negro youth and to the internal stability of our nation." Randolph was adamant. He pleaded with Truman: "We consider the matter so serious and urgent as to require a personal conference with the President."[15]

Randolph's feverish pace paid dividends later that month. On December 21 the Committee against Jim Crow publicized the statement of Emma Clarissa Clement of Louisville, Kentucky. The Golden Rule Foundation had named the seventy-two-year-old woman the "American Mother of 1946." She was the first African American to win such an honor. Clement voiced her own personal concern about the prospective social impact of UMT and urged immediate action by African American mothers against the UMT bill on Capitol Hill. Clement's critique was scathing. She grieved that "to us who had sons in the last war, nothing could be more of a betrayal of the ideals for which they fought. To mothers who for the first time would see their sons dragged off in peacetime and exposed to various types of discrimination, this piece of legislation is Public Enemy No 1." In the face of such a threat, Clement urged action: "Fortunately, we are not helpless. Our demands can be heard and can be effective."[16]

On December 28, the Committee against Jim Crow revealed a letter that Senator Robert A. Taft of Ohio had written them. In it Taft pledged his support for antisegregation amendments to the UMT bill. He confided, "I am opposed to the passage of legislation providing for universal military training, and I will vote against any such bill. However, I will support any amendment in that bill barring all racial distinctions."[17] Although Taft fundamentally disagreed with UMT for a variety of reasons, he could agree with opponents of the racial implications of UMT on one thing. Both Taft and Randolph understood that a sure way to kill UMT would be to force its supporters to take a stand on race. If they ignored the issue of segregation, they would open themselves to charges that they intended to create a government-sponsored extension of segregation. If they addressed the issue by barring segregation in UMT, they would most likely lose the support of southern Democrats, many of whom were staunch advocates of UMT. Either way, Taft and Randolph would limit the chances that UMT would become a reality.

With pressure from Randolph mounting, other African American leaders attempted to influence the public debate on UMT in a positive way. To many leaders in the NAACP, the solution was simple. In order to obtain NAACP support for UMT, there would have to be safeguards in place to end segregation and discrimination. As Jesse O. Dedmon put it, "If Congress proposed to pass legislation for compulsory peacetime military conscription, then this legislation should spell out in no uncertain terms that there would be no segregation and discrimination based on race or color."[18]

The perfect opportunity to present such views occurred in March 1948. As the momentum to pass UMT seemed to be hitting a crescendo, the Senate Committee on Armed Services held hearings on UMT from March 17 to April 3, 1948. They heard from hundreds of witnesses. One issue was how any UMT program would handle the issue of discrimination in the military. Gibson appeared before the committee on March 30 and passionately pleaded for UMT. Citing the "present pattern of aggression of the Soviet Union," Gibson argued that "the strength necessary to show our intention to stop aggression can be achieved only by adopting an integrated national security program. Such a program should certainly include UMT." Gibson articulated a vision of future war as quick and intense, with a battlefield that stretched to "every city, every factory, and every farm." With such frightening prospects on the horizon, Gibson warned that "these circumstances make it mandatory that all elements of our manpower pool be utilized to their maximum efficiency. Since universal military training will have to fill up the pool, all physically qualified youth must be trained. This means that Negroes, comprising as they do roughly 10 percent of the available manpower potential, must be trained and must be used. Not to do so would make a mockery of the whole program that is designed to prepare our country for all-out warfare."[19]

Gibson made a compelling case that full participation in UMT would require a new manpower system. He contended, "Now, this use must not be hedged about by quota restrictions and certainly not by segregation. This latter is a matter of necessity. The wartime experiences of the Army in utilizing Negro personnel reflect the absolute impossibility of measuring a man's value by the color of his skin." Gibson harkened back to his own experience as civilian aide to the secretary of war during World War II, in which he was able to observe thousands of troops in the United States and overseas. He contended that "the Army had come out of that experience with many convictions that were strongly held prior to the war now completely and thoroughly shaken." Gibson noted that the navy had recently adopted an official policy of integration and maintained, "That policy certainly must be a part of any system of universal military training."[20]

African American leaders Truman K. Gibson and A. Philip Randolph presented two divergent views on the desirability of UMT. Even though they never admitted it, they did agree on one fundamental point. Both men knew for certain that UMT would impact generations of African American youth. Resolving the issue of segregation in UMT became paramount for both men. Even though their approaches to the issue were different, they both highlighted the importance of the debate throughout African American audiences in America. Storm clouds were on the horizon though. International tensions were rising as the early uncertainty of the postwar period congealed into open tension between the United States and the Soviet Union. As a result, international events accelerated the campaign for UMT and provided it fresh momentum. The campaign was reaching its climax.

11 A Shock throughout the Civilized World

On the whole, I think that the old team, although its uniforms may be a little shopworn, is approaching the goal line and will score a touchdown.
—Archibald G. Thacher

Wearing a green carnation in his buttonhole, President Truman walked briskly into the great House chamber. In face of a cold audience of Representatives and Senators, he flipped open a brown notebook and read from it. Though he looked like a man who was in a hurry to be off to a St. Patrick's Day parade, the President had something to say; he said it as earnestly and forcefully as he could. He issued a call to arms.
—*Time*

As the cold chill of fall set in during 1947, supporters of UMT stayed warm with increasing optimism for their chances of success. Thacher confided to Wadsworth that "our deteriorating relations with Russia and some remarks of higher representatives undoubtedly constitute the most useful ammunition to support our cause." Thacher revealed that the Citizens Committee had prepared a pamphlet "in attractive and interesting form" that summarized the main analysis and recommendations of the Compton report. He proposed to "distribute [it] in thousands at low cost on various news stands."[1]

Other civilians joined the push. One key individual was Daniel A. Poling, president and editor of *Christian Herald*. After establishing contacts within the War Department and serving on the President's Advisory Commission on Universal Training, Poling authored a series of eighteen columns on UMT entitled "Americans All." Poling's first column hit newsstands on January 4, and the *New York Post* syndicate offered the articles to nine hundred papers throughout the country. Poling was a true zealot who saw his mission as reaching any "doubting Thomas" that failed to understand the merits of UMT. He remained active in his mission in other ways, evangelizing for UMT "several times each week" to target audiences such as the state teachers' meeting in New York State. He also maintained a symbiotic relationship with generals in the War Department, and UMT advocates in the War Department, such as Raymond S. McLain, War Department liaison with the President's Advisory Commission on Universal Training, actively sought his writings so they could use them in their own efforts to market UMT. More important, War Department personnel also passed information directly to Poling for him to use in his marketing efforts. Since Poling's area of expertise was religion, it was no surprise that much of this information intended to "set the moral tone for Universal Military Training." He accomplished this by promulgating the moral safeguards that the army would enact, such as "restrictions on prostitution and liquor sales or gifts to trainees in the vicinity of training stations." Poling intended such provisions to overcome the many objections to UMT on religious grounds.[2]

By no means did Poling limit his advocacy of UMT to religious groups exclusively. His extensive connections made it possible for him to articulate the "moral tone" of UMT to high-ranking civic leaders as well. For example, when one evening Representative Charles Taft of Cincinnati, Ohio, questioned Poling on the moral impact of UMT on America's youth, Poling not only personally countered with the successes of the Fort Knox program but also relayed the loss of Taft's support to McLain. In return, McLain praised Poling for doing "one of the most outstanding jobs on the question of Universal Training" and felt certain that he would "be of great help on the question of raising the prestige of the Armed Forces in the estimation of the people." Poling's participation was critical to the marketing effort that the War Department pursued.[3]

As the New Year rang in, hopes were high for UMT. Most involved realized that 1948 was the year of decision. During the course of the year, peacetime selective service would have to be either renewed or scrapped. If it were scrapped, UMT would be the only available alternative. Its renewal, on the other hand, would prove problematic for establishment of UMT.

Compounding this legislative urgency was an overwhelming sense of international crisis. The year 1948 witnessed dramatic and tumultuous changes throughout the world. Poland, Hungary, Bulgaria, and Romania all were Soviet satellites by 1948. A Communist coup in Czechoslovakia on February 25 resulted in the first war scare of three that occurred throughout the year. The US Congress passed the Marshall Plan in March, greatly aiding Western Europe but exacerbating Cold War tensions between the United States and the Soviet Union. Also in March, Belgium, France, Great Britain, Luxembourg, and the Netherlands signed the Brussels Treaty, a collective security arrangement that foreshadowed the formation of the North Atlantic Treaty Organization (NATO) the following year. David Ben-Gurion declared the creation of the state of Israel on May 14, and President Truman immediately recognized Israel. The Arab-Israeli War quickly erupted, with intense fighting continuing throughout the year. The Soviet Union initiated the Berlin blockade in June, and the United States quickly countered with the successful Berlin Airlift. In China, a civil war raged. Chinese Communist forces led by Mao Zedong made steady gains throughout the year against the Nationalist Party of Chiang Kai-shek. A Communist victory in China appeared ever more likely. On the Korean peninsula, the Democratic People's Republic of Korea, led by Kim Il Sung, increasingly fell under the sway of the Soviet Union. In response, the United States backed Syngman Rhee as president of the Republic of Korea, and tensions in Korea assumed international significance. Meanwhile, in Japan, Gen. Douglas MacArthur and US occupation officials worked feverishly to revive the struggling Japanese economy and to ensure that Communism would not make inroads there as well. Overall, fear of conflict with the Soviet Union heightened the angst among many Americans and greatly softened the traditional resistance to preparedness measures that prevailed in calmer times.[4]

In fact, the year began with UMT advocates riding a rising wave of optimism. Supporters from all quarters weighed in. The Hearst newspapers announced on January 2 that "our straightest thinkers, both in and out of uniform, agree that a trained citizenry is the firmest foundation for peace. The Hearst Newspapers applaud this wise agreement, and urge upon the Congress prompt adoption of a universal military training program." The American Legion, under the leadership of James F. O'Neil, national commander, pronounced the week of January 6–12, 1948, as "Universal Military Training Week in the United States and each separate state." O'Neil even requested that President Truman officially sanction the observance nationally. Although Truman demurred, he promised O'Neil that he would urge Congress to pass UMT in his state-of-the-union message during that week. Even Thomas Dewey, governor of New York and leading Republican presidential prospect, announced his unequivocal support for UMT and also proclaimed Universal Military Training Week. Dewey informed reporters that UMT was a signal of American resolve to aggressive nations and a deterrent of future conflict. He insisted, "I repeat now what I have urged before, that we must provide universal military training for all able-bodied young American men. A nation so trained is of itself one of the strongest bulwarks against war." After lamenting that American leaders previously permitted "the illusion that free nations would fall easy victims to aggressors," Dewey concluded that UMT would correct this illusion and ensure that America was prepared and that other nations knew it.[5]

Even with such optimistic support, serious obstacles to UMT still existed. Most important, the priorities of the new Republican majority in Congress focused on tax reductions rather than expensive preparedness measures such as UMT. On January 2, Joseph W. Martin, speaker of the House, listed individual income tax reduction as "one of the very first" items the House would consider when it reconvened. When asked about Truman's reluctance to accept a major tax reduction, since Truman had already vetoed two previous ones in the earlier session, Martin quipped, "You never can tell; when the lamplight is held out the sinner may return and we welcome him." Martin characterized a tax cut as "absolutely essential" and explained that it would allow workers to keep more of their pay, promote business growth and productivity, and curb inflation.[6]

Another complication combined with the predisposition of leading Republicans in Congress to seek a tax cut before any action on UMT. Leading Republicans also voiced concern that the military services were pursuing independent strategic visions without an overall coordinated plan. Chan Gurney, a key Republican senator from South Dakota and chairman of both the armed services legislative and military appropriations committees, warned Truman that the apparent lack of strategic coordination concerned him and his Republican colleagues: "The 1948 budget, of course, largely was prepared before unification, and is only loosely coordinated. We have no firm estimates on the cost of UMT or what its place will be in the over-all security picture. We would like some fairly concrete recommendations by the end of next month."[7] To Gurney, the concern over strategic coordination dealt ultimately with economy. If each of the services pursued a completely independent strategy, there would be obvious and costly redundancies that would place a heavy burden on the overall economy. Reducing such excesses would ensure a more efficient, and less onerous, defense establishment.

The two apprehensions Martin and Gurney voiced, tax reductions and strategic coordination leading to economy, were related. Government spending, especially on defense, had increased dramatically since the late thirties. For example, the *Washington Post* estimated that over the span of a decade, the defense spending share of the federal budget doubled from 14 percent to 28 percent. In addition, defense spending in 1948 represented a shared cost of seventy-four dollars a year for everyone in the country compared to only eight dollars a year for everyone only ten years earlier.[8] The trend of significant increases in defense spending, even after victory in World War II, worried Republican leaders. As a result, they approached UMT cautiously and saw in part an expansion of government control and spending that could ultimately lead to higher taxes, increased inflation, or both.

Truman wasted no time in delivering what he had promised to UMT supporters. On January 6 he delivered his budget message to Congress for fiscal year 1949. Truman once again exhorted Congress to act on UMT and tried to force their hand by providing the seed money to begin the program. He declared: "In anticipation of early approval by the Congress of a program of universal training along the lines recommended by the Advisory Commission on Universal Training, I have included 400 million dollars in the expenditure estimate for the fiscal year 1949. This is the first-year cost of a program which in full operation will cost about 2 billion dollars annually." Truman followed his budget message the next day with his state-of-the-union message for 1948. In it, Truman placed UMT at the foundation of his proposed national security program. He informed Congress: "There are many elements in a balanced national security program, all inter-related and necessary, but Universal Training should be the foundation for them all. A favorable decision by the Congress at an early date is of world importance. I am convinced that such action is vital to the security of this Nation and to the maintenance of its leadership."[9]

Optimism spread like wildfire. Leaders within the American Legion mobilized in order to pressure lawmakers. John T. Taylor, director of the Legion's National Legislative Commission, urged Congressman Leo E. Allen (R-IL), chairman of the House Rules Committee, to act. Taylor proclaimed that "the Congress, including Members of your Committee, is aware that 35 national women's organizations with more than 2,000,000 members went on record unanimously here last week for Universal Military Training." Taylor did not stop there. He informed Allen that "sixty more national organizations including some of our most prominent fraternal and civic associations—with total membership of 11,000,000— are waging a campaign for Universal Military Training through the National Security Committee." Taylor blasted Allen for what he considered an un-American tactic of barring the UMT bill from open debate before the entire House: "Every group in America, except one has expressed its views on Universal Military Training or had full opportunity to do so. That one exception is Congress itself! Only Congress in this entire nation has been denied the fundamental American right of free expression, and it has been and is being denied this right by one Committee. That Committee is the House Rules Committee of which you are its distinguished chairman."[10]

The motivation for Allen's decisive move to hold the UMT bill captive within the House Rules Committee was essentially political. The context of the 1946 midterm election illuminates exactly why. In that pivotal midterm, Republicans gained solid control of both the House of Representatives (246–188) and the Senate (51–45) for the first time since 1928. It was on this high tide that Republicans entered the political fray in 1948. They were confident, perhaps even cocky, and willing to assert their newfound influence against the Truman administration. Republicans remained assured that they would repeat their recent success in the upcoming 1948 election by gaining an even larger majority in Congress and the presidency for the first time in five elections. Stifling the UMT bill, albeit through parliamentary procedures, provided Republicans a significant victory against a cornerstone of the Truman administration's postwar security agenda and held little political risk for the majority party.[11]

Sensing rising fortunes for proponents of UMT, some critics also increased their efforts early in 1948. A National Youth Assembly against UMT took place in Washington, DC, on February 15–16. Approximately fifteen hundred youth from throughout the country gathered at Turner's Arena for the first day's events. Rev. John Darr, chairman of the event, argued that "UMT became a major part of our government's program last year" and went on to outline specific developments in 1947, such as the Compton commission and the Towe bill. Darr took specific aim at the army's role in the process, claiming that "throughout the summer the Army carried on a huge propaganda campaign for the adoption of UMT." The following day the event moved to the Metropolitan Baptist Church, where attendees received greetings from Henry A. Wallace and thirty AFL and CIO labor leaders "expressing their opposition to UMT and support for the assembly." Wallace warned the youth that "U.M.T. is only part of a great and fearful program, which heads the world towards a third world war." Wallace included the Truman Doctrine, the European Recovery Plan, and the Taft–Hartley bill as "part of the same fearful plan." The thirty labor leaders representing both the AFL and the CIO weighed in to support the youth assembly. In addition, Robert W. Kenny, former attorney general of California and president of the National Lawyers Guild, addressed the crowd, referring to the campaign for UMT as "Operation Goosestep" and urging opposition.[12]

Other events also countered the rising momentum of UMT. On March 4, 1948, the Congressional Committee on Expenditures in the Executive Departments released its second report blasting the army's campaign for UMT. The report highlighted five areas where the army overstepped its bounds by openly advocating its own policy on UMT. The report revealed that "evidence indicates that members of the Armed Forces ranking from five-star generals to privates, first-class, were filling speaking engagements from coast to coast, participating in panel discussions, and making radio addresses in support of the universal military training program." The committee discovered that "in some instances, activities were the result of invitations which had been deliberately engineered or inspired by Army personnel and are, therefore, improper and illegal propaganda activity." The second violation the committee unearthed was the activity of the Women's Interest Unit within the Department of the Army. The committee recounted "that at a meeting and luncheon, the latter paid for out of funds of the Department of the Army, of the advisory committee of the Women's Interest Unit, the implied suggestion was made by various Army Department officers that the women should educate the public to acceptance of UMT, and that the tone of the whole meeting was in the nature of propaganda for UMT. Your committee, from the evidence, finds that these accusations were justified."[13]

In addition, the committee learned "that the Army advisory committees in communities throughout the country have been prompted unduly to agitate in favor of universal military training." The committee also reported that "evidence presented at the hearing showed that some members had been urged to make speeches advocating universal military training, and that outline talks and other suggested material on this subject were forwarded to members of the advisory committees without solicitation." Moreover, the committee found "that the *UMT Pioneer,* published at Fort Knox, has been designed more to influence outside readers in favor of UMT than for the benefit of the men in the unit, and that this paper, of much more attractive design and make-up than the average camp paper, was, in fact, given wide circulation outside the camp. Your committee reports the evidence shows that this paper is far superior to the average camp newspaper and that many of the articles were written with an apparent appeal, not to the trainee, but to sell the virtue of universal military training." Finally, the committee determined "that propaganda pamphlets and other material had been prepared and were being distributed in a wholesale manner to members of the Army advisory committees, the advisory committee of the Women's Interest Unit, and others."[14]

It would be tempting to analyze the investigation as simply partisan politics. However, complaints to Congress over the active role the War Department engaged in had increased for some time. Several members of the investigation were actually staunch supporters of UMT. Wadsworth himself participated in the investigation. In fact, some questioned whether his involvement in the investigation meant that he had changed his mind on UMT. To them, Wadsworth emphatically denied that he had. Instead, he discussed the fact that "there is a law upon the federal statute books forbidding the use of federal funds by officers and employees of the executive branch of the government in activities calculated or intended to influence action of the Congress on any piece of legislation or policy." Wadsworth characterized the law merely as "an attempt on the part of the Congress to keep the bureaucracy within bounds." Acknowledging that "complaints" were reaching Congress that "the War Department was violating this law in its efforts to gain support for universal military training," Wadsworth explained that even a staunch supporter such as himself felt that "it was the duty of our committee to investigate these charges." He regretted that "we found, to our dismay, that the War Department had employed certain civilians at government salaries to do nothing else than to boost universal military training." In addition to this finding, which resulted in the dismissal of the civilian employees, Wadsworth also conceded that "we also found that officials of the [War] Department had incurred rather heavy traveling expenses at the cost of the government in organizing and attending meetings." Without directly labeling these activities propaganda, Wadsworth admitted that "some of these expenditures might be said to have fallen within the twilight zone—between the legitimate and the illegitimate."[15]

As tensions mounted, other preparedness options surfaced that offered alternatives to UMT. An important one was strategic airpower. On March 1 the Congressional Aviation Policy Board, also known as the Brewster–Hinshaw board after its chairman, Owen Brewster, senator from Maine, and vice-chairman Carl Hinshaw, representative from California, released its recommendations. The report portrayed the international scene in apocalyptic terms: "It is folly to pretend that the world does not live under a sense of impending tragedy. Deliberately and continuously we are faced with the possibility of aggressive attack. The deadly character of the new weapons makes war an open invitation to mass annihilation." Several features of the report were important. First, Brewster and Hinshaw recommended a level of defense spending heretofore unimaginable. Previous defense plans envisioned total government spending of under $38 billion per year. In stark contrast, the Brewster–Hinshaw board envisioned two possible plans, both totaling more than $40 billion per year over the same period. In addition to calling for massive defense spending levels, their report also focused heavily on strategic airpower as the future of the American defense establishment. They wrote: "Anything less than complete supremacy in air power is self-deception." Interestingly, the board did not rule out UMT. Instead, they recommended capping government spending at $25 billion, exclusive of defense spending, the Marshall Plan, and UMT.[16]

The following day, Marshall met with members of the Senate Armed Services Committee behind closed doors to highlight the urgency of the European situation and to urge prompt enactment of UMT as a response. Chan Gurney, chairman of the committee, and five other members met with Marshall in his office for over an hour. As Gurney explained to reporters, "In view of all the things that have happened lately in the international field, including Czechoslovakia and the critical situation in Finland, our committee decided we wanted to talk to Marshall." What they heard was foreboding. Marshall described a deteriorating European situation and its implications for the United States. He urged the senators to enact UMT as a response. Reports of the meeting indicated that "Marshall had lost none of his confidence and faith in the proposed UMT program that he had voiced previously, both as Chief of Staff of the Army and as Secretary of State." Gurney divulged that "we asked for his viewpoint of UMT and heard him reaffirm vehemently his belief that the training program should be approved at this time."[17]

On March 8, Secretary of Defense James Forrestal and his top three subordinates, Secretary of the Army Kenneth Royall, Secretary of the Navy John Sullivan, and Secretary of the Air Force Stuart Symington, met with the Senate Armed Services Committee behind closed doors. Their hope was that the distinguished group would provide high-ranking endorsement to the campaign to make UMT a "companion measure" to the European Recovery Program (ERP) and to emphasize its necessity to the committee. In fact, reports indicated that the secretaries claimed UMT was "not only necessary but mandatory." The top military authorities explained to the committee that UMT would allow America to mobilize much faster in case of attack. Gurney revealed that the military brass claimed it would take eighteen months to mobilize without UMT but only six months if the measure were enacted. Initially, Forrestal's drive was effective. On the same day, the committee voted unanimously to hold public hearings on UMT, something they were hesitant to do previously. Upon hearing the news of the progress, Forrestal remarked, "Events are making progress for us." Although he declined to elaborate, Forrestal clearly alluded to the momentum that international tensions provided to the UMT campaign. Even so, the fate of UMT was still anything but certain. As one member of the committee remarked, "It appears that the choice lies between UMT and a return of the peacetime draft." Such a choice would prove problematic for proponents of UMT.[18]

On March 17, 1948, President Truman addressed a joint session of Congress on events taking place in Europe and their relevance to the United States. In his address, Truman warned that the Communist takeover of Czechoslovakia required increased preparedness measures on the part of the United States. He told Congress, "The tragic death of the Republic of Czechoslovakia has sent a shock throughout the civilized world." Once Truman explained the rationale for increased preparedness measures, he informed Congress and the American people of his desired response. He asked Congress for three specific items. First, he wanted quick passage of the European Recovery Plan, also known as the Marshall Plan. He informed Congress, "That program is the foundation of our policy of assistance to the free nations of Europe. Prompt passage of that program is the most telling contribution we can now make toward peace." The second item Truman requested was "prompt enactment of universal training legislation." He argued, "Universal training is the only feasible means by which the civilian components of our armed forces can be built up to the strength required if we are to be prepared for emergencies. Our ability to mobilize large numbers of trained men in time of emergency could forestall future conflict and, together with other measures of national policy, could restore stability to the world." The sense of crisis that the administration fostered required a return to the underlying military utility of UMT as a long-range preparedness measure. Even so, Truman still touted its value as a deterrent. He assured Congress, "I am convinced that the decision of the American people, expressed through the Congress, to adopt universal training would be of first importance in giving courage to every free government in the world."[19]

The third and final policy Truman urged Congress to pass was "the temporary reenactment of selective service legislation in order to maintain our armed forces at their authorized strength." Sensing that critics would complain about his asking for both UMT and selective service at the same time, Truman explained the logic behind the request: "There is no conflict between the requirements of selective service for the regular forces and universal training for the reserve components. Selective service is necessary until the solid foundation of universal training can be established. Selective service can then be terminated and the regular forces may then be maintained on a voluntary basis." Truman closed by fostering a sense of urgency because of the international situation: "The recommendations I have made represent the most urgent steps toward securing the peace and preventing war."[20]

Two points regarding Truman's message of March 17 are crucial. First, the order of his request is revealing. Truman asked for UMT before selective service. To Truman, the more valuable of the two policies was UMT, because it was viewed as a viable long-range solution to the manpower and financial constraints expected in the postwar world. In addition, he saw UMT as more beneficial to the nation than selective service. He advocated UMT because of its supposed positive impact on American society in terms of national health, literacy, and citizenship. Second, Truman asked for selective service only as a bridge to the enactment of a working UMT system. In fact, his request for temporary reenactment of selective service was only necessary until the "solid foundation" of UMT was established. Ultimately, his plan was to let selective service expire, rely on UMT to create a trained citizenry, and then fill the smaller professional army "on a voluntary basis."[21]

The same day, the Senate Armed Services Committee began full public hearings on UMT. Marshall addressed the committee. Acknowledg-

ing his "own concern over the accelerated trend in Europe," he continued, saying that "in the short years since the end of hostilities this trend
has grown from a trickle into a torrent." As he recounted, all of the Balkan
states except Greece had "lost all semblance of national independence."
Even worse, "two friendly nations—first Hungary and last week Czechoslovakia—have been forced into complete submission to the Communist control." Marshall provided a two-part solution for the committee
to enact. First, he advocated the ERP as "a fundamental requirement for
the strengthening of the western nations of Europe." He also advocated
UMT. He felt there were limitations to the ERP: "This economic program in the existing situation is not a complete answer. It is said that one
cannot buy peace and prosperity with dollars. . . . There is something
more for the United States to do." That something was to enact UMT.
In making his plea, Marshall did not fail to address the other options
that were available. He discussed a "temporary application" of selective
service and a "reconsideration" of strategic airpower as "necessary," but
his preference was clear. As he recommended to the committee, "First
of all, I am convinced that the decision of the American people to adopt
the democratic procedure of universal training would strengthen every
free government." Marshall closed his argument by reiterating that he
felt these two items, ERP and UMT, "are necessary now, I think, to the
maintenance of peace in the world."[22]

At the start of May, the fate of UMT hung in the balance. Three distinct
legislative options surfaced. The original UMT bill, known as the Towe
bill because its sponsor was Harry L. Towe (R-NJ), still languished in the
House Rules Committee after approval by the House Armed Services
Committee the previous July. The chairman of the House Rules Committee, Leo E. Allen (R-IL), adamantly refused to allow the bill onto the floor
of the House and showed little sign of relenting. The Towe bill required
registration of all men between the ages of eighteen and twenty. Once
screened, all physically qualified men would be inducted for six months
of military training combined with service in the reserves. The Towe bill
represented the legislative expression of the UMT ideal. It was universal
in reach and military in application.[23]

With the Towe bill in captivity, the House Armed Services Committee, chaired by Walter G. Andrews (R-NY), completed a separate draft
bill that introduced a new obstacle for UMT passage. The bill uncou-
pled selective service and UMT. It provided for a temporary draft but no

UMT. The House bill sought "to put 700,000 more men in uniform over the next two years," requiring all men eighteen through thirty years old to register and men nineteen through twenty-five years old to be liable for induction for two years of military service, most likely overseas. The House bill sought selective service alone as the solution to the nation's military manpower shortages, primarily based on the urgency of international events.[24]

The Senate bill was a compromise measure that provided for both selective service and a modified version of UMT. It called for a year of training for men between the ages of eighteen and nineteen and one-half years old, although the plan was not universal in scope but rather a selective military training program. In addition, it established selective service for all men between the ages of nineteen and one-half and twenty-five years old. The day after Andrews announced completion of the House bill, Chan Gurney (R-SD), chairman of the Senate Armed Services Committee, announced that his committee had modified their draft bill to allow men nineteen years old to be classified under selective service as opposed to the selective training plan. Gurney blamed the modification on the revival of the draft. He commented, "We have learned there is not enough available manpower between 19 ½ and 25 to fill the expected needs of the two-year draft plan." He acknowledged that numerous exemptions—including World War II service, reserve membership, or marriage—compelled the use of more young draftees in order to ensure adequate numbers.[25]

Amidst the confusion resulting from three different bills addressing military manpower, President Truman attempted to keep pressure on lawmakers to produce some form of UMT legislation. Addressing the National Health Assembly in Washington, DC, he passionately urged UMT. Once again he painted UMT in much broader strokes than did his generals. At the meeting Truman portrayed compulsory health insurance and UMT as two pillars of a comprehensive national health program that would benefit the nation immensely. Lamenting the fact that as many as one-third of World War II draftees were deemed "not to be fit for service," Truman characterized the situation as "a most disgraceful thing" and argued that UMT would alleviate such health problems. In fact, Truman testified that his own experience in the National Guard in the early twenties illustrated the link between military training and improved health.[26]

"We Must be Ready to Back Up What We Say."
(Cartoon by Clifford K. Berryman, March 18, 1948;
Courtesy Center for Legislative Archives)

Others chimed in as well. Owen J. Roberts, spokesman for a preparedness group known as the National Security Committee and a former Supreme Court justice, decried the Senate's bill as "an ill-conceived
compromise dictated by the political expediency of an election-minded
Congress." In particular, Roberts lambasted the compromise bill's "in-
tolerable inequities," claiming that anything but a "real" UMT program
would permit the government to "draft one boy and permit two or more
of his neighbors to escape any responsibility." Roberts attacked Republican leaders Robert A. Taft and Joseph W. Martin as purposely evad-
ing a direct vote on UMT because they feared that it might harm their
prospects "for the Republican (Presidential) nomination." Reinforcing
Roberts's rhetoric, Towe threatened to attach a UMT amendment to the
House draft bill when it reached the floor. It was reported that he planned

to amend the draft bill to ensure that UMT would be implemented immediately following the expiration of the initial two-year draft.[27]

The same week, Senator Robert A. Taft, chairman of the Senate Republican Policy Committee, called a two-week halt to progress on all three military manpower bills before Congress. Taft sought to ensure that Republicans coordinated their policy on all issues relating to preparedness. The result was that the Senate Republican Policy Committee gave clear and coordinated preference to the seventy-group air force over both selective service and UMT. Such a development further hurt the chances that some form of UMT legislation would pass.[28]

Two days later the House Armed Services Committee released its report accompanying its own selective service bill. The majority members used heightened rhetoric to connect the need for a draft to international tensions directly. They declared, "The Soviet Union may now be willing to risk a showdown," a possibility that the group characterized as "new and ominous." In addition to using international tensions as tinder to ignite action on selective service, the group also warned against basing preparedness exclusively on air power. As the group admonished, "A powerful Air Force is not a panacea for security. A seventy-group Air Force is not a substitute for selective service." The majority concluded that although volunteer methods could maintain the proper force levels for both the air force and the navy, they certainly could not for the army.[29]

On May 24 the Senate Armed Services Committee executed an astounding reversal. Sensing that time was running out on the current session, and feeling that some solution had to be reached to stabilize military manpower levels, they suddenly dropped their plan for a modified UMT program and replaced the compulsory selective training plan with a voluntary program instead. Under the new program, a maximum of 161,000 eighteen-year-old males would be permitted to volunteer for training within the continental United States and then join reserve units near their homes for the next four to six years. Successful completion of the voluntary military training program exempted youths from the two-year draft. This final legislative blow to UMT came the same week that George Gallup, director of the American Institute of Public Opinion, reported, "The weight of public opinion today is in favor of Universal Military Training rather than a temporary draft. Although Congress has postponed consideration of UMT, more than twice as many voters favor that program as favor selective service." In fact, Gallup characterized his findings as consistent with several years of high levels of public support for the concept of UMT. He exclaimed, "The preference of voters for a permanent system of peacetime military training is hardly surprising in view of past surveys which have consistently found approval of the idea since the early days of World War II."[30]

At the end of May, it became apparent to even the most diehard proponents that UMT would not become a reality. The Towe bill was still captive in the House Rules Committee, the House Armed Services Committee refused to link UMT and selective service in their bill, and the Senate Armed Services Committee modified their compromise measure providing for selective service and selective military training to contain only limited voluntary military training. With little over two weeks left in the session, attention quickly shifted to the draft.

As June began, there were serious doubts whether agreement could even be reached on the draft. The Senate version still had the voluntary military training plan and authorized the draft for five years, whereas the House version planned no military training program and a two-year draft. After a grueling twelve-hour session that lasted late into the evening on June 8, the Senate voted 47–33 to reduce its draft to two years. Other amendments were offered, including a last-ditch effort to include a compulsory UMT plan in the draft bill. Sponsored by George W. Malone (R-NV), the amendment sought to restore the Senate draft bill back to its original form with selective service and limited selective military training. Senators debated Malone's amendment most of the day on June 9 but eventually rejected it by a voice vote late in the session. The following day, the senators wrapped up their work on the draft bill by decisively passing the measure with a vote of 78–10.[31]

The decisive action by senators spurred their colleagues in the House to action. The House Rules Committee had bottled up the house draft bill ever since the House Armed Services Committee approved it on May 7. There was much doubt whether there was even enough time to consider the bill before the established end of the congressional session on June 19. The ending date was especially problematic in an election year, as both parties needed to leave Washington, DC, to attend their national conventions and nominate presidential candidates. On June 14, the House Rules Committee released the House draft bill to the floor for debate. What followed was four days of rancorous debate, including numerous amendments and filibustering by congressional supporters of Henry A. Wallace, who made every effort to kill the bill completely, or at least delay it past the session deadline of June 19. However, on June 18 the House draft bill came up for final vote and passed easily on a vote of 283–130.[32]

The final version of the draft bill required men between eighteen and twenty-five years old to register but only allowed for the induction of men between nineteen and twenty-five years old. The period of service was twenty-one months. The bill also retained the voluntary military training program in which up to 161,000 eighteen-year-olds annually could participate in military training in the continental United States for one year and then transition into the reserves. Any youth pursuing this option was exempted from the draft. Also, enlistment by youths in the National Guard would preclude them from being drafted later.[33]

The editorial staff of the *New York Times*, a newspaper known to advocate UMT, characterized the compromise draft bill as "not what the National Defense Department asked for, but it is a much better bill than it seemed possible would be gotten out of the Committee and through Congress." They lamented that the voluntary limited training program enacted was "only a pale shadow of the training program that was incorporated in the Universal Military Training bill that was bottled up in the House Rules Committee, but it is a step in the right direction." In the end, they hoped that the draft, as they had claimed UMT would, "will give notice to the world that we intend, as a people, to live up to our responsibilities."[34]

The immediate impact of the draft bill was interesting. The highly public debate over it spurred enlistment in the National Guard and to a lesser degree the Organized Reserves. In fact, at the end of May the National Guard had been at a total strength of only 250,000, compared to its total authorized strength of 341,000, but once it became clear that enlistment in the National Guard exempted one from the draft, enlistments surged. In fact, in less than a month the National Guard eclipsed its authorized strength and continued recruiting above its authorized strength. Kenneth Royall, secretary of the army, ordered units to stop further recruiting to avoid a budget deficit the following year.[35]

With both the Senate and the House bills passed, Congress smoothed out the differences between them in just one day. On June 19 the compromise draft bill proceeded on a roundabout journey first to the Republican National Convention, to be signed by Arthur H. Vandenberg, president pro tem of the Senate, and Joseph W. Martin, speaker of the House. The official bill arrived at the White House on June 23. The following day, at a little before six in the evening, and with only his executive clerk present, President Truman signed it into law.[36]

During the spring of 1948, rising international tensions changed the fortunes of UMT. As tensions around the globe mounted, the campaign for UMT surged forward. Advocates of all types joined in the campaign and clamored for speedy enactment of UMT as the solution to the dangers of conflict. However, a paradox prevented that crescendo from pushing their proposal towards enactment. At the critical moment, the campaign became captive to its own rhetoric. By inciting fears of conflict as a justification for preparedness, advocates of UMT were forced to admit that long-term preparedness measures such as UMT contributed little to immediate national security. Even if enacted without delay, UMT would still take several years to make a significant contribution to national security. The inflated sense of fear that pushed UMT forward also limited its chances of success. Selective service was revived to become the primary preparedness measure that could immediately contribute to national security. Critics of UMT seized that point and forced advocates to concede that if the world was such a dangerous place, then what was needed immediately was selective service, not UMT. The hopes of implementing UMT as a long-range solution to the nation's preparedness program were sacrificed in order to achieve some fix, even if it was viewed by preparedness advocates as short-term and second-best.

12   The Paradox of Preparedness

> Our failure to provide for Universal Military Training in 1920 and the tragic
> repetition of that error [following World War II] . . . are largely responsible for
> the call we must make on our young men today. I am convinced that it would
> not now be necessary to interrupt the normal course of their lives if we had
> taken the conservative, wise action—an effort that was defeated largely by
> emotional rather than logical reactions.
> —George C. Marshall

> But whatever is the best way to solve the problem, the country hasn't
> been sold as yet on the necessity for urgency on a "training" program while
> the draft is in operation. If there's an "emergency," the draft is supposed to
> take care of it, says the observing public, and, if that isn't enough, the reserve
> powers in the law can be invoked to bring back into service some of the
> draftees who have served their time. That's an inequitable set-up but it hasn't
> been argued out.
> —*New York Herald Tribune*

The summer of 1948 witnessed the end of the campaign for Universal Military Training after World War II. The defeat of UMT and the ascendance of selective service in its place hold important implications for subsequent American history. To begin with, 1948 was a presidential election year, and the Truman administration feverishly conducted its election campaign. Presidential advisor Clark M. Clifford and Attorney James Rowe had already outlined a detailed plan for the campaign in a confidential memorandum for the president entitled "The Politics of 1948." In it, Clifford and Rowe recommended among other things that the Truman campaign focus on civil rights to offset recent Republican forays into the issue. Clifford noted, "The Republicans know how vulnerable the Democratic Party is insofar as the negro vote is concerned." He anticipated "a flourish of oratory" on civil rights by Republicans highlighting the importance of civil rights without their actually taking any radical action. Clifford and Rowe argued persuasively that allowing the anticipated Republican approach to go unchallenged would be "a grave error," and they instead pressed Truman to "go as far as he feels he possibly could go in recommending measures to protect the rights of minority groups." They acknowledged that an aggressive stand on civil rights during the summer of 1948 might risk alienating Southern

Democrats on a contentious issue. However, they strongly urged doing so because it was well worth the risk. They contended: "This course of action would obviously cause difficulty with our Southern friends but that is the lesser of two evils."[1]

The issue of civil rights broadly and segregation in the military specifically remained contentious after the defeat of UMT. Shifting their previous critique against UMT to selective service, A. Philip Randolph and Grant Reynolds pleaded with Truman to institute the same civil rights reforms in selective service that they had argued for relative to UMT. As before, they sought concrete action on the part of the President: "Because Congress enacted, and you have now signed, a Selective Service bill devoid of any safeguards for Negro youth, we should like to request, at your earliest convenience, a conference with you to discuss the issuance of an executive order abolishing all *segregation* and discrimination from the armed forces." Although Truman demurred on meeting with them, the pair did not relent. They wrote Truman again on July 15 urging the issuance of an executive order.[2]

As a result of both the campaign strategy outlined in "The Politics of 1948" and the increased pressure to prevent segregation from occurring in either UMT or selective service, Truman took unprecedented action. On July 26 he issued two pivotal executive orders advancing civil rights as federal policy. Executive Order 9980 instituted fair employment practices within the federal government and established a board to enforce those fair employment practices.[3] More directly related to UMT, Executive Order 9981 created the President's Committee on Equality of Treatment and Opportunity in the Armed Services. The purpose of 9981 was clear. It sought to imbue the military with "the highest standards of democracy" and to ensure the "equality of treatment and opportunity for all those who serve in our country's defense." In order to accomplish this purpose, Truman issued a new, groundbreaking policy regarding American military manpower. He wrote, "It is hereby declared to be the policy of the President that there shall be equality of treatment and opportunity for all persons in the armed services without regard to race, color, religion, or national origin." He urged that "this policy shall be put into effect as rapidly as possible, having due regard to the time required to effectuate any necessary changes without impairing efficiency or morale." The order inaugurated a committee composed of seven members whom Truman would personally appoint.[4]

Even though the long-term consequences of Executive Order 9981 were significant, the immediate reaction to the order was less than stellar. Because the order did not specifically mention segregation, Randolph initially "denounced" the order "as a misleading move, made for political purposes and deliberately calculated to obscure the issue of segregation." Randolph's and Reynolds's divergent views and contentious relationship with Truman K. Gibson also resurfaced as a result of the order. Speaking for the Committee against Jim Crow in Military Service and Training, Reynolds communicated the group's "alarm" that President Truman might choose Gibson as one of the seven members of the committee. Other advocates of civil rights cautiously viewed the order as mere rhetoric, not unlike the Republican platform issued at the party's national convention on June 21 in Philadelphia. Reaction by army leadership was outright hostile. Immediately following the issuance of Executive Order 9981, Army Chief of Staff Omar Bradley made controversial remarks while visiting the UMT Experimental Unit at Fort Knox, Kentucky. When questioned about the order by reporters, Bradley flatly stated, "The Army will put men of different races in different companies. It will change that policy when the nation as a whole changes it."[5]

Bradley's remarks immediately became a lightning rod for debate. Secretary of the NAACP Walter White expressed grave concern at Bradley's comments, declaring, "We are deeply shocked at General Bradley's statement. This statement by the Chief of Staff less than 24 hours after the Commander in Chief of the Army, Navy and Air Force had issued an executive order to eliminate racial discrimination and inequality in the armed services is unbelievable. It is another illustration of how men who have been isolated in the Army for many years from contact with the outside world are unable to understand or even be aware of the growth of enlightened public opinion."[6]

Since Executive Order 9981 did not specifically mention segregation in the military, Truman quickly clarified the intent of the order by holding his own press conference. As the *New York Times* reported, "President Truman emphasized today that he expected all segregation of race to be abolished eventually from the Armed Services."[7]

While many echoed White's criticism of Bradley and applauded Truman's clarification regarding segregation, an unlikely ally quickly interpreted Bradley's controversial views more positively. Hanson W. Baldwin, outspoken critic of UMT, responded just over a week later with a spirited defense of Bradley's interpretation of Executive Order 9981. Baldwin characterized Bradley's remarks as "straight-forward and courageous" and argued that they contextualized segregation properly "as a national problem, rather than an Army problem." Baldwin went further, though. In an interesting twist, he directly related Bradley's resistance *against* Executive Order 9981 to the US Army's campaign *for* UMT that had just suffered defeat. Baldwin contended, "The Army is not, cannot, and must not be an instrument of social reform. A somewhat similar fallacious suggestion was advanced by well-meaning but utterly mistaken persons when universal military training was being debated. The trainees were not to be trained primarily in the military profession, but in civics and scholarship. The Army was to be an educational institution. This is not and never can be the Army's job if we are to have an Army. It is extremely dangerous nonsense to try to make the Army other than one thing, a fighting machine."[8]

President Truman officially appointed the members of the President's Committee on Equality of Treatment and Opportunity in the Armed Forces on September 18, 1948. The designated members included Charles H. Fahy (chairman), former solicitor general of the United States; Alphonsus J. Donahue, president of A. J. Donahue Corporation; Lester B. Granger, executive secretary of the National Urban League; Charles Luckman, president of Lever Brothers; Dwight R. G. Palmer, president of General Cable Corporation; John H. Sengstacke, publisher of the *Chicago Defender;* and William E. Stevenson, president of Oberlin College. The committee became known as the Fahy committee.

The Fahy committee worked feverishly for sixteen months from their first official meeting on January 12, 1949, until the release of their final report on May 22, 1950. They held sixteen meetings and issued ten reports to the president, including progress, interim, memorandum, and draft reports. Beginning with their first meeting, the Fahy committee examined Executive Order 9981 in minute detail. The committee members parsed, interpreted, and expanded upon every word and phrase in the order. They quickly agreed that they should approach their work from both social and military standpoints. As the members indicated in their final report, "At the outset of its deliberations the Committee was agreed that the problem with which it was charged was not merely one of simple justice. In addition to the factor of equality of treatment and opportunity was the factor of military efficiency, the making of a better armed service." The Fahy committee questioned sixty-seven senior leaders regarding desegregation of the military, including service secretaries, assistant service secretaries, chiefs of staff, military and civilian personnel experts, and representatives of civilian organizations. These in-depth proceedings produced 1,025 pages of testimony.[9]

On May 22, 1950, the committee released its final report, entitled *Freedom to Serve: Equality of Treatment and Opportunity in the Armed Services, a Report by the President's Committee.* The members unanimously declared that "the Committee appointed by the President has conducted such an inquiry and has made recommendations to the President, the Secretary of Defense, and the Secretaries of the three services. It was the judgment of the Committee that these recommendations, when put into actual practice, would bring an end to inequality of treatment and opportunity. All of the Committee's recommendations have been approved and accepted by the President, the Secretary of Defense and the service Secretaries. They are now in effect."[10]

The Truman administration distributed the report widely, delivering 7,587 copies of it throughout the federal government and to state governments, public organizations, libraries, and media outlets. On July 6, 1950, President Truman disbanded the Fahy committee, noting "that as these programs are carried out, there will be, within the reasonably near future, equality of treatment and opportunity in the Armed Services, with a consequent improvement in military efficiency. . . . Accordingly, I am relieving the Committee of its assignment as of today, while I am, at the same time, leaving in effect Executive Order No. 9981."[11]

In addition to Executive Order 9981, there were other important consequences of the failure of the campaign for UMT on subsequent American history. One was the fate of selective service after 1948. Even though UMT suffered ultimate defeat in that year, proponents of the plan advocated for it for several more years to little avail. George C. Marshall never abandoned the plan, continuing to argue for its value to both the army and American society. In April 1951, Marshall published an article entitled "The Obligation to Serve." In it, he demonstrated his strong support for UMT long after its chances for full enactment had faded. He used strong language, characterizing US national security planning as "a succession of feasts and famines" demonstrating to the world "our vacillations on preparedness." He lamented, "Our failure to provide for Universal Military Training in 1920 and the tragic repetition of that error [following World War II] . . . are largely responsible for the call we must make on our young men today. I am convinced that it would not now be necessary to interrupt the normal course of their lives if we had taken the conservative, wise action—an effort that was defeated largely by emotional rather than logical reactions."[12]

This last gasp of the campaign for UMT after World War II did result in a pyrrhic victory of sorts. When Congress reauthorized selective service during the summer of 1951, the army actually achieved recognition for the general principle of UMT, included the words *universal military training* in the title of the selective service law, and created some minor provisions of the envisioned UMT plan. Congress passed Public Law 51, the Universal Military Training and Service law, on June 19, 1951, establishing the National Security Training Corps and a National Security Training Commission composed of five members: James W. Wadsworth (chairman), William L. Clayton, Karl T. Compton, Thomas C. Kinkaid, and Raymond S. McLain. Marshall praised the passage of the law as "a step of historic significance," but in an extreme understatement he admitted that "the law does not contain all the provisions the Defense Department would have desired." However disappointed, Marshall remained "confident that Congress will enact the necessary supporting legislation to carry into actual effect the historic principles unified in the bill. The objective of a universally shared obligation for the defense of our country on a basis that we can support is now within our grasp, for the first time since George Washington began the pursuit of this goal a century and a half ago." As before, Congress would sorely disappoint him.[13]

In January 1952, Department of Defense officials retrospectively compared their preferred plan, including UMT and selective service, to the one chosen by Congress focusing on selective service. Assistant Secretary of Defense Anna M. Rosenberg, former member of the President's Advisory Commission on Universal Training, requested a detailed comparison of the two plans "for the use of General Marshall." In the resulting analysis, John G. Adams, assistant general counsel, demonstrated that the army's plan was to establish both UMT and selective service and then gradually transition from selective service to UMT. Such a stance supported earlier characterizations during the campaign for UMT, namely, that the army considered UMT the long-term solution to its manpower needs and selective service the temporary remedy. Adams argued "In short, if UMT cannot begin until after the draft completely ceases, the draft may continue throughout our lifetime and the size of the standing force never be reduced. I do not believe that this country can afford indefinitely the economic and social costs of Armed Forces as big as, or bigger than, those we have today. The prompt beginning of UMT and the gradual building of strong reserve forces form the only practical alternative." Adams's assessment echoed the army's consistent position throughout the campaign for UMT, namely, that selective service was simply a transitory means to an end. That end was UMT.[14]

Selective service almost immediately began suffering from numerous exemptions and deferments, the very situation that army leaders hoped to avoid with UMT. Lewis B. Hershey, director of selective service, complained early on that "thus, for every available registrant, four were deferred or exempted. Unless the liberal deferment provisions of the current legislation and regulations are tightened or unless inductions drop considerably, the time cannot be too far away when 18½ to 19 years of age will become for all practical purposes the only current source of military manpower."[15] Exemptions and deferments under selective service continued to increase, reaching their zenith during the Vietnam War. As a result, large segments of American society remained untouched by military service. Public resentment at the inequity of the selective service system fueled protest and eventually led to the creation of the All-Volunteer Force (AVF) in 1973. Clearly, the history of American society would have been significantly different in the 1950s and 1960s had Congress enacted UMT.

Finally, the implications of the campaign for UMT after World War II still reverberate today. Politicians, academics, and analysts currently debate the merits of national service in much the same way their predecessors debated UMT during the early Cold War.[16] Echoing the earlier public support for UMT, Americans today largely support the idea of national service. However, politics and cost prevent legislative action. At the center of both debates are contested notions of citizenship. The fundamental questions—both for UMT before and national service today—are what are the rights and obligations of citizenship and what is the appropriate balance between the two in American democracy? Following World War II, most Americans supported measures such as UMT that many today view as draconian. Following World War II, the prevailing view of citizenship focused on the obligations of individual citizens to American democracy. Today the balance is reversed. Many Americans concentrate on the rights of citizenship. Most conversations regarding citizenship today emphasize what the government owes its citizens. They rarely delve into what citizens owe their government. The campaign for UMT after World War II offers historical context regarding such contested notions of citizenship, the appropriate balance between rights and obligations in American democracy, and both the promises and the dangers inherent in national service today.

In the end, Congress forced the army to accept selective service, but army leaders always understood that arrangement to mean two fundamental things. First, they assumed that selective service would be accompanied by UMT. Second, they expected that selective service would gradually transition to UMT. In both respects, army leaders were profoundly let down. The campaign for UMT after World War II demonstrated what I characterize as the paradox of preparedness. Selective service and UMT were always in natural conflict. Selective service would put individuals into active units immediately, whereas UMT would develop entire reserve units over time. When crisis erupted, the army needed active forces without delay rather than reserve units later on. More broadly, in terms of policy, politics, and society, it is quite difficult to establish concurrently both effective long-term and short-term solutions to national security dilemmas. In fact, the two realms often work at cross-purposes. Prescient leaders must craft lasting national security responses during peacetime. However, the very existence of peace in American democracy often negates any sense of urgency and political pressure to accomplish radical changes. Likewise, during times of crisis national security threats often demand temporary answers with immediate results. These stopgap remedies frequently drain attention, momentum, and resources (both fiscal and political) away from the consideration and enactment of enduring answers.

The story of the campaign for UMT after World War II is in many ways a three-part play dealing with policy, politics, and society. It began with policy. Senior army leaders grappled with the daunting challenge of crafting a postwar policy in the face of great uncertainty. Even as the battles of World War II still raged, they attempted to create a viable army that would stand the test of the unknown and be well suited to a democracy—both economically and socially. As a result, the early story of the UMT campaign centered on military utility and the proposal's ability to improve mobilization and preparedness through the creation of a General Reserve. In the face of continued social resistance and political apathy to their plan, army leaders refused to consider strategic alternatives and instead became obsessed with UMT as a panacea for their problems. Strategic fixation impaired the US Army as it entered what would become the critical early Cold War period.

Politically, proponents of UMT—both inside the War Department and in Congress—slowly evolved their message. The changes were often subtle but substantial nonetheless. Over time, advocates of the plan shifted their rhetoric from military utility to the social benefits of UMT. These included improved public health, better citizenship, social leavening, and religious outreach. In many cases, the reason for the alteration was to overcome opposition to their plan from specific segments of American society. Each time an individual or group presented a potential drawback of UMT, political advocates countered with arguments about how UMT would improve rather than harm American society. This back-and-forth exchange caused a metamorphosis in the underlying rationale for UMT. As a result, many advocates changed their initial focus and muddied the waters of the overall debate. Attempts to point out the secondary benefits backfired for supporters of the plan and left their policy open for additional critiques and obstacles.

Due to the political shift from military utility to secondary benefits, the campaign for UMT ended up focusing on society. The most important question for both sides of the debate to answer became, "How would this policy impact American society?" Two factors were paramount. First, the debate hinged on what price Americans were willing to pay for security. The advocates of UMT proposed unprecedented changes in American society. In return they promised preparedness. Opponents remained unconvinced that such sweeping changes were necessary in order to secure America. Second, the logistical requirements of the War Department plan forced the UMT debate towards racial questions. The fact that the army plan proposed UMT camps located predominately in the South because of better year-round training weather guaranteed that race would be an issue. Questions such as whether UMT units would be segregated and how trainees would interact with the surrounding towns dominated the later phases of the campaign. At the heart of the issue was segregation. If UMT were to be enacted, it would in many ways overturn the dynamic that legal segregation was a unique Southern phenome-

non. Instead, every eighteen-year-old male—whether white or black—
from the North would be forced to travel to military training camps in
the South and experience it firsthand. In the end, such a price was too
high to pay.

The story of the campaign for UMT is instructive for several reasons.
First, it illustrates the complexities of military planning when so many
variables in the future are unknown. Even when there was great consensus—both within the army and within American society—about the
broad concept of UMT, the consensus shattered when the actual details
of a plan had to be settled. Second, it also highlights the fact that policy
in a democracy can never be created in a vacuum. Political and social
concerns do play an important role in ways that are not as relevant in
authoritarian regimes. Policies cannot be conceived simply for their
military effectiveness alone. Instead, military planners must realistically
incorporate other factors into their overall strategic calculus. Third, the
balance between freedom and security is a delicate one. Democracies
must be realistic about their security and ensure that it is adequate. At
the same time, they must ensure that they do not sacrifice fundamental
liberties in the pursuit of endless security. To do so endangers the very
thing security is meant to protect.

The campaign for UMT after World War II began as a quest to make
every citizen a soldier. Somewhere along the way it morphed into making every soldier a citizen. In the end, it became a cautionary tale about
how the best of intentions can often take unintended paths. Without
constant reevaluation, policies can become ends in and of themselves,
as opposed to simply means to ends. Following World War II, the US
Army pursued just such a course. It identified UMT as the policy to
achieve its postwar goals. In the face of steady resistance, army leaders
entrenched and fixated on UMT increasingly. Their strategic fixation
morphed UMT from a policy into an end. As a result, US Army postwar
planning suffered when UMT was defeated decisively in 1948.

Military leaders were not the only ones to fall victim to this phenomenon. Politicians throughout the Truman administration came to see
UMT as a way to alter American society. They sought to improve public
health, combat illiteracy, inculcate citizenship, and preach morality to
masses of American youth. In the process, they undermined the basic
strategic rationale behind UMT. Once that shift from mobilization to social improvement occurred, the concept of UMT was laid open to critics

who pointed out serious negative social implications of UMT—primarily its impact on race relations.

In the end, these two factors—the US Army's increasing obsession with UMT as a policy and the Truman administration's shift away from military utility to social benefits—made UMT critically vulnerable to a coalition of opponents who believed that America would be better off without it. A paradox also caused the defeat of UMT in the critical spring of 1948. The paradox of preparedness, as I term it, was that as international tensions rose, the more receptive Congress and the American public became to preparedness measures. However, the sense of crisis also ensured that the primary focus would be on short-term fixes such as selective service that could produce immediate results. If one's house is on fire, one needs a bucket of water now, not necessarily the best long-term water delivery solution. As the political rhetoric hyped the sense of urgency in the spring of 1948, boosters hoped that the result would be final acceptance of UMT as a preparedness measure. Instead, they found themselves captive to the crisis and forced to accept the tangible and immediately useful selective service as their bucket. The paradox of preparedness illustrated that the more proponents of UMT asked for what they wanted, the more they were backed into a corner to accept what they needed.

Appendix A Key Personalities

DEPARTMENT OF DEFENSE (CREATED 1947)
James V. Forrestal   Secretary of Defense, 1947–49

WAR DEPARTMENT
Robert P. Patterson   Secretary of War, 1945–47
Henry L. Stimson   Secretary of War, 1940–45
John J. McCloy   Under Secretary of War, 1941–45
Howard C. Petersen   Assistant Secretary of War, 1945–47
Truman K. Gibson   Civilian aide to the Secretary of War, 1943–45
William H. Hastie   Civilian aide to the Secretary of War, 1940–43
Omar N. Bradley   Army Chief of Staff, 1948–49
Dwight D. Eisenhower   Army Chief of Staff, 1945–48
George C. Marshall   Army Chief of Staff, 1939–45
Stephen G. Henry   Assistant Chief of Staff, G-1
Idwal H. Edwards   Assistant Chief of Staff, G-3
George J. Richards   Director, Budget Division
Frederick H. Osborn   Director, Information and Education Division
Wilton B. Persons   Chief, Legislative and Liaison Division
William R. Arnold   Army Chief of Chaplains
John M. Palmer   Special advisor to Army Chief of Staff
Ray E. Porter   Director, Special Planning Division, 1945–46
William F. Tompkins   Director, Special Planning Division, 1943–45
Gordon E. Textor   Deputy Director, Special Planning Division
Edward W. Smith   Executive for Reserve and ROTC Affairs
Walter L. Weible   Director of Military Training
W. E. Watters   Chief, Special Training Branch
Harold W. Kent   Executive Officer, Special Training Branch
Russell C. Stroup   Chaplain representative, Special Training Branch

ARMY GROUND FORCES
Jacob L. Devers   Commanding General, AGF
John M. Devine   Commanding General, UMTEU
George E. Lynch   Chief, UMT Branch

NAVY DEPARTMENT
James V. Forrestal   Secretary of the Navy, 1944–47
Ralph A. Bard   Under Secretary of the Navy, 1944–45

Louis E. Denfield	Chief of Naval Operations, 1947–49
Chester W. Nimitz	Chief of Naval Operations, 1945–47
Ernest J. King	Chief of Naval Operations, 1942–45
Randall Jacobs	Navy representative handling UMT

CONGRESS

Chan Gurney (R-SD)	Chairman, Senate Armed Services Committee
Edwin C. Johnson (D-CO)	Member, Senate Military Affairs Committee
Clifton A. Woodrum (D-VA)	House Select Committee on Postwar Military Policy
Andrew J. May (D-KY)	Chairman, House Military Affairs Committee
James W. Wadsworth (R-NY)	House Select Committee on Postwar Military Policy
Dewey J. Short (R-MO)	Member, House Military Affairs Committee
Harry L. Towe (R-NJ)	Sponsor of the Towe Bill
Leo E. Allen (R-IL)	Chairman, House Rules Committee
Robert A. Taft (R-OH)	Chairman, Senate Republican Policy Committee

STATE DEPARTMENT

George C. Marshall	Secretary of State, 1947–49
James F. Byrnes	Secretary of State, 1945–47
Edward R. Stettinius	Secretary of State, 1944–45
Joseph C. Grew	Under Secretary of State, 1944–45

AMERICAN LEGION

James F. O'Neal	National Commander, 1947–48
Paul H. Griffith	National Commander, 1946–47
John Stelle	National Commander, 1945–46
Edward N. Scheiberling	National Commander, 1944–45
Warren H. Atherton	National Commander, 1943–44

CITIZENS COMMITTEE FOR MILITARY TRAINING OF YOUNG MEN, INC.

Jay Cooke	President
Archibald G. Thacher	Chairman of the Board
Ernesta A. Barlow	Vice President

CRITICS OF UMT

A. Philip Randolph	Labor leader and civil rights activist
Robert M. Hutchins	Chancellor of the University of Chicago
Oswald G. Villard	American journalist and civil liberties leader

Norman M. Thomas   Socialist candidate for President
Hanson W. Baldwin   Military correspondent for the *New York Times*
Roscoe S. Conkling   Outspoken critic of UMT
George F. Zook   President, American Council on Education

PRESIDENT'S ADVISORY COMMISSION ON UNIVERSAL TRAINING

Karl T. Compton   Chairman; President of Massachusetts Institute of Technology
Joseph E. Davies   Former ambassador to the Soviet Union
Harold W. Dodds   President of Princeton University
Truman K. Gibson   Civilian aide to the Secretary of War
Daniel A. Poling   President and editor of *Christian Herald*
Anna M. Rosenberg   War Manpower Commission
Samuel I. Rosenman   Presidential speechwriter
Edmund A. Walsh   Founder of Georgetown School of Foreign Service
Charles E. Wilson   Chief Executive Officer of General Electric

Appendix B Timeline

1943

February 11   Introduction of Gurney-Wadsworth bill (S. 701–H.R. 1806)

1944

January 3   *Time* names George C. Marshall "Man of the Year" for 1943
January 11   Introduction of H.R. 3947 by Andrew J. May
August 25   War Department Circular No. 347
November 10   First meeting with labor leaders
December 16   George C. Marshall appointed to five-star rank
December 20   War Department orientation conference on UMT
December 29   Meeting with leading educators

1945

January 3   Introduction of H.R. 515 by Andrew J. May
January 10   Conference on Universal Military Training
January 10   Second meeting with labor leaders
January 11   Meeting of the Association of American Colleges
February 20   Citizens Committee for Military Training of Young Men, Inc.
April 12   President Truman assumes office
April 26   Meeting with national women's organizations
May   *The War and Navy Departments' Views on Universal Military Training*
May 3   Meeting with General Commission on Army and Navy Chaplains
May 15   Extension of Selective Service
June 4–19   Woodrum committee hearings
June 23   President Truman's "A Plan for Universal Military Training under Postwar Conditions"
July 5   Woodrum Committee report submitted to Congress
October 23   President Truman's message to Congress advocating UMT
October 24   Creation of the United Nations

1946

May 15   Extension of Selective Service
June   Special Planning Division is deactivated
October 31   "A.G.F. Detailed Plan, Universal Military Training"

November 20	Appointment of President's Advisory Commission on Universal Training
November 25	UMT Experimental Unit activated
December 19	Announcement of the President's Advisory Commission on UT

1947

January 6	First cycle of training at UMT Experimental Unit begins
May 29	Report of the President's Advisory Commission on UT
June 20, July 16	Investigation in relation to UMT, first session

1948

January 5	*Time* names George C. Marshall "Man of the Year" for 1947
January 6	President Truman's budget message for 1949
January 6–12	American Legion UMT week
January 7	President Truman's State of the Union message
January 14	Investigation in relation to UMT, second session
February 25	Communist coup in Czechoslovakia
March 17	President Truman's special message to Congress on Europe
April 4–11	National anti-UMT week
June 24	Passage of Selective Service Act
July 15	Third and final cycle of training at UMT Experimental Unit

Notes

Book Epigraph. US War Department, "UMT Brochure," spring 1945, box 345, folder 000.74 UMT Brochure, 42, Record Group 165, Records of the War Department General and Special Staffs, entry 479, Security Classified Correspondence, Reports, Memoranda, and Other Papers Relating to Universal Military Training, 1944–1948, National Archives.

Chapter 1

Epigraph. Thomas M. Johnson, "Army, Navy Ask Action; Explain Plans, Purpose of Military Training," *Washington Post,* 14 January 1945, B2. The words "a grave decision" in the quotation presented above are reflected in the title of this chapter. A similar practice is used in titles of the following chapters of this book.

1. Some form of UMT debate in America can be found throughout most of the twentieth century. Even so, the specific historical context of the campaign following World War II in which the army and the executive branch both championed UMT—albeit for different reasons—meant that the campaign was the summit of the various UMT campaigns and the only one with some possibility of success. For example, in the UMT campaign following World War I, senior army leaders were not convinced of the strategic rationale underlying UMT. In fact, Newton D. Baker, secretary of war, and Peyton C. March, army chief of staff, played pivotal roles in the campaign's failure.

2. For example, UMT was the national high school debate proposition for the academic year 1945–46. See *Peacetime Military Training: the Nineteenth Annual Debate Handbook,* in box 355, folder 095A, Record Group 165, Records of the War Department General and Special Staffs, entry 479, Security Classified Correspondence, Reports, Memoranda, and Other Papers Relating to Universal Military Training, 1944–1948, National Archives.

3. For more on military planning for World War II, see Charles E. Kirkpatrick, *An Unknown Future and a Doubtful Present: Writing the Victory Plan of 1941.* For more on military planning for the immediate postwar period, see Michael S. Sherry, *Preparing for the Next War: American Plans for Postwar Defense, 1941–1945.*

4. For a review of the literature, see William A. Taylor, "Every Citizen a Soldier: The U.S. Army's Campaign for Universal Military Training following World War II," PhD diss., George Washington University, 2010, 6–16. For articles on UMT, see John Sager, "Universal Military Training and the Struggle to Define American Identity during the Cold War," *Federal History Journal* 5 (January 2013): 57–74; Frank D. Cunningham, "Harry S. Truman and Universal Military Training, 1945,"

Historian 46 (Summer 1984): 397–415; Joe P. Dunn, "UMT: A Historical Perspective," *Military Review* 61 (January 1981): 11–18.

5. "Respectable Posture," *Time*, 3 March 1947.

6. "The Quarter's Polls," *Public Opinion Quarterly* 9 (Summer 1945): 251–53.

Chapter 2

Epigraphs. James W. Wadsworth to George Marvin, 8 July 1940, box 31, folder UMT September 13, 1935–July 1940, James Wadsworth Family Papers, Manuscript Division, Library of Congress, Washington, DC (hereafter cited as Wadsworth Papers); Montana citizen drafted in September 1917 to Edward R. Burke, box 355, folder 095B, Record Group 165, Records of the War Department General and Special Staffs, entry 479, Security Classified Correspondence, Reports, Memoranda, and Other Papers Relating to Universal Military Training, 1944–1948, National Archives.

1. Leonard Wood, "Citizenship Obligation: National Training for Defense," *Proceedings of the Academy of Political Science in the City of New York* 6 (July 1916): 157, 159; Halstead Dorey, "The Plattsburg Contribution to Military Training," *Proceedings of the Academy of Political Science in the City of New York* 6 (July 1916): 229. For an excellent analysis of the Plattsburg Movement, see J. Garry Clifford, *The Citizen Soldiers: The Plattsburg Training Camp Movement, 1913–1920.*

2. Wood, "Citizenship Obligation," 159, 163.

3. Ernest Lindley, "2 Proposals for Retaining the Power to Wage War," *Washington Post*, 23 January 1944, B2.

4. For Palmer's and Marshall's understanding of Upton's viewpoints and sway, see John M. Palmer to George C. Marshall, 4 August 1941, and George C. Marshall to John M. Palmer, 15 August 1941, box 87, folder 18; and John M. Palmer to George C. Marshall, 2 November 1944, box 87, folder 23, George C. Marshall Papers, George C. Marshall Research Library, Lexington, VA (hereafter cited as Marshall Papers). For a traditional interpretation of Upton's beliefs and influence, see Russell F. Weigley, "The Soldier, the Statesman, and the Military Historian," *Journal of Military History* 63 (October 1999): 807–22; Eliot A. Cohen, *Making Do with Less, or Coping with Upton's Ghost;* T. Harry Williams, *The History of American Wars;* Andrew J. Bacevich, "Emory Upton: A Centennial Assessment," *Military Review* 61 (December 1981): 21–28; Wallace E. Walker, "Emory Upton and the Officer's Creed," *Military Review* 61 (April 1981): 65–68; Stephen E. Ambrose, *Upton and the Army;* and Russell F. Weigley, *Towards an American Army.* For a reconsideration of Upton's views on citizen soldiers and democracy, see David J. Fitzpatrick, "Emory Upton and the Army of a Democracy," *Journal of Military History* 77 (April 2013): 463–90; and David J.

Fitzpatrick, "Emory Upton and the Citizen Soldier," *Journal of Military History* 65 (April 2001): 355–89.

5. John McAuley Palmer, *America in Arms: The Experience of the United States with Military Organization,* viiii, 125, 126, 136, 137, 149. The Manchu dynasty had recently been exiled from Peking, so the "exile" from Washington, DC of these General Staff officers seemed a similar fate. The later change in the Manchu law made attendance at schools such as General Staff College count as service with troops.

For a complete recounting of the story behind the National Defense Act of 1920, see James W. Wadsworth, memorandum, 25 June 1941, box 31, folder UMT June 10–October 22, 1941, Wadsworth Papers.

6. Palmer, *America in Arms,* viiii, 152, 153.

7. Biographical note, finding aid, Wadsworth Papers.

8. Ibid.

9. Palmer, *America in Arms,* 158, 159–75.

10. Ibid., 170–71; James W. Wadsworth, memorandum, 25 June 1941, p. 2, box 31, folder UMT June 10–October 22, 1941, Wadsworth Papers.

11. James W. Wadsworth to George Marvin, 8 July 1940, box 31, folder UMT September 13, 1935–July 1940, and James W. Wadsworth to Frances M. Nash, 22 October 1941, box 31, folder UMT June 10–October 22, 1941, Wadsworth Papers. The best example of the hope that the Great War was the last was the Kellogg-Briand Pact of 1928, which attempted to outlaw war.

12. James W. Wadsworth to Willard M. Richart, 13 September 1935, pp. 1–2, box 31, folder UMT September 13, 1935–July 1940, Wadsworth Papers.

13. Palmer, *America in Arms.* Besides *America in Arms,* Palmer's writings included *An Army of the People: The Constitution of an Effective Force of Trained Citizens; Statesmanship or War,* with an introduction by James W. Wadsworth Jr.; and *Washington, Lincoln, Wilson: Three War Statesmen.*

14. Palmer, *America in Arms,* 2, 3, 6. It is important to note that Emory Upton also based his views on an interpretation of the military policy of George Washington that stood in complete contrast to Palmer's interpretations. Essentially, Palmer argued that Washington wanted a citizen army reserve but never got it due to lack of training. Upton felt Washington never wanted a citizen army reserve. See Palmer, *America in Arms,* and Emory Upton, *The Military Policy of the United States.*

15. Palmer, *America in Arms,* 7, 12–14.

16. Ibid., 16, 21.

17. Ibid., 72, 75; Upton, *Military Policy of the United States.*

18. Palmer, *America in Arms,* 124, 126–27.

19. Ibid., 97.

20. Ibid.

21. George C. Marshall to Ellard A. Walsh, 13 November 1941, and George C. Marshall to John M. Palmer, 13 November 1941, box 87, folder 18; John M. Palmer, "Memorandum for General Marshall," 14 March 1942, p. 2, box 87, folder 19, Marshall Papers. The office was "study room no. 6."

22. Marshall to Walsh, 13 November 1941, box 87, folder 18; Palmer, "Memorandum for General Marshall," 14 March 1942, p. 2, and John M. Palmer to George C. Marshall, 26 March 1942, box 87, folder 19, Marshall Papers.

23. John M. Palmer, "Memorandum for the Committee on Civilian Components," 9 January 1948, p. 3, box 87, folder 33, and John M. Palmer to George C. Marshall, 11 August 1942, box 87, folder 19, Marshall Papers.

Chapter 3

Epigraphs. "Marshall Opposes Big Post-war Army but Favors Draft," *New York Times,* 2 September 1944, 1; James W. Wadsworth to Walt Horan, 7 September 1944, box 31, folder UMT September 1–14, 1944, James Wadsworth Family Papers, Manuscript Division, Library of Congress, Washington, DC.

1. For letters illustrating the close friendship and mutual respect between Palmer and Marshall, see John M. Palmer to George C. Marshall, 1 September 1938; George C. Marshall to John M. Palmer, 7 September 1938; John M. Palmer to George C. Marshall, 21 November 1938; George C. Marshall to John M. Palmer, 22 November 1938; George C. Marshall to John M. Palmer, 6 March 1939; and John M. Palmer to George C. Marshall, 15 December 1939, all in box 78, folder 16, George C. Marshall Papers, George C. Marshall Research Library, Lexington, VA. For their relationship in the Infantry Association, see John M. Palmer to George C. Marshall, 13 November 1944, box 87, folder 23, and on their wives' friendship, see John M. Palmer to George C. Marshall, 19 April 1941, box 87, folder 18, Marshall Papers.

2. "Military Training for All Urged," *Washington Post,* 10 March 1943, 10; "Postwar Soldiers," *New York Times,* 1 September 1943, 18; "Secretary Knox's Appeal for a Year's Training of Our Youth in Arms," *New York Times,* 15 January 1944, 9; "Schools Criticized by Army Educator," *New York Times,* 24 May 1944, 17.

3. John M. Palmer, "Memorandum for the Chief of Staff (through the Director, Special Planning Division), Subject: Army Organization as Pertaining to the 'Citizen Forces,'" 3 August 1944, pp. 1–2, 4, box 31, folder UMT September 1–14, 1944, James Wadsworth Family Papers, Manuscript Division, Library of Congress, Washington, DC (hereafter cited as Wadsworth Papers).

4. "Postwar Training Urged by Stimson," *New York Times,* 18 August 1944, 8; "Roosevelt Urges Training of Youth, but Puts Method Up to Public," *New York Times,*

19 August 1944, 1; "Stimson Approves a Postwar Draft," *New York Times,* 23 August 1944, 21.

5. Even though Marshall signed Circular No. 347, it is clear that Palmer authored it. His memorandum of August 3 is the draft of Circular No. 347. However, Palmer's role does not minimize Marshall's. He still agreed to sign it and promulgate it as his own. As army chief of staff, such actions lent critical momentum to the campaign for UMT. In addition, Marshall's support for UMT never wavered, even in later posts as secretary of state and secretary of defense as late as 1951.

For the text of Circular No. 347, see US President's Advisory Commission on Universal Training, *A Program for National Security, May 29, 1947: Report of the President's Advisory Commission on Universal Training,* 397–99. Also see George C. Marshall, "Circular No. 347," 25 August 1944, pp. 4–5, box 348, folder 020 Chief of Staff, Record Group 165, entry 479, National Archives (hereafter cited as RG 165). The four sections were I: General Hospital, II: Enlisted Men, III: Military Establishment, and IV: Military Information.

6. "Marshall Asks Safety; Limit Standing Army," *Washington Post,* 2 September 1944, 1. Also see "Marshall Opposes Big Postwar Army but Favors Draft," *New York Times,* 2 September 1944, 1.

7. Marshall, "Circular No. 347," 4–5.

8. Ibid.

9. Ibid., 5.

10. Ibid.

11. "Marshall Asks Safety; Limit Standing Army," 1; "Marshall Opposes Big Postwar Army but Favors Draft," 1; John M. Palmer to Clifton A. Woodrum, 7 September 1944, box 31, folder UMT September 1–14, 1944, Wadsworth Papers.

12. James W. Wadsworth to Walt Horan, 7 September 1944, and Walt Horan to James W. Wadsworth, 4 September 1944, box 31, folder UMT September 1–14, 1944, Wadsworth Papers. The 5th District of Washington included Spokane, Stevens, Pend Oreille, Ferry, Chelan, Okanogan, Douglas, and Lincoln counties.

13. John M. Palmer to George C. Marshall, 14 September 1944, and John M. Palmer to George C. Marshall, 25 September 1944, box 78, folder 21, Marshall Papers.

Chapter 4

Epigraphs. Henry L. Stimson to Archibald G. Thacher, 15 August 1944, box 349, folder 020 Secretary of War, Record Group 165, entry 479, National Archives (hereafter cited as RG 165); "Target No. 1: U.S.A.," *Collier's,* 10 February 1945, copy in box 345, folder 000.3 Pacifism, ibid.

1. Julian L. Schley, "Policy of Preparedness," *Military Engineer* 36 (July 1944): 220–23, located in box 355, folder 095 D, RG 165.

2. "Patterson Urges Military Training: Future Wars Will See Much Less Time to Prepare, He Declares at Norwich," *New York Times,* 7 August 1944, 13; "Wide Changes Due in Set-up of Army," *New York Times,* 25 April 1944, 15.

3. Henry L. Stimson to Archibald G. Thacher, 15 August 1944, box 349, folder 020 Secretary of War, RG 165; "Postwar Training Urged by Stimson," *New York Times,* 18 August 1944, 8.

4. Ray E. Porter, "War Department Statement on Universal Military Training to National Defense Committee of the American Legion," 16 November 1944, p. 7, box 348, folder 020 G-3, RG 165.

    The one possible exception to the military effectiveness argument was the plan of army leaders to attack illiteracy among UMT recruits. However, this was a qualified exception because army leaders saw literacy not solely as a social function but also as a military effectiveness tool enabling command and control among soldiers. See ibid., 4.

5. War Department, "Statement on Universal Military Training Prepared by Assistant Chief of Staff, G-3," 6 December 1944, pp. 2, 5, box 353, folder 080 Women's National Committee for UMT for Young Men, RG 165.

6. Joseph S. Bradley, "A Year with the Army," 15 December 1944, box 348, folder 020 G-3, RG 165.

7. Ibid., 4.

8. "Target No. 1: U.S.A.," *Collier's,* 10 February 1945, copy in box 345, folder 000.3 Pacifism, RG 165.

9. Ray E. Porter, statement to the Committee on Military Affairs, House of Representatives, Seventy-Ninth Congress, pp. 7–8, 9, 10, box 349, folder 020 Special Planning Division (II), RG 165.

10. Ibid., 10–11.

11. Ibid., 14–15.

12. Ibid.

13. Ibid., 17.

Chapter 5

Epigraphs. Walter L. Weible to Harry F. Hazlett, 27 April 1945, box 355, folder 095 H, Record Group 165, entry 479, National Archives (hereafter cited as RG 165); Harold W. Kent, "Universal Military Training? Yes," *Christian Advocate,* 28 June 1945, 14.

1. John J. McCloy, "The Plan of the Armed Services for Universal Military Training," *Annals of the American Academy of Political and Social Science* 241 (September 1945): 34.

2. American Forum of the Air, "Should We Have Universal Military Training in Peacetime?" 12 September 1944, pp. 1, 3, box 352, folder 080 Forum (General), RG 165.

3. Ibid., 9.

4. Ibid., 4, 5, 7.

5. Ibid., 5.

6. Ibid., 8.

7. The University of Chicago Round Table, "Should We Have Universal Military Training in Peacetime?" 26 November 1944, p. 16, box 352, folder 080 Forum (General), RG 165.

8. Ibid., 21–22. Although Robert Hutchins stated that the timing of action was the issue, his concurrent statement urging "that the international organization unite to abolish compulsory military training throughout the world" indicated his support of the Martin Resolution and seemed to make the timing less of an issue and to make preventing UMT at any time the real issue.

9. John J. McCloy, "Memorandum for the Director of the Bureau of Public Relations, Subject: Universal Military Training," 28 November 1944, box 349, folder 020 Public Relations, Bureau of, RG 165.

10. Walter L. Weible, "Memorandum for the Surgeon General," 27 December 1944, and Norman T. Kirk, "Memorandum for Major General Walter L. Weible, G.S.C., Headquarters, ASF, Room 2E614, The Pentagon, Subject: Lt. Col. Jay Cooke, 0–157627, Infantry," 29 December 1944, both in box 352, folder 080 Citizens Committee, Col. Cooke, RG 165. For the story's background, see Gretchen M. Thorp to Arden Freer, 29 December 1944, ibid.

11. Jay Cooke to Walter L. Weible, 8 December 1944, including handwritten memo attached to the front of the letter, and Jay Cooke to Walter L. Weible, 10 December 1944, both in box 352, folder 080 Citizens Committee, Col. Cooke, RG 165.

12. Jay Cooke to Walter L. Weible, 9 January 1945, including handwritten note in the margin of the letter, box 352, folder 080 Citizens Committee, Col. Cooke, RG 165.

13. Keith Morgan to Jay Cooke, 16 February 1945, pp. 1, 2, box 352, folder 080 Citizens Committee, Col. Cooke, RG 165.

14. "Certificate of Incorporation and By-Laws of Citizens Committee for Military Training of Young Men, Inc.," 20 February 1945, p. 3, box 353, folder 080 Citizens Committee * Thacher, A. G., RG 165.

15. Walter L. Weible to Jay Cooke, 19 February 1945, box 352, folder 080 Citizens Committee, Col. Cooke, RG 165.

16. Walter L. Weible to Jay Cooke, 20 February 1945, box 352, folder 080 Citizens Committee, Col. Cooke, RG 165.

17. Walter L. Weible to Jay Cooke, 2 March 1945, box 352, folder 080 Citizens Committee, Col. Cooke, RG 165. Representative works by Hanson W. Baldwin include *The Caissons Roll: A Military Survey of Europe* (New York: Alfred A. Knopf, 1938); *Great Mistakes of the War* (New York: Harper and Brothers, 1950); *Battles Lost and*

Won: Great Campaigns of World War II (New York: Harper and Row, 1966); and *Strategy for Tomorrow* (New York: Harper and Row, 1970).

18. Walter L. Weible to Jay Cooke, 5 March 1945, and Walter L. Weible to Jay Cooke, 20 March 1945, both in box 352, folder 080 Citizens Committee, Col. Cooke, RG 165.

19. The letter was sent to the following publications: *Air Force, Army Life and United States Army Recruiting News, Army Motors Magazine, Army Nurse, Army Ordnance, Army Transportation Journal, Cavalry Journal, Coast Artillery Journal, Field Artillery Journal, Fire Power, Infantry Journal, Military Engineer, Military Review, Military Surgeon,* and *Quartermaster Review.* See the list attached to Weible's letter. Walter L. Weible to fifteen editors of army journals, 17 March 1945, pp. 1–3, box 349, folder 020 Public Relations, Bureau of, RG 165.

20. "Memorandum for Lt Col Monaghan, Subject: Analytical Index of Materials Dealing with Universal Military Training," box 349, folder 020 Public Relations, Bureau of, RG 165.

21. Jay Cooke to newspapers, 4 April 1945, box 352, folder 080 Citizens Committee, Col. Cooke, RG 165. Cooke indicated directly to Weible that he had sent the letter to seventeen hundred newspapers and intended on sending another letter to thirty-five hundred smaller publications. Jay Cooke to Walter L. Weible, 6 April 1945, ibid.

22. Jay Cooke to Walter L. Weible, 6 April 1945, box 352, folder 080 Citizens Committee, Col. Cooke, RG 165.

23. Harold W. Kent to Douglas Parmentier, 16 April 1945, box 349, folder 020 Public Relations, Bureau of, RG 165.

24. Archibald G. Thacher to Walter L. Weible, 20 April 1945, and Walter L. Weible to Archibald G. Thacher, 7 May 1945, both in box 353, folder 080 Citizens Committee * Thacher, A. G., RG 165. See extensive testimony attached to the letter Thacher to Weible, 20 April 1945. For more on Thatcher's role in the 1940 campaign for the draft, see Clifford and Spencer, *The First Peacetime Draft,* 27–28, 30, 73, 77, 116, 144–45, 227.

25. A. D. Surles, "Memorandum for: Major General Walter L. Weible, Headquarters, Army Service Forces, 2 E 614, Subject: Film on Universal Military Training," 10 April 1945, box 349, folder 020 Public Relations, Bureau of, RG 165.

26. *The War and Navy Departments' Views on Universal Military Training,* brochure, May 1945, in box 349, folder 020 Special Planning Division (II), RG 165. The Navy Department and the Army Air Forces—as well as the US Air Force later on—did not view UMT as central to their postwar plans. Many young recruits viewed these two organizations as more technical and cutting edge than the army. Such a recruiting draw, combined with the fact that both organizations required far less manpower than the army, meant that the navy and the AAF drew sufficient

volunteers to fill their ranks with less need to resort to compulsion. As a result, both organizations were willing to halfheartedly press for UMT as long as doing so did not endanger their own organizational goals.

27. Ibid., 1.
28. Ibid.
29. Ibid., 6.
30. Ibid., 19.
31. Ibid., 19, 20, 21. The two military service exemptions were for individuals who had served on active duty during World War II and people who enlisted in the regular forces.
32. Ibid., 31. For an excellent table illustrating the training and service requirements of other nations at the time, see ibid., 36.
33. Ibid., 31.
34. Ibid., 32.
35. War Department Budget Officer, "War Expenditures by Fiscal Years," 8 May 1945, box 348, folder 020 Budget Officer, RG 165.
36. Ibid. These estimates include not only direct costs associated with fighting the war, but also continuing costs such as pensions and interest that were incurred as a result of the war.
37. William F. Tompkins, "Memorandum for Major General Walter L. Weible, Office, Assistant Secretary of War, Subject: Costs of the Armed Forces in Peace and War, 1895–1945," 27 March 1945, box 348, folder 020 Budget Officer, RG 165. The $1.75 billion was in addition to the approximate $3.845 billion per year of all other activities within the War Department, for a total estimated cost of the postwar military establishment of $5.595 billion per year. See Ray E. Porter, "Memorandum for the Deputy Chief of Staff, Subject: Reduction in Estimated Cost of Universal Military Training," 15 February 1946, ibid.
38. Ray E. Porter, "Memorandum for the Director, Bureau of Public Relations, Subject: Release of Film 'War Comes to America' to Civilian Agencies," 23 August 1945, box 349, folder 020 Public Relations, Bureau of, RG 165.
39. Ray E. Porter, "Memorandum for Acting Director, Bureau of Public Relations, Subject: Film on Universal Military Training," 16 November 1945, box 349, folder 020 Public Relations, Bureau of, RG 165.
40. McCloy, "Plan of the Armed Services for Universal Military Training," 33, 34.
41. Ibid., 26.
42. Ibid., 27.
43. Ibid.
44. William F. Tompkins, "Future Manpower Needs of the Armed Forces," *Annals of the American Academy of Political and Social Science* 241 (September 1945):

59, 60. Some outside the War Department did advocate volunteer forces, most notably Hanson W. Baldwin.

45. McCloy, "Plan of the Armed Services for Universal Military Training," 28.

46. Ibid.

47. Ibid.

48. Ibid., 32.

49. Ibid., 30, 31; Tompkins, "Future Manpower Needs," 60. Later in his article, McCloy used the number of 620,000 trainees for the Army, similar to Tompkins's 600,000 figure.

The estimate of 750,000–800,000 trainees annually was based on the average number of male births in the United States from 1928 to 1937: 1.1 million per year. Approximately 93 percent of these births reached the age of eighteen. Most planners assumed that 25 percent of the available pool would not be eligible due to "physical or mental defects." That number came out to 767,250 trainees per year. See Rainer Schickele and Glenn Everett, "The Economic Implications of Universal Military Training," *Annals of the American Academy of Political and Social Science* 241 (September 1945): 103, 105.

50. Schickele and Everett, "The Economic Implications of Universal Military Training," 102, 104. For this position Schickele pointed to Hanson Baldwin's article "Conscription for Peacetime?" *Harper's,* March 1945.

51. The actual figure was $1.047 billion per year. Schickele and Everett, "The Economic Implications of Universal Military Training," 105–6 and Table 2. Schickele's estimates assumed a pay rate of $30 per month. In 1945 the minimum military pay rate had risen to $50 per month. Some people felt UMT trainees would be paid at the lower rate; others felt they would be paid at the higher rate.

52. Ibid., 107–8, 109, Table 3, 110.

53. Ibid., 112.

Chapter 6

Epigraphs. *Yank,* 28 May 1945, 2, located in box 345, folder 000.76 Newspapers and Magazines; Edwin C. Johnson, *Standard and Times* (Philadelphia), 1 December 1944, quoted in "The Case against Peacetime Conscription," 11, box 345, folder 000.3 Religion—Organizations; and Roscoe S. Conkling, *The Case against Compulsory Peacetime Military Training* (Post War World Council, 1945), 5, located in box 355, folder 095 Conkling, Lt. Col. Roscoe S., all in Record Group 165, entry 479, National Archives (hereafter cited as RG 165).

1. "Short Hand Notes on Proceedings of Pacifist Conference," 17 November 1944, pp. 2, 3, box 345, folder 000.3 Pacifism, RG 165.

2. "Memorandum for the Assistant Secretary of War, Attn: Walter L. Weible, Subject:

Universal Military Training," 24 November 1944, p. 1, box 345, folder 000.3 Pacifism, RG 165.

3. Ibid., 1, 2.

4. Ibid., 2.

5. Ibid.

6. "Agenda for Off-the-Record Meetings of National Phase Groups on the Subject of Universal Military Training," p. 1, and Howard C. Petersen, "Memorandum for Mr. McCloy, Assistant Secretary of War, Subject: Secretary's Meeting with Labor Leaders," 6 November 1944, p. 1, both in box 345, folder 004 Labor, RG 165.

7. Petersen, "Memorandum for Mr. McCloy," 1, 2.

8. Henry L. Stimson to T. C. Cashen, 30 October 1944, box 345, folder 004 Labor, RG 165. Also see Henry L. Stimson to A. Johnson, 1 January 1945; to T. C. Cashen, 1 January 1945; to D. B. Robertson, 1 January 1945; to A. F. Whitney, 1 January 1945; to H. W. Fraser, 1 January 1945; to Philip Murray, 1 January 1945; and to William Green, 1 January 1945, all ibid. For a list of those present at the 10 November 1944 meeting with labor leaders, see "Friday, November 10, 1944," 10 November 1944, ibid.

9. A. H. Raskin, "Memorandum for General Weible, Subject: Labor Attitude toward Universal Military Training," 21 December 1944, p. 1, box 345, folder 004 Labor, RG 165.

10. Ibid., 2.

11. Douglas Parmentier, "Memorandum for the Director, Subject: Principal Points Raised by Labor Representatives at Meeting in War Department," 10 January 1945, box 345, folder 004 Labor, RG 165.

12. Dillon Anderson, "Memorandum for Major General Wilton B. Persons, Subject: Labor Leaders' Conference on Universal Military Training," 11 January 1945, pp. 1–2, box 345, folder 004 Labor, RG 165.

13. It is interesting to note that Irvine's data revealed that the two states most overrepresented were Virginia and Texas. They had 138 and 110 officers, respectively, over their proportional representations. For specific state numbers, see W. W. Irvine, "Memorandum for the Assistant Secretary of War, Subject: Proportion of Regular Army Officers from Southern States," 5 February 1945, box 345, folder 004 Labor, tab B, RG 165.

14. "Summary of Study of Personnel in the Overhead of Organizations Devoted to International Peace and In Some Respect Opposed to Universal Military Training," pp. 1, 8, box 345, folder 000.3 Pacifism, RG 165.

15. John J. McCloy to Douglas MacArthur, 17 January 1945, box 345, folder 000.3 Religion (General), RG 165.

16. Russell C. Stroup, "Memorandum for Walter L. Weible," 22 February 1945; Wal-

ter L. Weible, "Memorandum for William R. Arnold," undated, but response required by 1 March 1945; and Walter L. Weible, "Memorandum for the Chief of Chaplains," 14 February 1945, all in box 345, folder 000.3 Religion (General), RG 165.

17. Stroup, "Memorandum for Walter L. Weible."

18. "A Survey of the Position of the Churches Relative to UMT," p. 1, box 345, folder 000.3 Religion (General), RG 165. Stroup's assumption does not include the "out-and-out Pacifists," whose views, the survey argued, could not be modified significantly but whose resistance could possibly be blunted by exempting "so-called 'conscientious objectors' from the year of military training substituting for them some other sort of training" (ibid., 2).

19. "Suggestions for Service Command and Supervisory Chaplains," pp. 1, 2, box 345, folder 000.3 Religion (General), RG 165.

20. Ibid., 2.

21. "Survey of the Position of the Churches Relative to UMT," 4.

22. "Number of Members of Major Religious Denominations"; Russell C. Stroup, "Memorandum for Walter L. Weible, Subject: The Attitude of the Roman Catholic Church toward UMT"; and "Memorandum on Meeting with Russell C. Stroup, Jewish Welfare Board National Office," 14 May 1945, all in box 345, folder 000.3 Religion (General), RG 165.

23. "Memorandum for Walter L. Weible, Subject: Report on Conference with Bishop Page and Others," box 345, folder 000.3 Religion (General), RG 165.

24. Joseph R. Koch to Walter L. Weible, 26 April 1945, box 345, folder 000.3 Religion (General), RG 165.

25. Walter L. Weible to Sherman Miles, 10 May 1945, box 345, folder 000.3 Religion (General), RG 165.

26. Franklin C. Fry to Walter L. Weible, 11 May 1945, box 345, folder 000.3 Religion (General), RG 165.

27. Ibid.; Franklin C. Fry to Russell C. Stroup, 18 May 1945, box 345, folder 000.3 Religion (General), RG 165.

28. Russell C. Stroup to Franklin C. Fry, box 345, folder 000.3 Religion (General), RG 165.

29. Harold W. Kent, "Statement on Universal Military Training—International Peace—The Church," p. 6, box 345, folder 000.3 Religion (General), RG 165. For the published version, see *Christian Advocate,* 28 June 1945. Also see Harold W. Kent, "Universal Military Training? Yes," box 355, folder 095 C, RG 165.

30. Luther Miller, excerpt from testimony, p. 3, box 345, folder 000.3 Religion (Protestant), RG 165.

31. Ibid.

32. Roscoe S. Conkling, *The Case against Compulsory Peacetime Military Training*, 24 March 1945, pp. 3, 5, box 355, folder 095 Conkling, Lt. Col. Roscoe S., RG 165.

For an example of Conkling's attack, see the repeated comparisons that he made throughout between UMT in America and the military regimes under Hitler, Mussolini, and Tojo (ibid.). There were other aspects to his attack, however. For example, he feared the impact of taking one full year away from the educational development of eighteen-year-olds. As he wrote, "Who dares say that the interruption of a year or more of military training 'to obey and not to think' during the brave, free, persevering youth of the young Edison or Bell, Lake, Holland, Fulton, or the Wright brothers would still have yielded us the incandescent lamp and sound reproduction, the telephone, the submarine and the airplane?" (ibid., 23). Even so, the main gist of Conkling's argument always centered on militarism in America.

33. Ibid., 6.

34. Ibid., 10.

35. Ibid., 21, 34.

36. Ibid., 10; Roscoe S. Conkling to Harry S. Truman, 21 May 1945, box 355, folder 095 Conkling, Lt. Col. Roscoe S., RG 165.

37. Conkling, *Case against Compulsory Peacetime Military Training*, 11, 34.

38. H. C. Holdridge, "Statement Presented to the Military Affairs Committee of the House of Representatives Opposing the Army Program of Compulsory Military Training," pp. 2–4, box 355, folder 095 H, RG 165. Holdridge's personal connection to the army ran deep. His son also graduated from West Point and served in the army.

39. Ibid., 5–6.

40. Ibid., 15.

41. Ibid., 9.

42. George F. Zook, "Statement on Compulsory Military Training," 20 November 1945, p. 1, box 352, folder 080 American Council on Education, RG 165. For more on the organization, see American Council on Education, "A Brief Statement Regarding the American Council on Education," October 1943, box 352, folder 080 American Council on Education, RG 165.

43. Zook, "Statement on Compulsory Military Training," 1, 2.

44. Ibid., 3.

Chapter 7

Epigraphs. Harry S. Truman, "A Plan for Universal Military Training under Postwar Conditions," 23 June 1945, p. 3, PSF: Subject File, 1940–1953, box 126, folder Military: Universal Training, Harry S. Truman Papers, Harry S. Truman Presidential

Library, Independence, MO (hereafter cited as Truman Papers); Woodrum Committee, "Universal Military Training," 5 July 1945, p. 3, box 89, folder National Defense—Universal Military Training (folder 1), George M. Elsey Papers, Harry S. Truman Presidential Library, Independence, MO (hereafter cited as Elsey Papers).

1. James W. Wadsworth, "H.Res. 465," pp. 1–2, box 29, folder Postwar Military Policy Woodrum Committee July 21, 1942–March 17, 1944, James Wadsworth Family Papers, Manuscript Division, Library of Congress, Washington, DC.

2. "Suggested Agenda for the Committee on Post-war Military Policy," box 29, folder Postwar Military Policy Woodrum Committee April 4–27, 1944, Wadsworth Papers.

3. Dwight D. Eisenhower to Clifton Woodrum, 2 June 1945, pp. 1, 2, box 348, folder 020 Chief of Staff, Record Group 165, entry 479, National Archives (hereafter cited as RG 165).

4. "Draft Statement for Mr. Grew to Women's Conference on Universal Military Training," 26 April 1945, p. 4, box 351, folder 040 State, Department, RG 165.

5. Julius C. Holmes to Walter L. Weible, 15 June 1945, and "Form Letter from Secretary of State to Organizations Concerned with Dumbarton Oaks Proposals and Universal Military Training," p. 1, both in box 351, folder 040 State, Department, RG 165.

6. "Form Letter from Secretary of State," 1–2.

7. Truman, "Plan for Universal Military Training under Postwar Conditions," 2.

8. Ibid.

9. Ibid.

10. Ibid., 2, 3. There was an interesting irony evident in Truman's views on senior military leaders. He could at the same time idolize Marshall and view him as the epitome of professionalism while disdaining "brass hats" in general.

11. "Universal Military Training, 79th Congress, 1st Session, House of Representatives, Report No. 857," 5 July 1945, pp. 1–3, box 89, folder National Defense—Universal Military Training (folder 1), Elsey Papers.

12. Wilton B. Persons, "Memorandum for the Chief of Staff," 1 August 1945, box 348, folder 020 Chief of Staff, Marshall, RG 165.

13. Henry L. Stimson, "Statement by the Secretary of War at the Cabinet Meeting," 7 September 1945, pp. 1–4, PSF: Subject File, 1940–1953, box 126, folder Military: Universal Training, Truman Papers. The only other issue discussed after the UMT discussion was health care. "Proposed Agenda for Cabinet Meeting," 7 September 1945, in ibid.

14. Stimson, "Statement by the Secretary of War at the Cabinet Meeting," 1, 3–4.

15. Harry S. Truman, address to Congress, 13 September 1945, pp. 1–6, PSF: Subject File, 1940–1953, box 126, folder Military: Universal Training, Truman Papers.

16. Harold L. Ickes to Harry S. Truman, 6 September 1945; Fred M. Vinson to Harry S. Truman, 11 September 1945; Philip B. Fleming to Harry S. Truman, 19 September 1945; and Henry A. Wallace to Harry S. Truman, 5 September 1945, PSF: Subject File, 1940–1953, box 126, folder Military: Universal Training, Truman Papers.

17. Secretary of War, "Memorandum for the President," 21 September 1945, p. 1, box 349, folder 020 Special Planning Division, RG 165; Robert P. Patterson, "Memorandum for the President," 21 September 1945, pp. 1, 2, 3, PSF: Subject File, 1940–1953, box 126, folder Military: Universal Training, Truman Papers.

18. George M. Elsey, handwritten note, 15 October 1945, box 90, folder National Defense—Universal Military Training (folder 2), Elsey Papers.

19. Harry S. Truman, "Text of the President's Message to the Congress on Universal Military Training," 23 October 1945, pp. 1–4, PSF: Historical File, 1924–1953, box 196, folder Universal Military Training, Truman Papers.

20. "Draft of Statement for Secretary of State," 2 November 1945, p. 1, box 351, folder 040 State, Department, RG 165.

21. Ibid., 2.

22. Ibid., 2–3.

23. Ibid., 5–6.

24. American Legion, "A Brief Outline of the American Plan of Universal Training for National Security," June 1946, p. 1, box 20, folder Bureau of the Budget: Universal Military Training, James E. Webb Papers, Harry S. Truman Presidential Library, Independence, MO.

25. Ibid., 2, 3.

Chapter 8

Epigraphs. John M. Devine, "Opening Conference, UMT Cadre Courses," p. 1, box 129, folder Cadre Instruction, Record Group 337, Records of Headquarters Army Ground Forces, entry 26F, National Archives (hereafter cited as RG 337, entry 26F); "The Nation: Respectable Posture," *Time,* 3 March 1947; American Legion National Headquarters, "The Fort Knox Experiment," January 1948, box 131, folder Dept of the Army Plan for UMT, inside cover, RG 337, entry 26F.

1. Jacob L. Devers, "Memorandum on Universal Military Training to Unit Commanders, Army Ground Forces," 9 November 1945, Xerox 996, pp. 5–6, Marshall Foundation National Archives Project, George C. Marshall Research Library, Lexington, VA. The seventeen-week period could vary from as little as nine weeks to as many as twenty-six weeks depending on the specialty. However, the seventeen-week period was the contemplated average for most trainees.

2. Ibid.

3. "Music Program," p. 1, box 8, folder Staff Studies—Ft. Knox, KY, Records of the

President's Advisory Commission on Universal Training, RG 220, Records of Temporary Committees, Commissions, and Boards, Harry S. Truman Presidential Library, Independence, MO (cited hereafter as RG 220, PACUT).

4. "A.G.F. Detailed Plan, Universal Military Training, Demonstration Unit (Experimental), 12 Annexes," 31 October 1946, pp. 1, 2, annex 9, box 6, folder A.G.F. Detailed Plan Universal Military Training, RG 337, entry 91.

5. John M. Devine to J. B. Sweet, 19 November 1946, box 6, folder 320 UMT, WD Plan for UMT 1946, ibid.

6. C. P. Hall, "Memorandum to Commanding General, Army Ground Forces, Fort Monroe, Virginia, Subject: Detailed Plan for Demonstration Unit for Training under a Universal Military Training Program, WDGOT 353 UMT," 13 November 1946, p. 1, ibid.; Jacob L. Devers, "Lecture on AGF Plan for UMT, Restricted, Regarded by Authority of CG, AGF," 25 November 1947, p. 5, box 134, folder Lecture on AGF Plan for UMT, RG 337, entry 26F; Jesse O. Dedmon, "Hearings Before the Committee on Armed Services, United States Senate, Eightieth Congress, Second Session, on Universal Military Training," 17, 18, 22, 23, 24, 25, 29, 30, and 31 March; 1, 2, and 3 April 1948, p. 664, box 131, folder Hearings Before the Committee on Armed Services, RG 337, entry 26F.

7. "Army to Test Code to Rule Trainees," *New York Times,* 27 December 1946, 17.

8. "The Cavalcade of UMT," 6 July 1947, p. 12, box 131, RG 337, entry 26F; Hanson W. Baldwin, "Army to Extend UMT Experiment with First Camp Called a Success," *New York Times,* 17 May 1947, 3; "Group at Fort Knox for Training," *New York Times,* 4 January 1947, 26. Private Whetzel's father, Lester G. Whetzel Sr., had been drafted in World War II and had served in the Seabees. *UMT Pioneer,* 18 January 1947, p. 1, box 14, folder Publications—PACUT, RG 220, PACUT.

9. "To Advise on Training," *New York Times,* 27 January 1947, 5; John M. Devine, "Opening Conference, UMT Cadre Courses," pp. 9–10, box 129, folder Cadre Instruction, RG 337, entry 26F.

10. Gilbert P. Bailey, "'Umties'—First Soldier of the 'New Army,'" *New York Times,* 23 February 1947, SM11.

11. John M. Devine, "Letter of Transmittal to the Commanding General, AGF, Interim Report, U.M.T. Experimental Unit," 1 August 1947, box 1, folder UMT General Orders, and John M. Devine, "Interim Report, U.M.T. Experimental Unit," 1 August 1947, p. 2, box 1, folder UMT General Orders, RG 337, entry 91. The whole report is in the latter document.

12. Devine, "Interim Report," 27, 29, 30, 32.

13. Ibid., 4.

14. Ibid., 4, 5.

15. Ibid., 5.

16. Ibid., 10–11, 26.
17. Ibid., 11, 25–26.
18. Ibid., 11.
19. Ibid., 15.
20. Ibid., 19, 20, 27.
21. Hanson W. Baldwin, "Army to Extend UMT Experiment with First Camp Called a Success," *New York Times,* 17 May 1947, 3.
22. Hanson W. Baldwin, "Army's Youth Unit Called a Success," *New York Times,* 18 May 1947, 50.
23. "The Cavalcade of UMT," 6 July 1947, p. 41, box 131, RG 337, entry 26F.
24. *UMT Pioneer,* 18 January 1947, p. 1, box 14, folder Publications—PACUT, RG 220, PACUT.
25. Ibid.
26. Hanson W. Baldwin, "Army's Youth Unit Called a Success," *New York Times,* 18 May 1947, 50.
27. Ray T. Maddocks, "Universal Military Training as Applied in the 3d Armored Division," foreword, box 136, RG 337, entry 26F.
28. Ibid., 1.
29. Ibid., 5, 6–14, 16.

Chapter 9

Epigraphs. Harry S. Truman, "Informal Remarks of the President to His Advisory Commission on Universal Training," press release, 20 December 1946, PSF: Historical File, 1924–1953, box 196, folder Universal Military Training, Harry S. Truman Papers, Harry S. Truman Presidential Library, Independence, MO (hereafter cited as Truman Papers); US President's Advisory Commission on Universal Training, *A Program for National Security: Report of the President's Advisory Commission on Universal Training* (hereafter cited as *Program for National Security*), 89.

1. Robert P. Patterson, "Memorandum for the President of the United States, Subject: Advisory Council on Universal Military Training," 7 October 1946, pp. attachment, 2, 4, OF 109-B, box 641, folder O.F. 109-B President's Advisory Commission on Universal Training (1946–1947), Truman Papers.

For clarification, Davies represented "International Affairs"; Dodds represented "Education"; Walsh, Poling, and Rosenman represented "Religion"; Compton represented "Science"; Rosenberg represented "Labor"; Wilson represented "Industry"; and Gibson represented "Minorities." The explicit assignment of each committee member to represent a specific segment of society was dropped in the actual letter sent by Truman to each committee member. Even so, the intention of correlating each member to a particular group opposing UMT remained. Harry H. Vaughan to distribution list, 20 November 1946, OF 109-B, box 641, folder O.F. 109-B President's Advisory Commission on Universal Training (1946–1947), Truman Papers. For an example of the actual letter sent, see Harry S. Truman to Joseph E. Davies, 20 November 1946, ibid.

2. Levi K. Ziegler to Harry S. Truman, 4 January 1947, OF 109-B, box 641, folder O.F. 109-B President's Advisory Commission on Universal Training (1946–1947), and Harry S. Truman to Franklin I. Sheeder, 7 February 1947, PSF: Subject File, 1940–1953, box 126, folder Military: Universal Training, Truman Papers.

    In 1943, Warner Brothers made *Mission to Moscow* into a popular movie with the same title, starring Walter Huston.

3. Harry S. Truman, "Informal Remarks of the President to his Advisory Commission on Universal Training," press release, 20 December 1946, PSF: Historical File, 1924–1953, box 196, folder Universal Military Training, Truman Papers.

4. Ibid.

5. Harry S. Truman to Arthur J. Altmeyer, 15 January 1947, OF 109-B, folder O.F. 109-B President's Advisory Commission on Universal Training (1946–1947), Truman Papers.

6. Karl T. Compton to Harry S. Truman, 3 January 1947; Karl T. Compton to Harry S. Truman, 9 January 1947, p. 1; and Harry S. Truman to Karl T. Compton, 17 January 1947, p. 4, all in PSF: Subject File, 1940–1953, box 126, folder Military: Universal Training, Truman Papers; *Program for National Security*, 99 (For a complete list of all individuals consulted by the commission, see 104–10.).

7. William H. Hastie, transcript of testimony, 25 January 1947, p. 671, box 11, folder PACUT—Minutes of Sixth Meeting, Records of the President's Advisory Commission on Universal Training, RG 220, Records of Temporary Committees, Commissions, and Boards, Harry S. Truman Presidential Library, Independence, MO (cited hereafter as RG 220, PACUT).

    Although Hastie appeared with Jesse O. Dedmon, Hastie presented the vast majority of the testimony. In fact, Dedmon added only one comment to Hastie's testimony, voicing the hope that the experiences of World War II "would be such that the military—the Army, the Navy, Marine Corps—would change some of the policies that they had had previously. Unfortunately, we have been shown by their actions that they intend to continue certain patterns that have been in vogue in the various services." Jesse O. Dedmon, transcript of testimony, 25 January 1947, p. 675, box 11, folder PACUT—Minutes of Sixth Meeting, RG 220, PACUT.

8. Karl T. Compton, transcript of testimony, 25 January 1947, and Hastie, transcript of testimony, 25 January 1947, p. 679, box 11, folder PACUT—Minutes of Sixth Meeting, RG 220, PACUT.

9. James Patton, transcript of testimony, 1 February 1947, pp. 901, 903, box 11, folder PACUT—Minutes of Seventh Meeting, RG 220, PACUT.

10. Ibid., 900–917.

11. Elizabeth Smart, transcript of testimony, 21 February 1947, pp. 1288, 1289, box 11, folder PACUT—Minutes of Tenth Meeting, RG 220, PACUT.

12. Ibid., 1289–90.

13. Ibid., 1290, 1294, 1302–3.

14. Bernard Brodie, "The Atomic Bomb and Universal Training: A Survey of Published Opinion," February 1947, pp. 1, 2–3, box 4, folder Commission Kit—Thirteenth Meeting, RG 220, PACUT.

15. Ibid., 4, 7; William L. Borden, *There Will Be No Time: The Revolution in Strategy*, 63–65, quoted in Brodie, "The Atomic Bomb and Universal Training," 5–7.

16. Brodie, "The Atomic Bomb and Universal Training," 8; W. A. Gerhard, untitled article, *Infantry Journal*, October 1946, 41, quoted in Brodie, "The Atomic Bomb and Universal Training," 8–9.

17. Gerhard, untitled article, *Infantry Journal*, 41.

18. Brodie, "The Atomic Bomb and Universal Training," 9.

19. Ibid., 9–10; Bernard Brodie, *The Absolute Weapon: Atomic Power and World Order*, 94, quoted in Brodie, "The Atomic Bomb and Universal Training," 11.

20. Walter Lippman, "Why We Are Disarming Ourselves," *Infantry Journal* (December 1946), 41, quoted in Brodie, "The Atomic Bomb and Universal Training," 16–17.

21. Hanson W. Baldwin, transcript of testimony, 12 April 1947, p. 1681, box 12, folder PACUT—Minutes of Twelfth Meeting, RG 220, PACUT.

22. Ibid., 1683, 1685, 1687–97.

23. *Program for National Security*, 7, 89; Harry S. Truman to Arthur H. Vandenberg, 4 June 1947, and Harry S. Truman to Joseph W. Martin, 4 June 1947, PSF: Historical File, 1924–1953, box 196, folder Universal Military Training, Truman Papers.

24. "An Analysis of the Report of the President's Advisory Commission on Universal Training," 7 July 1947, pp. 3, 5, 13, 16, 17, 20, box 9, folder Universal Military Training, the President's Advisory Commission on, Samuel I. Rosenman Papers.

Chapter 10

Epigraphs. Truman K. Gibson, "Hearings before the Committee on Armed Services, United States Senate, Eightieth Congress, Second Session, on Universal Military Training," 17, 18, 22, 23, 24, 25, 29, 30, 31 March; 1, 2, 3 April 1948, p. 644, box 131, Record Group 337, Records of Headquarters Army Ground Forces, National Archives, entry 26F (hereafter cited as RG 337, entry 26F); Committee against Jim-crow in Military Service and Training, "Negro Leaders Hit Truman Civil Rights Message on Army Segregation: Demand End of 'Bi-partisan Conspiracy' for

Jimcrow Draft," press release, 5 February 1948, box 17, folder Committee to End 'Jim Crow' in the Armed Services; Circulars, Memoranda, and Lists (2), A. Philip Randolph Papers, Manuscript Division, Library of Congress, Washington, DC (hereafter cited as Randolph Papers).

1. William H. Hastie, "The Negro and the Postwar Military Policy," pp. 1, 2, box II: G18, folder UMT 1945–1948, NAACP Collection, part II: Veterans Affairs File, 1940–1950, Manuscript Division, Library of Congress (hereafter cited as NAACP Collection).

2. Ibid., 1, 3–4, 5.

3. Ibid., 6.

4. "Negroes Threatened by UMT Segregation," p. 2, box II: G18, folder UMT 1945–1948, NAACP Collection.

5. Ibid., 2–3. For details on the proposed UMT stations, see John E. Pederson, "Memorandum To: Distribution List, Subject: Annex VI to Army Ground Forces Plan for UMT," 11 April 1947, pp. 1–21, box 4, folder Proposed UMT Stations, RG 337, entry 91. The distribution list included all commanding generals of armies, all commandants of schools, and all presidents of AGF boards. The proposed UMT stations were Fort Devens, Fort Dix, Camp Edwards, Camp Atterbury, Fort Meade, Fort Indiantown Gap, Camp Pickett, Camp Breckinridge, Fort Benning, Camp Rucker, Camp Gordon, Camp Chaffee, Camp Polk, Fort Bliss, Fort Custer, Camp McCoy, Fort Riley, Fort Leonard Wood, Camp Cooke, Fort Lewis, and Camp Roberts.

6. Biographical note, finding aide, Truman K. Gibson Papers, Manuscript Division, Library of Congress, Washington, DC.

7. William Worthy to A. Philip Randolph, 14 August 1947, box 17, folder Committee to End 'Jim Crow' in the Armed Services, Correspondence (1), Randolph Papers.

8. Ibid.

9. A. Philip Randolph to Roy Wilkins, 2 October 1947, box 17, folder Committee to End 'Jim Crow' in the Armed Services, Correspondence (1), Randolph Papers.

10. Committee against Jim Crow in Military Service and Training, "Negroes Threatened by U.M.T. Segregation," and A. Philip Randolph and Grant Reynolds, "Committee against Jimcrow in Military Service and Training memorandum," 30 October 1947, both in box 17, folder Committee to End 'Jim Crow' in the Armed Services, Circulars, Memoranda, and Lists (1), Randolph Papers.

   For information on Reynolds, see Charles J. Patterson, "Committee against Jim Crow in Military Service and Training," press release, 23 November 1947, pp. 1–2, box 17, folder Committee to End 'Jim Crow' in the Armed Services, Circulars, Memoranda, and Lists (1), Randolph Papers.

11. A. Philip Randolph to Brotherhood locals and women's auxiliaries, 12 November 1947, box 17, folder Committee to End 'Jim Crow' in the Armed Services, Correspondence (1), Randolph Papers.

12. A. Philip Randolph to Truman K. Gibson, 16 November 1947, box 17, folder Committee to End 'Jim Crow' in the Armed Services, Correspondence (1), Randolph Papers.

13. Patterson, "Committee against Jim Crow in Military Service and Training," 23 November 1947, box 17, folder Committee to End 'Jim Crow' in the Armed Services, Circulars, Memoranda, and Lists (1), Randolph Papers.

14. A. Philip Randolph and Grant Reynolds to the editor, *New York Times,* 10 December 1947, box 17, folder Committee to End 'Jim Crow' in the Armed Services, Circulars, Memoranda, and Lists (1), Randolph Papers.

15. A. Philip Randolph and Grant Reynolds to Harry S. Truman, 10 December 1947, and A. Philip Randolph to Harry S. Truman, 28 December 1947, both in box 17, folder Committee to End 'Jim Crow' in the Armed Services, Correspondence (1), Randolph Papers.

16. Committee against Jimcrow in Military Service and Training, "American Mother of 1946 Calls UMT Bill 'Public Enemy No 1,'" press release, 21 December 1947, box 17, folder Committee to End 'Jim Crow' in the Armed Services, Circulars, Memoranda, and Lists (1), Randolph Papers.

17. Committee against Jimcrow in Military Service and Training, "Taft Pledges Support to UMT Anti-segregation Amendments; President's Committee on Civil Rights Members Urges Testimony by Negro Veterans," press release, 28 December 1947, box 17, folder Committee to End 'Jim Crow' in the Armed Services, Circulars, Memoranda, and Lists (1), Randolph Papers.

18. NAACP, "NAACP Opposes Universal Military Training without Proper Safeguards in Regard to Negro Personnel," press release, 31 March 1948, part II: Veterans Affairs File, 1940–1950, box II: G18, folder UMT 1945–1948, NAACP Collection.

19. Gibson, "Hearings on Universal Military Training," 642–43, 644.

20. Ibid., 644.

Chapter 11

Epigraphs. Archibald G. Thacher to James W. Wadsworth, 9 October 1947, p. 2, box 31, folder UMT June 20–November 24, 1947, James Wadsworth Family Papers (hereafter cited as Wadsworth Papers); "National Affairs: Call to Arms," *Time,* 29 March 1948.

1. Thacher to Wadsworth, 9 October 1947, 1, 2.

2. Daniel A. Poling to Raymond S. McLain, 26 November 1947; Daniel A. Poling to Theodore A. Huntley, 5 December 1947; and Theodore A. Huntley to Daniel A. Poling, 1 December 1947, all in box 355, folder Daniel A. Poling, Record Group 165, entry 479, National Archives.

3. Daniel A. Poling to Raymond S. McLain, 15 December 1947, and Raymond S. McLain to Daniel A. Poling, 18 December 1947, both in ibid.

4. The sense of international crisis was acute enough to compel the Central Intelligence Agency to evaluate whether the passage of UMT and/or selective service would "cause the USSR to resort to military action within the next sixty days." The report concluded that neither option would do so. Central Intelligence Agency, "Special Evaluation No. 28, Soviet Reaction to U.S. Adoption of Universal Military Training and/or Selective Service," 16 March 1948, Xerox 3557, p. 1, Marshall Foundation National Archives Project, George C. Marshall Research Library, Lexington, VA.

5. Display ad, *New York Times,* 2 January 1948, 10; James F. O'Neil to Harry S. Truman, 6 November 1947, OF 109-B, box 641, folder O.F. 109-B President's Advisory Commission on Universal Training (1946–1947), Harry S. Truman Papers, Harry S. Truman Presidential Library, Independence, MO; "Dewey in Training Plea," *New York Times,* 5 January 1948, 9. Norman Thomas immediately criticized Dewey's proclamation in a letter to the editor. He pointedly asked, "Since when has it been the business of the Governor of the State of New York to use his official position to proclaim 'a week,' whatever that means, in support of a particular proposal before Congress? Has he not, as Governor, other and far different function?" Norman Thomas, "Naming of Weeks Criticized," *New York Times,* 8 January 1948, 24.

6. John D. Morris, "Tax Slash is High on House Agenda, Martin Promises," *New York Times,* 3 January 1948, 1.

7. John G. Norris, "Congress Wants to See Defense Blueprint before Acting on Two Major Military Issues," *Washington Post,* 4 January 1948, M4.

8. Ibid.

9. George M. Elsey, "Occasions of Formal Recommendation to Congress of Universal Training by the President," 1 August 1950, box 90, folder National Defense — Universal Military Training (folder 3), George M. Elsey Papers, Harry S. Truman Presidential Library, Independence, MO (hereafter cited as Elsey Papers).

10. John T. Taylor to Leo E. Allen, 22 January 1948, p. 2, box 31, folder UMT January 21–22, 1948, Wadsworth Papers.

11. There were exceptions to this general trend. James W. Wadsworth (R-NY) was one of the most ardent supporters of UMT, Harry L. Towe (R-NJ) was the sponsor of the UMT bill, and governor of New York and Republican presidential nominee Thomas E. Dewey also vocally supported UMT.

12. National Youth Assembly against Universal Military Training, press release, 15 February 1948; "Text of Wallace Greeting to National Youth Assembly," press release, 16 February 1948; and National Youth Assembly against Universal Military Training, press release, 16 February 1948, all in box 65, folder Universal Mil-

itary Training, D.N.C. Chairman, J. Howard McGrath Papers, Harry S. Truman Presidential Library, Independence, MO.

Initial press releases of the event refer to 2,000–2,500 attendees. Subsequent press releases refer to the lower number of 1,500 consistently. A list of the thirty labor leaders is in "Text of Statement by 30 AFL and CIO Leaders in Support of National Youth Assembly against Universal Military Training," 16 February 1948, box 65, folder Universal Military Training, D.N.C. Chairman, McGrath Papers.

13. "Investigation of Participation of Federal Officials of the Department of the Army in Publicity and Propaganda, as It Relates to Universal Military Training," 4 March 1948, p. 2, box 90, folder National Defense—Universal Military Training (folder 3), Elsey Papers.

14. Ibid.

15. James W. Wadsworth to Charles P. Morse, 17 April 1948, pp. 1–2, box 31, folder UMT March–April, 1948, Wadsworth Papers. For Wadsworth's characterization of "at least three" of the members of the committee as "heartily in favor of [UMT]," see ibid., 2. For the interpretation that Wadsworth had changed his mind, see Charles P. Morse to James W. Wadsworth, 15 April 1948, box 31, folder UMT March–April, 1948, Wadsworth Papers.

16. Charles Hurd, "Air Force of 35,000 Planes Is Urged by Congress Board," *New York Times,* 2 March 1948, 1.

Plan A would provide instant retaliation upon a major enemy. It planned to spend $41.30 billion in fiscal year 1949, peak at $47.20 billion in fiscal year 1952, and level off at $45.37 billion in fiscal year 1954 and thereafter. Plan B would only allow the United States to hold off an enemy until mobilization could be completed. It planned to spend $40.96 billion in fiscal year 1949, peak at $45.42 billion in fiscal year 1951, and level off at $41.47 billion in fiscal year 1954. Both plans represented massive increases in defense spending.

17. John G. Norris, "Marshall Urges UMT Passage before Senate Services Group," *Washington Post,* 3 March 1948, 13; "Marshall Urges Senate Push UMT," *New York Times,* 3 March 1948, 4.

18. C. P. Trussell, "Hearings on UMT to Begin in Senate," *New York Times,* 9 March 1948, 1; "Forrestal to Urge UMT," *New York Times,* 8 March 1948, 15; John G. Norris, "Committee Acts on Urgent Plea of Military Leaders," *Washington Post,* 9 March 1948, 4. Ten of the thirteen members were present at the meeting.

19. Harry S. Truman, "President's Address to Congress," press release, 17 March 1948, pp. 2, 3, 4, box 90, folder National Defense—Universal Military Training (folder 3), Elsey Papers.

20. Ibid., 4.

21. Ibid.

22. "Secretary Marshall's Plea for Universal Military Training," *New York Times,* 18 March 1948, 6.

23. "The Draft and UMT," *New York Times,* 5 May 1948, 24.

24. Robert C. Albright, "Draft Bill Is Completed by House Committee," *Washington Post,* 1 May 1948, 1.

25. Samuel A. Tower, "Senators Propose Only Youths of 18 Get Year Training," *New York Times,* 2 May 1948, 1. The Senate bill contemplated training 161,000 eighteen-year-olds annually. Army UMT plans envisioned training 800,000 eighteen-year-olds annually.

26. William L. Laurence, "Truman Asks UMT as Aid to Health," *New York Times,* 2 May 1948, 1.

27. Jay Walz, "Roberts Condemns Congress 'Politics' on Defense Plans," *New York Times,* 3 May 1948, 1; "Surprise Maneuver May Start House UMT Debate This Week," *Washington Post,* 3 May 1948, 2.

28. C. P. Trussell, "Taft Moves for GOP Accord in Congress on All Defense," *New York Times,* 6 May 1948, 1.

29. Samuel A. Tower, "Soviet Willingness for Test Growing, House Group Fears," *New York Times,* 9 May 1948, 1. There were five dissenting members, two Republicans and three Democrats. The dissenting members were Dewey Short (R-MO), C. W. Bishop (R-IL), James J. Heffernan (D-NY), Philip J. Philbin (D-MA), and Franck R. Havenner (D-CA). The dissenting members issued a scathing report arguing that the draft would result in a huge tax burden and cede to the government excessive control over both industry and labor "that could destroy our democracy."

30. C. P. Trussell, "Senators Abandon Draft of Youths 18," *New York Times,* 25 May 1948, 1; John G. Norris, "Training Plan Dropped for Youths 18," *Washington Post,* 25 May 1948, 1; George Gallup, "UMT Still a Top-heavy Favorite," *Washington Post,* 30 May 1948, B3.

31. C. P. Trussell, "Senate Cuts Draft from 5 to 2 Years; Votes Alien Force," *New York Times,* 9 June 1948, 1; John G. Norris, "Two-Year Draft Law Limit Voted by Senate," *Washington Post,* 9 June 1948, 1; C. P. Trussell, "Senate Refuses To Put Draft Call Up to President," *New York Times,* 10 June 1948, 1; John G. Norris, "Standby Plan for Draft Is Defeated in Senate," *Washington Post,* 10 June 1948, 1; C. P. Trussell, "Bill Wins, 78 to 10," *New York Times,* 11 June 1948, 1. Senator Malone's UMT amendment was originally sponsored by both himself and Senator Chapman Revercomb (R-WV). However, Revercomb withdrew his support for the amendment when he discovered that UMT would not replace the draft but rather exist alongside it.

For a detailed list of how individual senators voted on reducing the term of the draft, see "Senate Vote on Draft Bill," *Washington Post,* 9 June 1948, 3. For a detailed list of how individual senators voted on the final bill, see "Senate's Roll-call Vote on Draft Bill Passage," *New York Times,* 11 June 1948, 2. For a good summary of the Senate bill, see "The Draft Bill in Brief as Passed by the Senate," *New York Times,* 11 June 1948, 2.

32. C. P. Trussell, "Draft Bill Freed in a Sudden Move for Vote by House," *New York Times,* 15 June 1948, 1; John G. Norris, "Measure Comes Up Today after Being Cleared by Vote of 6 to 4," *Washington Post,* 15 June 1948, 1; John G. Norris, "Marcantonio Says Every Delaying Tactic to Be Used to Stop Passage," *Washington Post,* 17 June 1948, 1; John G. Norris, "Opponents Cripple Bill by Series of Changes," *Washington Post,* 18 June 1948, 1. For a detailed list of how individual representatives voted, see "Roll Call Vote on Draft Bill," *Washington Post,* 19 June 1948, 4.

33. "Main Points in Compromise Draft Bill," *New York Times,* 20 June 1948, 34.

34. "The Compromise Draft Bill," *New York Times,* 20 June 1948, E8.

35. "Enlistments Increase," *New York Times,* 19 June 1948, 17; "Draft Act Causes Rush of Recruits," *New York Times,* 22 June 1948, 14; Frank Wilder, "Boards Could Be Set Up Within 2 Weeks After Authorization," *Washington Post,* 22 June 1948, 1; "Enlistment Rush Goes On," *New York Times,* 23 June 1948, 20; "Rush to Join Guard Continues in State," *New York Times,* 24 June 1948, 12; Harold B. Hinton, "Guard over Quota, Enlistments Go On," *New York Times,* 24 June 1948, 12; Anthony Leviero, "Draft Bill Signed by Truman; Youths Register in Six Weeks," *New York Times,* 25 June 1948, 1; John G. Norris, "Draft-swollen Guard Units Ordered to Stop Recruiting," *Washington Post,* 26 June 1948, 10.

36. Anthony Leviero, "Draft Bill Signed by Truman; Youths Register in Six Weeks," *New York Times,* 25 June 1948, 1; John G. Norris, "Truman Signs Bill for Draft of Men 19–25," *Washington Post,* 25 June 1948, A1; Harold B. Hinton, "Guard over Quota, Enlistments Go On," *New York Times,* 24 June 1948, 12.

Chapter 12

Epigraphs. George C. Marshall, "The Obligation to Serve," *Army Information Digest* 6, no. 4 (April 1951), reproduced as Xerox 3289, p. 7, Marshall Foundation National Archives Project, George C. Marshall Research Library, Lexington, VA; David Lawrence, "U.M.T. Defeat Called Sign That U.S. Won't Face Facts," *New York Herald Tribune,* 6 March 1952, reproduced as Xerox 2610, p. 1, Marshall Foundation National Archives Project.

1. Clark M. Clifford, "Confidential Memorandum for the President," 19 November 1947, pp. 39, 40, box 22, folder Confidential Memo to the President [Clark-Rowe memorandum of November 19, 1947, 1 of 2], Clark M. Clifford Papers, Harry S. Truman Presidential Library, Independence, MO.

2. Grant Reynolds and A. Philip Randolph to Harry S. Truman, 29 June 1948, and Grant Reynolds and A. Philip Randolph to Harry S. Truman, 15 July 1948, both in Student Research File (B File), Desegregation of the Armed Forces, #20A, box 1, folder The Truman Administration's Civil Rights Program: The Desegregation of the Armed Forces, [1 of 17], Truman Library.

3. Congress of Industrial Organizations Political Action Committee, *A Look at Truman's Record on Civil Rights,* brochure, 1948, p. 4, box 21, folder Publications, 1948 [1 of 2], Clark M. Clifford Papers. For more on Executive Order 9980, see James C. Evans, "Memorandum for the Record, Subject: Federal Fair Employment Policy—Executive Order 9980," 20 July 1949, p. 1, box 4, folder Evans, James C., Records of the President's Committee on Equality of Treatment and Opportunity in the Armed Services, RG 220, Records of Temporary Committees, Commissions, and Boards, Truman Library (cited hereafter as RG 220, PCETO).

4. Harry S. Truman, Executive Order 9981, 26 July 1948, p. 1, Staff Member and Office Files: Philleo Nash Files, box 31, folder Executive Order 9981 (Working Papers and Final [draft] Order), Harry S. Truman Papers, Truman Library. Truman officially appointed the committee members on September 18, 1948. See Eben A. Ayers, "President's Committee on Equality of Treatment and Opportunity in the Armed Services," press release, 18 September 1948, Student Research File (B File), Desegregation of the Armed Forces, #20A, box 1, folder The Truman Administration's Civil Rights Program: The Desegregation of the Armed Forces, [2 of 17], Truman Library.

5. "Randolph Terms Order Misleading, Says Ignore It," *Baltimore Afro American,* 27 July 1948, p. 1, copy in box 12, folder Committee against Jim Crow [in Military Service and Training] Hearing—Exhibits I and II [2 of 2, newspaper clippings], RG 220, PCETO; Grant Reynolds to David Niles, 6 August 1948, Student Research File (B File), Desegregation of the Armed Forces, #20A, box 1, folder The Truman Administration's Civil Rights Program: The Desegregation of the Armed Forces, [1 of 17], Truman Library; "Bradley on Segregation," *New York Herald Tribune,* 28 July 1948, 1. Also see "Army to Keep Segregation, Bradley Says," *Washington Post,* 28 July 1948, 1; "Gen. Bradley Backs Segregation in Army at Company Level," *Washington Evening Star,* 28 July 1948, copy in box 12, folder Committee against Jim Crow [in Military Service and Training] Hearing—Exhibits I and II [2 of 2, newspaper clippings], RG 220, PCETO.

For a typical negative reaction to EO 9981, see "Civil Rights Orders," *Baltimore Sun,* 27 July 1948, 1. For a more positive reaction, see Anthony Leviero, "Truman Orders End of Bias in Forces and Federal Jobs; Addresses Congress Today," *New York Times,* 27 July 1948, copy in box 12, folder Committee against Jim Crow [in Military Service and Training] Hearing—Exhibits I and II [2 of 2, newspaper clippings], RG 220, PCETO.

When President Truman met with the committee for the first time on January 12, 1949, he could not remember when he issued the order or even that he had issued it in the summer. As he remarked to the committee members, "Well, gentlemen, I issued an Executive Order, last spring, or fall—I forget the date of it. . . ." Harry S. Truman, "Meeting of the President and the Four Service Secretaries with the President's Committee on Equality of Treatment and Opportunity in the Armed Services," transcript, 12 January 1949, box 2, folder January 12, 1949—Meeting with the President, RG 220, PCETO. This is an anecdotal example of how historical events such as Executive Order 9981 accrued their significance over time as a result of their cascading consequences rather than immediately.

6. "NAACP Hits Bradley," *Washington Post,* 29 July 1948, copy in box 13, folder Army [1 of 2, 1944–September 1949], RG 220, PCETO.

7. "Army Segregation to Go, Says Truman," *New York Times,* 30 July 1948, 1. Also see "Truman Sees Extension of Equality Rule, Looks to Ending of Race Segregation in Armed Forces," *Baltimore Sun,* 30 July 1948, copy in box 12, folder Committee against Jim Crow [in Military Service and Training] Hearing—Exhibits I and II [2 of 2, newspaper clippings], RG 220, PCETO.

8. Hanson W. Baldwin, "Segregation in the Army: Gen. Bradley's View is Held to Put Morale Above Compulsory Change," *New York Times,* 8 August 1948, copy in box 13, folder Army [1 of 2, 1944–September 1949], RG 220, PCETO.

9. "Inventory of the Fahy Committee Files," box 1, folder Inventory of the Fahy Committee Files, and Fahy Committee, "Plan of Argument," pp. 1–33, box 1, folder Fahy, Charles [Chairman, March-December, 1949, 1 of 2], both in RG 220, PCETO; US President's Committee on Equality of Treatment and Opportunity in the Armed Services, *Freedom to Serve: Equality of Treatment and Opportunity in the Armed Services, A Report by the President's Committee,* 1, 3 (cited hereafter as *Freedom to Serve*), copy in box 4, folder Final Printed Copy, RG 220, PCETO. For a detailed list of the various witnesses that appeared before the Fahy Committee, see "Appearances," pp. 83–88, box 12, folder Appearance of Witnesses before the Fahy Committee, RG 220, PCETO.

10. Even though the Fahy Committee had seven original members, only five members signed the final report. Alphonsus J. Donahue died in July 1949, and Charles Luckman "has not actively participated in the work of the Committee." *Freedom to Serve,* vii, xii.

11. "Distribution Report," Staff Member and Office Files: Philleo Nash Files, box 32, folder President's Committee on Equality of Treatment and Opportunity in the Armed Services, Truman Papers; Harry S. Truman to Charles Fahy, 6 July 1950, box 1, folder Fahy, Charles [Chairman, March-December, 1949, 2 of 2], RG 220, PCETO.

12. George C. Marshall, "The Obligation to Serve," *Army Information Digest* 6, no. 4 (April 1951), reproduced as Xerox 3289, pp. 1, 3, 7, Marshall Foundation National Archives Project.

13. Lewis B. Hershey, "Annual Report of the Director of Selective Service for the Fiscal Year 1952 to the Congress of the United States Pursuant to the Universal Military Training and Service Act as Amended," 3 January 1953, p. 2, and George C. Marshall, "Statement by General Marshall on Enactment of UMTS Law," 19 June 1951, p. 1, both in Xerox 2610, Marshall Foundation National Archives Project.

14. John G. Adams, "Memorandum for the Honorable Anna M. Rosenberg," 11 January 1952, Xerox 2610, pp. 1, 2, Marshall Foundation National Archives Project.

15. Hershey, "Annual Report of the Director of Selective Service," 63.

16. See William A. Galston, "Our National Responsibilities," *U.S. News & World Report,* November 2010, 8; US Congress, Senate, Committee on Health, Education, Labor, and Pensions, *The Next Generation of National Service: Hearings of the Committee on Health, Education, Labor, and Pensions,* 111th Cong., 1st sess., 10 March 2009.

Bibliography

A Note on Sources

The National Archives at College Park, Maryland, houses the official military records for the time period relevant to this book. Record Group 147, Records of the Selective Service System, 1940–, offered valuable comprehension of the Military Selective Service Act of 1948. Record Group 165, Records of the War Department General and Special Staffs, entry 479, Security Classified Correspondence, Reports, Memoranda, and Other Papers Relating to Universal Military Training, 1944–1948, was instructive in providing an overall view of War Department efforts on UMT, primarily from 1943 to 1946. Specifically, it provided insight into the strategic rationale behind UMT, War Department policy, and the early marketing efforts of the War Department. Record Group 337, Records of Headquarters Army Ground Forces, 1916–1954, entry 26F, made known the work of the Universal Military Training Branch, primarily from 1946 to 1948. This record group documented later army efforts on UMT, especially more advanced planning once many of the details had been determined. Entry 91 charted the UMT Experimental Unit at Fort Knox, Kentucky, primarily from 1946 to 1949. This entry highlighted the detailed planning for the unit that occurred as well as the difficulties experienced during the unit's activation. It also illuminated the unique nature of the unit as the model for a nationwide UMT program and hence its public relations function.

The Manuscript Division of the Library of Congress in Washington, DC, houses various papers of individuals and organizations involved in the UMT story. Particularly instructive were the James Wadsworth Family Papers. These papers revealed the lifelong devotion of James W. Wadsworth Jr. to the cause of preparedness in general and UMT specifically. They also illustrated the close personal and professional relationship and mutual respect that Wadsworth and John M. Palmer held for one another. The Truman K. Gibson Papers chronicled Gibson's life in general and more specifically his role in the fight for racial equality from within the War Department. The NAACP Collection evidenced the part that race played in the UMT story and the close linkage between UMT and an extension of military segregation. The A. Philip Randolph Papers shed light on the vocal opposition of some African American leaders to UMT and the reasons for it. They also allowed an insider's view on the Committee against Jim Crow in Military Service and Training and its vociferous campaign against UMT.

The Harry S. Truman Presidential Library in Independence, Missouri, houses Record Group 220, Records of Temporary Committees, Commissions, and Boards. The records of the President's Committee on Civil Rights demonstrated the advocacy for civil rights within federal policy, while the records of the President's Committee on Equality of Treatment and Opportunity in the Armed Services specifically focused on racial equality within the military. They clarified the background to Truman's Executive Order 9981 and how that pivotal event related to the UMT campaign. The records of the President's Advisory Commission on Universal Training revealed the inner working of the commission, including its shift from military utility to social benefits. The Truman library also houses a large collection of records on both President Truman and his inner circle of political advisors. Most helpful among these were the Charles Fahy Papers, the Clark M. Clifford Papers, the George M. Elsey Papers, the J. Howard McGrath Papers, the Philleo Nash Papers, and the Samuel I. Rosenman Papers.

The George C. Marshall Research Library in Lexington, Virginia, houses the George C. Marshall Papers. These records illuminated Marshall's close friendship with John M. Palmer and the critical role Marshall played in the campaign for UMT. The Marshall Foundation National Archives Project augmented the Marshall papers with extensive material underscoring Marshall's advocacy of UMT. Other helpful collections at the Marshall library were the George M. Elsey Papers and the Hanson W. Baldwin Papers.

A wide array of other sources was also helpful in this study. A large collection of legislative hearings was available that shed light on the public debate over UMT during the mid-1940s. Multiple government reports, including *A Program for National Security, May 29, 1947: Report of the President's Advisory Commission on Universal Training*, described the UMT campaign in minute detail. Numerous books from the time period explored UMT specifically. Central among these were the works of John McAuley Palmer. Both supporters and detractors published contributions in a wide array of journals. Articles of multiple newspapers followed the debate at the local, regional, and national levels. National magazines such as *Time* also commented specifically on UMT. Nearly one hundred *Time* articles between 1943 and 1948 dealt particularly with UMT.

Finally, opinion polls outlined public support for UMT throughout the period. Poll data exist in the military records at the National Archives as well as through published sources such as *Public Opinion Quarterly*. These sources provided public opinion data organized into a number of useful categories. They presented public opinion data for different regions of the United States, for various age groups, and for diverse education levels in addition to other interesting categories. I have used public opinion data cautiously. I have presented only interpretations that could be validated by multiple sources. Nevertheless, it was clear from the records that military planners advocating UMT had such poll data and interpreted it. As a result, public opinion formed an important part of their conception of UMT as well as an important tool that they utilized in their campaign for UMT. Public opinion data also revealed the irony that general agreement on national policy does not necessarily translate into concrete action. Even when overwhelming accord existed on the broad issue of UMT, the devil was in the details. The consensus on UMT as a general issue splintered when actual plans had to be crafted to convert the concept into reality.

Archives, Collections, and Manuscripts

NATIONAL ARCHIVES, COLLEGE PARK, MARYLAND
RG 147 Records of the Selective Service System, 1940
RG 165 Records of the War Department General and Special Staffs
RG 319 Records of the Army Staff
RG 337 Records of Headquarters Army Ground Forces

LIBRARY OF CONGRESS, MANUSCRIPT DIVISION, WASHINGTON, DC
A. Philip Randolph Papers
Hanson W. Baldwin Papers
James Wadsworth Family Papers
NAACP Collection
Truman K. Gibson Papers

HARRY S. TRUMAN LIBRARY, INDEPENDENCE, MISSOURI
Harry S. Truman Papers
President's Secretary's Files
White House Central Files: Confidential File
White House Central Files: Official File
Staff Member and Office Files: Philleo Nash Files
Staff Member and Office Files: David H. Stowe Files
Charles Fahy Papers
Clark M. Clifford Papers
George M. Elsey Papers
J. Howard McGrath Papers
James E. Webb Papers
Philleo Nash Papers
Samuel I. Rosenman Papers
RG 220 Records of Temporary Committees, Commissions, and Boards
President's Advisory Commission on Universal Training
President's Committee on Civil Rights
President's Committee on Equality of Treatment and Opportunity in the Armed
    Services

GEORGE C. MARSHALL RESEARCH LIBRARY, LEXINGTON, VIRGINIA
George C. Marshall Papers
Marshall Foundation National Archives Project
George M. Elsey Papers
Hanson W. Baldwin Papers

Government Documents

Devan, Samuel A., and Bernard Brodie. *Universal Military Training.* Library
of Congress Legislative Reference Service. Public Affairs Bulletin no. 54.
Washington, DC: Government Printing Office, 1947.

Quattlebaum, Charles A. *Universal Military Training and Related Proposals:
Selected Data Basic to a Consideration of the Issues.* Library of Congress
Legislative Reference Service. Public Affairs Bulletin no. 43. Washington, DC:
Government Printing Office, 1946.

Upton, Emory. *The Military Policy of the United States.* Washington, DC:
Government Printing Office, 1904.

US Congress. House. *Investigation of War Department Publicity and Propaganda
in Relation to Universal Military Training: Hearings Before the United States
House Committee on Expenditures in the Executive Departments, Subcommittee
on Publicity and Propaganda.* 80th Cong., 1st sess., June 20, July 16, 1947.

———. *Investigation of War Department Publicity and Propaganda in Relation to
Universal Military Training: Hearings Before the United States House Committee
on Expenditures in the Executive Departments, Subcommittee on Publicity and
Propaganda.* 80th Cong., 2nd sess., January 14, 1948.

———. *Subcommittee Hearings on Universal Military Training (H.R. 4121): Hearings
Before the United States House Committee on Armed Services.* 80th Cong., 1st
sess., July 14, 16, 17, 1947.

———. *Universal Military Training: Hearings Before the United States House
Committee on Armed Services.* 80th Cong., 1st sess., June 11, 18, 19, 27, July 7, 9–11,
1947.

———. *Universal Military Training, Part 1: Hearings Before the United States House
Committee on Military Affairs.* 79th Cong., 1st sess., November 8, 13, 15, 16, 19–21,
26–30, December 3, 6, 7, 10–14, 17–19, 1945.

———. *Universal Military Training, Part 1: Hearings Before the United States House
Select Committee on Postwar Military Policy.* 79th Cong., 1st sess., June 4–9,
11–16, 19, 1945.

———. *Universal Military Training, Part 2: Hearings Before the United States House
Committee on Military Affairs.* 79th Cong., 2nd sess., February 18–21, 1946.

US Congress. Senate. *Universal Military Training: Hearings Before the United*

States Senate Committee on Armed Services. 80th Cong., 2nd sess., March 17, 18, 22–25, 29–31, April 1–3, 1948.

———. *Universal Military Training, Statements by Officials of the American Legion Which Organization Sponsored the Bill: Hearings Before the United States Senate Committee on Armed Services.* 81st Cong., 1st sess., March 3, 1949.

US Library of Congress. General Reference and Bibliography Division. *Universal Military Training: A Selected and Annotated List of References.* Compiled by Frances Neel Cheney. Washington, DC: Government Printing Office, 1945.

US President's Advisory Commission on Universal Training. *A Program for National Security, May 29, 1947: Report of the President's Advisory Commission on Universal Training.* Washington, DC: Government Printing Office, 1947.

US President's Committee on Equality of Treatment and Opportunity in the Armed Services. *Freedom to Serve: Equality of Treatment and Opportunity in the Armed Services, a Report by the President's Committee.* Washington, DC: Government Printing Office, 1950.

Books and Dissertations

Acacia, John. *Clark Clifford: The Wise Man of Washington.* Lexington: University Press of Kentucky, 2009.

Allison, William T., Jeffrey Grey, and Janet G. Valentine. *American Military History: A Survey from Colonial Times to the Present.* 2nd ed. New York: Pearson, 2012.

Ambrose, Stephen E. *Eisenhower: Soldier and President.* New York: Simon & Schuster, 1990.

———. *Upton and the Army.* Baton Rouge: Louisiana State University Press, 1964.

Bach, Morten. "None So Consistently Right: The American Legion's Cold War, 1945–1950." PhD diss., Ohio University, 2007.

Bailey, Beth. *America's Army: Making the All-Volunteer Force.* Cambridge, MA: Harvard University Press, 2009.

Barlow, Jeffrey G. *Revolt of the Admirals: The Fight for Naval Aviation, 1945–1950.* Washington, DC: Brassey's, 1998.

Berkowitz, Edward D. *Mr. Social Security: The Life of Wilbur J. Cohen.* Lawrence: University Press of Kansas, 1995.

Bernstein, Barton J., ed. *Politics and Policies of the Truman Administration.* Chicago: Franklin Watts, 1970.

———, and Allen J. Matusow, eds. *The Truman Administration: A Documentary History.* New York: Harper & Row, 1966.

Borden, William L. *There Will Be No Time: The Revolution in Strategy.* New York: Macmillan, 1946.

Boyer, Paul. *By the Bomb's Early Light: American Thought and Culture at the Dawn of the Atomic Age.* Chapel Hill: University of North Carolina Press, 1985.

Brewer, Susan A. *Why America Fights: Patriotism and War Propaganda from the Philippines to Iraq.* Oxford: Oxford University Press, 2009.

Brodie, Bernard, ed. *The Absolute Weapon: Atomic Power and World Order.* New York: Harcourt, Brace and Company, 1946.

Busch, Andrew E. *Truman's Triumphs: The 1948 Election and the Making of Postwar America.* Lawrence: University Press of Kansas, 2012.

Bynum, Cornelius L. *A. Philip Randolph and the Struggle for Civil Rights.* Urbana: University of Illinois Press, 2010.

Capozzola, Christopher. *Uncle Sam Wants You: World War I and the Making of the Modern American Citizen.* Oxford: Oxford University Press, 2008.

Caraley, Demetrios. *The Politics of Military Unification: A Study of Conflict and the Policy Process.* New York: Columbia University Press, 1966.

Chambers, John W. *To Raise an Army: The Draft Comes to Modern America.* New York: Free Press, 1987.

Clifford, J. Garry. *The Citizen Soldiers: The Plattsburg Training Camp Movement, 1913-1920.* Lexington: University Press of Kentucky, 1972.

———, and Samuel R. Spencer. *The First Peacetime Draft.* Lawrence: University Press of Kansas, 1986.

Coffman, Edward M. *The Regulars: The American Army, 1898-1941.* Cambridge, MA: Belknap Press, 2004.

Cohen, Eliot A. *Making Do with Less, or Coping with Upton's Ghost.* Carlisle Barracks, PA: US Army War College, 1995.

———. *Citizens and Soldiers: The Dilemmas of Military Service.* Ithaca, NY: Cornell University Press, 1985.

Cray, Ed. *General of the Army: George C. Marshall, Soldier and Statesman.* New York: Cooper Square Press, 1990.

Culver, John C., and John Hyde. *American Dreamer: A Life of Henry A. Wallace.* New York: Norton, 2000.

Cunningham, Frank D. "The Army and Universal Military Training, 1942-1948." PhD diss., University of Texas at Austin, 1976.

Dallek, Robert. *Harry S. Truman.* New York: Times Books, 2008.

———. *Franklin D. Roosevelt and American Foreign Policy, 1932-1945.* Oxford: Oxford University Press, 1979.

Davies, Robert B. *Baldwin of the Times: Hanson W. Baldwin, A Military Journalist's Life, 1903-1991.* Annapolis, MD: Naval Institute Press, 2011.

Davis, Vincent. *Postwar Defense Policy and the United States Navy, 1943-1946.* Chapel Hill: University of North Carolina Press, 1966.

Derthick, Martha. *The National Guard in Politics.* Cambridge, MA: Harvard University Press, 1965.

Donald, Aida D. *Citizen Soldier: A Life of Harry S. Truman.* New York: Basic Books, 2012.

Donaldson, Gary A. *The Making of Modern America: The Nation from 1945 to the Present.* Lanham, MD: Rowman & Littlefield, 2009.

———. *Truman Defeats Dewey.* Lexington: University Press of Kentucky, 1999.

Dorwart, Jeffrey M. *Eberstadt and Forrestal: A National Security Partnership, 1909–1949.* College Station: Texas A&M University Press, 1991.

Doubler, Michael D. *Civilian in Peace, Soldier in War: The Army National Guard, 1636–2000.* Lawrence: University Press of Kansas, 2003.

Dudziak, Mary L. *Cold War Civil Rights: Race and the Image of American Democracy.* Princeton, NJ: Princeton University Press, 2000.

Eden, Lynn R. "The Diplomacy of Force: Interest, the State, and the Making of American Military Policy in 1948." PhD diss., University of Michigan, 1985.

Eiler, Keith E. *Mobilizing America: Robert P. Patterson and the War Effort, 1940–1945.* Ithaca, NY: Cornell University Press, 1997.

Elsey, George M. *An Unplanned Life.* Columbia: University of Missouri Press, 2005.

Fitzpatrick, Edward A. *Universal Military Training.* New York: McGraw-Hill, 1945.

Flynn, George Q. *Conscription and Democracy: The Draft in France, Great Britain, and the United States.* Westport, CT: Greenwood Press, 2002.

———. *The Draft, 1940–1973.* Lawrence: University Press of Kansas, 1993.

Ford, Nancy G. *The Great War and America: Civil-Military Relations during World War I.* Westport, CT: Praeger Security International, 2008.

Friedberg, Aaron L. *In the Shadow of the Garrison State: America's Anti-Statism and Its Cold War Grand Strategy.* Princeton, NJ: Princeton University Press, 2000.

Friedman, Norman. *The Fifty Year War: Conflict and Strategy in the Cold War.* Annapolis, MD: Naval Institute Press, 2000.

Gaddis, John L. *Strategies of Containment: A Critical Appraisal of Postwar American National Security Policy during the Cold War.* Oxford: Oxford University Press, 1982.

———. *The United States and the Origins of the Cold War, 1941–1947.* New York: Columbia University Press, 1972.

Gambone, Michael D. *The Greatest Generation Comes Home: The Veteran in American Society.* College Station: Texas A&M University Press, 2005.

Gerhardt, James M. *The Draft and Public Policy: Issues in Military Manpower Procurement, 1945–1970.* Columbus: Ohio State University Press, 1971.

Giangreco, D. M., and Kathryn Moore. *Dear Harry . . . Truman's Mailroom, 1945–1953*. Mechanicsburg, PA: Stackpole Books, 1999.

Gibson, Truman K., Jr., with Steve Huntley. *Knocking Down Barriers: My Fight for Black America*. Evanston, IL: Northwestern University Press, 2005.

Gilroy, Curtis L., Barbara A. Bicksler, and John T. Warner. *The All-Volunteer Force: Thirty Years of Service*. Dulles, VA: Brassey's, 2004.

Gole, Henry G. *The Road to Rainbow: Army Planning for Global War, 1934–1940*. Annapolis, MD: Naval Institute Press, 2003.

Gregory, Raymond F. *Norman Thomas: The Great Dissenter*. New York: Algora Publishing, 2008.

Hamby, Alonzo L. *Man of the People: A Life of Harry S. Truman*. New York: Oxford University Press, 1995.

Hammond, Paul. *Organizing for Defense: The American Military Establishment in the Twentieth Century*. Princeton, NJ: Princeton University Press, 1961.

Hanson, Thomas E. *Combat Ready? The Eighth U.S. Army on the Eve of the Korean War*. College Station: Texas A&M University Press, 2010.

Heller, Francis H., ed. *Economics and the Truman Administration*. Lawrence: University Press of Kansas, 1981.

Herzog, Jonathan P. *The Spiritual-Industrial Complex: America's Religious Battle against Communism in the Early Cold War*. Oxford: Oxford University Press, 2011.

Higgs, Robert. *Crisis and Leviathan: Critical Episodes in the Growth of American Government*. Oxford: Oxford University Press, 1987.

Hogan, Michael J. *A Cross of Iron: Harry S. Truman and the Origins of the National Security State, 1945–1954*. Cambridge: Cambridge University Press, 1998.

Holley, I. B. *General John M. Palmer, Citizen Soldiers, and the Army of a Democracy*. Westport, CT: Greenwood Press, 1982.

Hoopes, Townsend, and Douglas Brinkley. *Driven Patriot: The Life and Times of James Forrestal*. Annapolis, MD: Naval Institute Press, 1992.

Horowitz, David A. *Beyond Left and Right: Insurgency and the Establishment*. Urbana: University of Illinois Press, 1997.

House, Jonathan M. *A Military History of the Cold War, 1944–1962*. Norman: University of Oklahoma Press, 2012.

Karabell, Zachary. *The Last Campaign: How Harry Truman Won the 1948 Election*. New York: Alfred A. Knopf, 2000.

Keene, Jennifer D. *Doughboys, the Great War, and the Remaking of America*. Baltimore: Johns Hopkins University Press, 2001.

Keiser, Gordon W. *The U.S. Marine Corps and Defense Unification, 1944–1947: The Politics of Survival*. Washington, DC: National Defense University Press, 1982.

Kennedy, David M., ed. *The Modern American Military*. Oxford: Oxford University Press, 2013.

———. *Over Here: The First World War and American Society*. Oxford: Oxford University Press, 1980.

Kersten, Andrew Edmund. *A. Philip Randolph: A Life in the Vanguard*. Lanham, MD: Rowman & Littlefield, 2007.

Kirkpatrick, Charles E. *An Unknown Future and a Doubtful Present: Writing the Victory Plan of 1941*. Honolulu, HI: University Press of the Pacific, 2005.

Klarman, Michael J. *From Jim Crow to Civil Rights: The Supreme Court and the Struggle for Racial Equality*. Oxford: Oxford University Press, 2004.

Kofsky, Frank. *Harry S. Truman and the War Scare of 1948: A Successful Campaign to Deceive the Nation*. New York: St. Martin's Press, 1993.

Koistinen, Paul A. C. *State of War: The Political Economy of American Warfare, 1945–2011*. Lawrence: University Press of Kansas, 2012.

Korb, Lawrence J. *The Joint Chiefs of Staff: The First Twenty-Five Years*. Bloomington: Indiana University Press, 1976.

Krehbiel, Nicholas A. *General Lewis B. Hershey and Conscientious Objection during World War II*. Columbia: University of Missouri Press, 2011.

Lewis, Adrian R. *The American Culture of War: The History of U.S. Military Force from World War II to Operation Iraqi Freedom*. London: Routledge, 2007.

Lingeman, Richard. *The Noir Forties: The American People from Victory to Cold War*. New York: Nation Books, 2012.

Linn, Brian M. *The Echo of Battle: The Army's Way of War*. Cambridge, MA: Harvard University Press, 2007.

MacGregor, Morris J. *Integration of the Armed Forces, 1940–1965*. Washington, DC: US Army Center of Military History, 1981.

Mansoor, Peter R. *The GI Offensive in Europe: The Triumph of American Infantry Divisions, 1941–1945*. Lawrence: University Press of Kansas, 1999.

Marble, Sanders, ed. *Scraping the Barrel: The Military Use of Substandard Manpower, 1860–1960*. Bronx, NY: Fordham University Press, 2012.

McCullough, David. *Truman*. New York: Simon & Schuster, 1992.

McGuire, Phillip, ed. *Taps for a Jim Crow Army: Letters from Black Soldiers in World War II*. Santa Barbara, CA: ABC-Clio, 1983.

Mershon, Sherie, and Steven Schlossman. *Foxholes and Color Lines: Desegregating the U.S. Armed Forces*. Baltimore: Johns Hopkins University Press, 1998.

Miller, William L. *Two Americans: Truman, Eisenhower, and a Dangerous World*. New York: Alfred A. Knopf, 2012.

Millett, Allan R., and Peter Maslowski. *For the Common Defense: A Military History of the United States of America*. Rev. ed. New York: The Free Press, 1994.

Mills, Nicolaus. *Winning the Peace: The Marshall Plan and America's Coming of Age as a Superpower.* Hoboken, NJ: John Wiley & Sons, 2008.

Moskos, Charles C. *A Call to Civic Service: National Service for Country and Community.* New York: The Free Press, 1988.

Neal, Steve. *Harry and Ike: The Partnership that Remade the Postwar World.* New York: Simon & Schuster, 2001.

Neiberg, Michael S. *Making Citizen-Soldiers: ROTC and the Ideology of American Military Service.* Cambridge, MA: Harvard University Press, 2000.

Odom, William O. *After the Trenches: The Transformation of U.S. Army Doctrine, 1918–1939.* College Station: Texas A&M University Press, 1999.

Olson, James C. *Stuart Symington: A Life.* Columbia: University of Missouri Press, 2003.

Palmer, John McAuley. *America in Arms: The Experience of the United States with Military Organization.* Fighting Forces Series. Washington, DC: *Infantry Journal,* 1941.

———. *An Army of the People: The Constitution of an Effective Force of Trained Citizens.* New York: G. P. Putnam's Sons, 1916.

———. *Statesmanship or War.* Introduction by James W. Wadsworth Jr. New York: Doubleday, Page & Company, 1927.

———. *Washington, Lincoln, Wilson: Three War Statesmen.* Garden City, NY: Doubleday, Doran & Company, 1930.

Patterson, James T. *Grand Expectations: The United States, 1945–1974.* Oxford: Oxford University Press, 1996.

———. *Mr. Republican: A Biography of Robert A. Taft.* Boston: Houghton Mifflin, 1972.

Perry, Mark. *Partners in Command: George Marshall and Dwight Eisenhower in War and Peace.* New York: Penguin, 2007.

Pfeffer, Paula F. *A. Philip Randolph, Pioneer of the Civil Rights Movement.* Baton Rouge: Louisiana State University Press, 1990.

Phillips, Kimberley L. *War! What Is It Good For? Black Freedom Struggles and the U.S. Military from World War II to Iraq.* Chapel Hill: University of North Carolina Press, 2012.

Pietrusza, David. *1948: Harry Truman's Improbable Victory and the Year That Transformed America.* New York: Union Square Press, 2011.

Reynolds, David. *From World War to Cold War: Churchill, Roosevelt, and the International History of the 1940s.* Oxford: Oxford University Press, 2006.

Rostker, Bernard. *I Want You! The Evolution of the All-Volunteer Force.* Santa Monica, CA: Rand Corporation, 2006.

Scahill, Jeremy. *Blackwater: The Rise of the World's Most Powerful Mercenary Army.* New York: Nation Books, 2007.

Schifferle, Peter J. *America's School for War: Fort Leavenworth, Officer Education, and Victory in World War II.* Lawrence: University Press of Kansas, 2010.

Segal, David R. *Recruiting for Uncle Sam: Citizenship and Military Manpower Policy.* Lawrence: University Press of Kansas, 1989.

Shenk, Gerald E. *"Work or Fight!" Race, Gender, and the Draft in World War One.* New York: Palgrave Macmillan, 2005.

Sherry, Michael S. *Preparing for the Next War: American Plans for Postwar Defense, 1941–1945.* New Haven, CT: Yale University Press, 1977.

Sherwin, Martin J. *A World Destroyed: Hiroshima and Its Legacies.* 3rd ed. Stanford, CA: Stanford University Press, 2003.

Spalding, Elizabeth E. *The First Cold Warrior: Harry Truman, Containment, and the Remaking of Liberal Internationalism.* Lexington: University Press of Kentucky, 2006.

Sparrow, James T. *Warfare State: World War II Americans and the Age of Big Government.* Oxford: Oxford University Press, 2011.

Stentiford, Barry M. *The American Home Guard: The State Militia in the Twentieth Century.* College Station: Texas A&M University Press, 2002.

Stoler, Mark A. *Allies and Adversaries: The Joint Chiefs of Staff, the Grand Alliance, and U.S. Strategy in World War II.* Chapel Hill: University of North Carolina Press, 2000.

———. *George C. Marshall: Soldier-Statesman of the American Century.* Boston: Twayne Publishers, 1989.

———. *The Politics of the Second Front: American Military Planning and Diplomacy in Coalition Warfare, 1941–1943.* Westport, CT: Greenwood Press, 1977.

Sweeney, Jerry K., ed. *A Handbook of American Military History: From the Revolutionary War to the Present.* 2nd ed. Lincoln: University of Nebraska Press, 1996.

Swomley, John M. "A Study of the Universal Military Training Campaign, 1944–1952." PhD diss., University of Colorado at Boulder, 1959.

Trauschweizer, Ingo. *The Cold War U.S. Army: Building Deterrence for Limited War.* Lawrence: University Press of Kansas, 2008.

Unger, David C. *Emergency State: America's Pursuit of Absolute National Security at All Costs.* New York: Penguin Press, 2012.

Vogel, Steve. *The Pentagon: A History.* New York: Random House, 2008.

Ward, Robert D. "The Movement for Universal Military Training in the United States, 1942–1952." PhD diss., University of North Carolina at Chapel Hill, 1957.

Weigley, Russell F. *The American Way of War: A History of United States Military Strategy and Policy.* Bloomington: Indiana University Press, 1973.

———. *History of the United States Army.* Enlarged ed. Bloomington: Indiana University Press, 1984.

———. *Towards an American Army: Military Thought from Washington to Marshall.* New York: Columbia University Press, 1962.

Williams, T. Harry. *The History of American Wars.* New York: Alfred A. Knopf, 1981.

Winton, Harold R. *Corps Commanders of the Bulge: Six American Generals and Victory in the Ardennes.* Lawrence: University Press of Kansas, 2007.

Wolk, Herman S. *Planning and Organizing the Postwar Air Force, 1943-1947.* Washington, DC: Office of Air Force History, 1984.

Articles

Bacevich, Andrew J. "Emory Upton: A Centennial Assessment." *Military Review* 61 (December 1981): 21-28.

Bailey, Beth. "The Army in the Marketplace: Recruiting an All-Volunteer Force." *Journal of American History* 94 (June 2007): 47-74.

Clifford, John G. "Grenville Clark and the Origins of Selective Service." *Review of Politics* 35 (January 1973): 17-40.

Coffman, Edward M. "The Duality of the American Military Tradition: A Commentary." *Journal of Military History* 64 (October 2000): 967-80.

Cooling, B. Franklin. "Civil Defense and the Army: The Quest for Responsibility, 1946-1948." *Military Affairs* 36 (February 1972): 11-14.

Cram, W. A. "Universal Training for War and Peace." *School Review* 53 (September 1945): 401-8.

Cunningham, Frank D. "Harry S. Truman and Universal Military Training, 1945." *Historian* 46 (Summer 1984): 397-415.

Curzon, Myron W. "The Nation's Military Security." *Scientific Monthly* 62 (January 1946): 66-70.

Davenport, Roy K. "Implications of Military Selection and Classification in Relation to Universal Military Training." *Journal of Negro Education* 15 (Autumn 1946): 585-94.

Dorey, Halstead. "The Plattsburg Contribution to Military Training." *Proceedings of the Academy of Political Science in the City of New York* 6 (July 1916): 229-33.

Dunn, Joe P. "UMT: A Historical Perspective." *Military Review* 61 (January 1981): 11-18.

Earhart, Mary. "The Value of Universal Military Training in Maintaining Peace." *Annals of the American Academy of Political and Social Science* 241 (September 1945): 46-57.

Elliott, Allen R. "The Plus Values of Military Training." *Journal of Criminal Law and Criminology* 35 (January 1946): 324-25.

Fitzpatrick, David J. "Emory Upton and the Army of a Democracy." *Journal of Military History* 77 (April 2013): 463–90.

———. "Emory Upton and the Citizen Soldier." *Journal of Military History* 65 (April 2001): 355–89.

Forman, Sidney. "Thomas Jefferson on Universal Military Training." *Military Affairs* 11 (Autumn 1947): 177–78.

Graham, Robert A. "Universal Military Training in Modern History." *Annals of the American Academy of Political and Social Science* 241 (September 1945): 8–14.

Grandstaff, Mark R. "Making the Military American: Advertising, Reform, and the Demise of an Antistanding Military Tradition, 1945–1955." *Journal of Military History* 60 (April 1996): 299–323.

Hershey, Lewis B. "Procurement of Manpower in American Wars." *Annals of the American Academy of Political and Social Science* 241 (September 1945): 15–25.

Holborn, Hajo. "Professional Army versus Military Training." *Annals of the American Academy of Political and Social Science* 241 (September 1945): 123–30.

Hoskins, Halford L. "Universal Military Training and American Foreign Policy." *Annals of the American Academy of Political and Social Science* 241 (September 1945): 58–66.

McCloy, John J. "The Plan of the Armed Services for Universal Military Training." *Annals of the American Academy of Political and Social Science* 241 (September 1945): 26–34.

Miller, Karen. "'Air Power Is Peace Power' The Aircraft Industry's Campaign for Public and Political Support, 1943–1949." *Business History Review* 70 (Autumn 1996): 297–327.

Modell, John, and Timothy Haggerty. "The Social Impact of War." *Annual Review of Sociology* 17 (1991): 205–24.

Moskos, Charles C., Jr. "Racial Integration in the Armed Forces." *American Journal of Sociology* 72 (September 1966): 132–48.

Nelson, Anna K. "Anna M. Rosenberg, an 'Honorary Man.'" *Journal of Military History* 68 (January 2004): 133–62.

Perri, Timothy J. "The Evolution of Military Conscription in the United States." *Independent Review* 17 (Winter 2013): 429–39.

Platt, Kenneth B. "What Is National Defense?" *Scientific Monthly* 62 (January 1946): 71–78.

Sager, John. "Universal Military Training and the Struggle to Define American Identity during the Cold War." *Federal History Journal* 5 (January 2013): 57–74.

Schickele, Rainer, and Glenn Everett. "The Economic Implications of Universal Military Training." *Annals of the American Academy of Political and Social Science* 241 (September 1945): 102–12.

Spiller, Roger. "Military History and Its Fictions." *Journal of Military History* 70 (October 2006): 1081–97.

Sprout, Harold. "Trends in the Traditional Relation between Military and Civilian." *Proceedings of the American Philosophical Society* 92 (October 1948): 264–70.

Stone, Marshall H. "Universal Military Service in Peacetime." *Science* 103 (May 1946): 579–81.

Thacher, Archibald G., and W. Randolph Montgomery. "The Relation of the Militia Clause to the Constitutionality of Peacetime Compulsory Universal Military Training." *Virginia Law Review* 31 (June 1945): 628–66.

Thomas, Norman. "Arming against Russia." *Annals of the American Academy of Political and Social Science* 241 (September 1945): 67–71.

Tompkins, William F. "Future Manpower Needs of the Armed Forces." *Annals of the American Academy of Political and Social Science* 238 (March 1945): 56–62.

Tresidder, Donald B. "My Hands to War." *Journal of Higher Education* 16 (October 1945): 343–50.

Trow, William C. "The Case against Compulsory Military Training." *Journal of Criminal Law and Criminology* 35 (January 1946): 325–26.

Villard, Oswald G. "Universal Military Training and Military Preparedness." *Annals of the American Academy of Political and Social Science* 241 (September 1945): 35–45.

Walker, Wallace E. "Emory Upton and the Officer's Creed." *Military Review* 61 (April 1981): 65–68.

Weigley, Russell F. "The Soldier, the Statesman, and the Military Historian." *Journal of Military History* 63 (October 1999): 807–22.

Wood, Leonard. "Citizenship Obligation: National Training for Defense." *Proceedings of the Academy of Political Science in the City of New York* 6 (July 1916): 157–65.

Ylvisaker, Hedvig. "Public Opinion toward Compulsory Peacetime Military Training." *Annals of the American Academy of Political and Social Science* 241 (September 1945): 86–94.

Index

Page numbers in italic refer to photos and figures.
Page numbers followed by an asterisk denote citation appears only in Appendix A.

134–35, 193n1; and Executive Order 9981, 163; and President's Advisory Commission on Universal Training, 135, 137; and Randolph, 137–38, 163; and struggle for racial equality in War Department, 205 (*see also* race relations); and support of UMT, 135, 141. *See also* Manuscript Division of the Library of Congress: Truman K. Gibson Papers

Granger, Lester B., 164

Great Britain, 144

Greece, 154

Green, William, 68, 70, 71

Grew, Joseph C., 89–90

Griffith, Paul H., 173*

Gurney, Chan, 146, 151–52, 155

Haislip, Wade H., 113

Hall, C. P., 105

Harper's (magazine), 50, 51

Harry S. Truman Presidential Library (Independence, Missouri), 205–206: Charles Fahy Papers, 206; Clark M. Clifford Papers, 206; George M. Elsey Papers, 206; J. Howard McGrath Papers, 206; Philleo Nash Papers, 206; Samuel I. Rosenman Papers, 206; records of the President's Committee on Civil Rights, 205–206; records of the President's Committee on Equality . . . , 206

Hastie, William H., 194n7; and appearance before President's Advisory Commission, 122, 132; and Jesse O. Dedmon, 193n7; as representative of NAACP position, 132–33; and segregation, 122–23, 133

Havenner, Franck R., 200n29

Hay, Alice, 19

Hay, John, 19

Hearst newspapers, 145

Heffernan, James J., 200n29

Henry, Stephen G., 172*

Hershey, Lewis B., 167

Hilldring, John H., 25

Hinshaw, Carl, 151

Hitler, Adolf, 101

Holdridge, H. C., 84–86

Holmes, John Haynes, 74

Holmes, Julius C., 90

Horan, Walt, 32

Hull, Warren, 113

Hungary, 144, 154

Hunt, Lester M., 71

Hutchins Report, 129–30

Hutchins, Robert M., 46–47, 183n8. *See also* Hutchins Report

Ickes, Harold L., 97

Infantry Journal, 126

Iowa State College, 65

Irvine, W. W., 73, 187n13

Israel, 145

Jacobs, Randall, 70

Jim Crow. *See under* race relations: and discrimination

Johnson, A., 70

Johnson, Edwin C., 129

Johnson, Parks, 113

Joint Chiefs of Staff (JCS), 121–22

Kellogg-Briand Pact (1928), 179n11

Kenny, Robert W., 149

Kent, Harold W., 48, 49: and BPR, 53; and religious implications of UMT, 80

Kim Il Sung, 145

King, Ernest J., 70

Kinkaid, Thomas C., 166

Kirk, Norman T., 47

Knox, Frank, 27

Koch, Joseph R., 78

Korea, 145

About the Author

William A. Taylor is assistant professor of security studies at Angelo State University in San Angelo, Texas. After graduating from the United States Naval Academy with honors and distinction, he participated in the Navy's highly selective Voluntary Graduate Education Program through which he earned an MA in history from the University of Maryland. He also completed an MA in security studies at Georgetown University, graduating with honors. He then earned an MPhil and PhD in history from George Washington University. Taylor won the ABC-Clio research grant from the Society for Military History, the George C. Marshall/Baruch fellowship, the Harry S. Truman Library Institute research grant, and the Angelo State University Faculty Research Enhancement Program grant to research *Every Citizen a Soldier.* Taylor maintains research interests in military manpower, military history, civil-military relations, security studies, grand strategy, and defense policy. He is active in a number of professional organizations and has contributed to various professional journals and research projects. In addition to his academic credentials, Taylor served as an officer in the United States Marine Corps for more than six years, holding posts in III Marine Expeditionary Force, Expeditionary Force Development Center, and Marine Corps Combat Development Command.